SUCKLING AT MY MOTHER'S BREASTS

SUNY SERIES IN WESTERN ESOTERIC TRADITIONS
David Appelbaum, editor

Suckling at My Mother's Breasts

The Image of a Nursing God in Jewish Mysticism

ELLEN DAVINA HASKELL

Published by State University of New York Press, Albany

© 2012 State University of New York

For information, contact State University of New York Press, Albany, NY
www.sunypress.edu

Production by Kelli Williams LeRoux
Marketing by Kate McDonnell

Library of Congress Cataloging-in-Publication Data

Haskell, Ellen Davina.
  Suckling at my mother's breasts : the image of a nursing God in Jewish
mysticism / Ellen Davina Haskell.
      p. cm. — (SUNY series in Western esoteric traditions)
  Includes bibliographical references and index.
  ISBN 978-1-4384-4381-2 (hardcover : alk. paper)
  1. Cabala—History. 2. God (Judaism)—Love. 3. Mysticism—Judaism.
4. Rabbinical literature—History and criticism. 5. Bible. O.T.—Criticism,
interpretation, etc. I. Title.

  BM526.H388 2012
  296.8'33—dc23

                                        2011045769

                      10 9 8 7 6 5 4 3 2 1

For my parents, with love.

Contents

Hebrew and Aramaic Transliterations

In order to make my material accessible to nonspecialists, I have adopted the following simplified transliteration system. In cases where common words like "Kabbalah" do not match this system, I retain the common usage.

Consonants

': *Alef* (except at beginning of words, where absent)
b: *Bet*
g: *Gimel*
d: *Dalet*
h: *He'*
v: *Vav*
z: *Zayin*
ḥ: *Ḥet*
t: *Tet*
y: *Yud*
k/kh: *Kaf*
l: *Lamed*
m: *Mem*
n: *Nun*
s: *Samekh*

': *Ayin* (except at beginning of words, where absent)
p/f: *Pe'*
tz: *Tzade*
q: *Quf*
r: *Resh*
sh/s: *Shin*
t: *Tav*

Vowels

a: *Qamatz, Patah, Hataf patah*
e: *Sheva'* (silent *sheva'* is unmarked), *Tzereh, Tzereh yud, Segol, Hataf segol*
i: *Hiriq, Hiriq yud*
o: *Holam, Holam vav, Hataf qamatz*
u: *Shuruq, Qubutz*

INTRODUCTION

Kabbalistic Images, Relationality, and a Breastfeeding God

This is the *Shekhinah* who was in the Temple and all the children of the world used to suckle from her. . . . And the *Shekhinah* rested upon them in the Temple, like a mother covering over her children. And all the faces used to shine while blessings were found above and below, and there was not a day on which blessings and rejoicings were not found. And Israel rested in safety in the land, and all the world used to be nourished because of them.
—Sefer ha-Zohar 1:203a[1]

A Divine Nursing Mother

As the kabbalists developed their theology in the twelfth and thirteenth centuries, they experimented with new ways to understand the relationships between God, themselves, and the world around them. While earlier Jewish devotion focused on male anthropomorphisms that described God as King, Father, and Judge, the kabbalists expressed their divine relationships through a broader variety of images. Perceiving the divine as a dynamic complex of ten aspects known as *sefirot*, these mystics boldly incorporated feminine figures, natural images, and even cultural artifacts into their literature, significantly expanding their available models for approaching deity. Each image complemented and corrected the others, generating a poetic theology whose distinctive metaphors allowed the kabbalists to ground their understanding

1

of a distant and abstract divinity in the language of daily life and experience.[2]

One of the most unusual of these images was the depiction of God as a nursing mother. Identifying two of the *sefirot* (the third and the tenth) as feminine to establish gender balance within divinity was one of Kabbalah's most innovative theological choices. In their formative writings, the mystics present God as a protective mother covering her children, as a pregnant being who births and nurses spiritual infants, as a breastfeeding mother whose healing milk spreads mercy through the divine world, and even as a breasted patriarch continuously suckling the universe with supernal love. These vivid images all convey the kabbalistic principle that both the *sefirot* and the human world are sustained by an overflow of divine energy.[3] While the kabbalists often use the term suckling (*yeniqah*) to describe divine energy's transmission, the term can occur without feminine context, applying equally to a child suckling milk from its mother and to the action by which young plants draw moisture from the earth. Depicting God as a nursing mother refines divine suckling by appealing to a distinctive set of social, physical, and emotional experiences surrounding motherhood and the parent-child relationship.

The textual excerpt that begins this introduction, *Sefer ha-Zohar* (*The Book of Splendor*) 1:203a, demonstrates some of the ways in which nursing imagery encourages an intimate and emotionally nuanced relationship with God. In this late thirteenth-century text, a feminine aspect of God interacts with all the world's inhabitants during an idealized Jewish past. This feminine aspect of God, *Shekhinah* (Divine Presence), is the aspect of God closest to human experience. She is shown residing in the ancient Temple before its destruction, engendering a perfected world in which divine energy flows out from the Temple to the Israelite people and ultimately into "all the children of the world." Although this passage makes a theological statement about ideal world order and its dependence on God's Presence abiding in Jerusalem, it also provides social and emotional nuance for its teaching. By depicting God as a nursing mother who nourishes the world, the passage reminds its reader that human beings are utterly dependent on the divine for their well-being. God is the source of blessings, nourishment, nurture, and safety. Humanity rejoices in its dependence, and a child's love for its mother illuminates the faces of those who exist in this ideal relationship. Motherly love is ascribed to *Shekhinah* as She protectively covers Her Israelite children. The passage's divine overflow theology is nuanced by engaging sociocultural implications of the love between mothers and infants to construct an emotionally positive relationship of nurture and reliance between God and human beings. This preliminary look at Zohar 1:203a demonstrates mothering imagery's potential for developing complex relationships between God and humanity. (Chapter 3 contains a broader look at this interesting text.)

Divine nursing imagery's most distinguishing feature is its intensive engagement with relationality—by which I mean a focus on the connections, associations, and relationships that occur between human beings and the things that exist in our perceived environment. These things may include other human beings, the divine, and even plants and inanimate objects. The nursing metaphor foregrounds and asserts the quality of relation because it never deals exclusively with an individual, speaking instead to the connection between its participants: the mother who breastfeeds and the child who suckles from her. It is predominantly a social image, providing an engaging model for the kabbalist who wishes to enter into a specifically defined relationship with God. This model establishes an intimate, familial bond between divinity and humanity, redefining the relationship between the two in terms of tenderness, rather than dominion. In this sense, the image of God as a suckling mother serves not only as a tool for theological teaching, but also as a unique entrée into a direct and emotional response to God.

Suckling, Nursing and Breastfeeding

At this point, it may be helpful to offer some observations about the term *suckling* and explain how it will be used in this study. English, Hebrew, and Aramaic all make grammatical distinctions between the action of a child who suckles and the action of a woman who gives suck to a child. English speakers tend to avoid the term *give suck* when speaking of human beings, reserving the term for animals (when we use it at all). To say that a woman "gives suck" sounds archaic and even vulgar in contemporary English usage, in which "expressing milk" has become the most common phrase associated with a woman passing milk from her breasts. However, "expressing milk" is not a helpful phrase for my purposes, since milk's presence or absence in relation to suckling language is an important marker for tracing the nursing divine's development over time. For these reasons (and to avoid redundancy), I have chosen to incorporate words like *nursing* and *breastfeeding* into my translations and analyses—using the term *suckle* in a general sense that encompasses both the causative *hif'il* and the active *pa'al* forms of the root *y.n.q.* (suckle). The identities of suckling's givers and receivers should remain clear from context.[4]

Project Goals and Considerations

This project examines the image of a breastfeeding God in three phases of Jewish literature: the classical rabbinic writings of the fifth through the twelfth centuries, the early kabbalistic literature of the late twelfth through the early thirteenth centuries, and the late thirteenth-century mystical classic *Sefer ha-Zohar*. Through close reading of these texts in relation to their cultural and historical contexts, I will support the following claims: 1) that the kabbalistic image of the breastfeeding divine developed organically from prior Jewish sources and from its medieval environment;, 2) that the breastfeeding divine was a valuable image for cultivating a relationship with God, a relationship that was not reliant on associations with sexuality or rulership;, and 3) that as such, the breastfeeding divine made a distinctive contribution to the broad spectrum of imagery that the kabbalists explored in their search for a full and meaningful relationship with divinity. The mode of divine and human relationality constructed through the nursing divine does not stand alone, but rather complements and corrects alternative models for thinking about God, forming a distinctive thread in the rich tapestry of kabbalistic theology.

Focusing on the image of God as a nursing mother in these textual settings also engages interrelated issues of theology, culture, and the history of Biblical interpretation. In addition to defining a kabbalistic model of divine relationality and its effect on the mystics' self-understanding, the nursing divine provides insight into the relationship between kabbalistic theology and medieval Jewish family life in southern France and northern Spain where Kabbalah originated. Nursing is grounded in domestic life, evoking associations with motherhood and nurture. Medieval European Jews also considered nursing a married woman's legal obligation, as a recent study by Elisheva Baumgarten demonstrates. While breastfeeding children or providing a wet-nurse were included in a married woman's legal obligations to her husband, Jews in medieval Spain believed that it was preferable for a mother to fulfill this obligation herself.[5] Chapter 1, which contains several rabbinic stories about breastfeeding mothers transmitting positive spiritual qualities to their children, provides insight into the cultural assumptions underlying such advice.[6]

The image of God breastfeeding also opens questions of cultural interaction between Judaism and Christianity. While scholars have suggested recently that European Christian Marian theology directly influenced Kabbalah's female divine figures, conversations between Jews and Christians in the period imply this influence is not unidirectional.[7] Tracing the nursing mother image to a clear source in classical rabbinic texts further complicates the issue of influence. Discovering a long tradition of Jewish reflection on breastfeeding lessens the tendency to read medieval instances as rooted solely in adoption of Christian themes. For example, during the twelfth century, Christians began to interpret the Song of Songs from a Marian perspective, reading it as a love song between Jesus and his holy mother. This choice marked a shift from earlier Christian readings of the Song that cast it as a dialogue between Jesus and a feminized Church.[8] When Rabbi Ezra of Gerona composed the first kabbalistic commentary on the Song in the early thirteenth century, his work made a similar shift.[9] Instead of reading the text as a love song between God and Israel, he relocated it to the heavens and created an internal divine dialogue between *Shekhinah* and the masculine *sefirot*. Both Christian and Jewish commentaries on the Song contain extensive breastfeeding imagery.[10]

While Ezra may have been aware of and inspired by these Christian readings, he also had a large body of earlier Jewish sources at his disposal, and many of these contained suckling images as well. Rabbinic texts composed in the fifth through the twelfth century frequently used suckling as a metaphor for spiritual transmission, and these sources would have been equally inspiring. Babylonian Talmud *Eruvin* 54b teaches about Torah, " 'Her breasts will satisfy you at all times' (Proverbs 5:19). Why are the words of Torah compared to a breast? As with this breast, that every time the child touches it, he finds milk in it, so it is with the words of Torah. Every time that a man reasons in them, he finds pleasure in them."[11] This passage's eroticism coheres with the Song of Song's sensuously holy aesthetic, and Ezra applies a similar motif to *Shekhinah* in his commentary. Ezra's *Shekhinah* announces,

"'I am a wall and my breasts are like towers. [Then I was in his eyes as one who finds peace.]' (Song 8:10).[12] She is proud that she will be like a fortified wall, to strengthen [herself] with her faith and with the two Torahs; the Written Torah and the Oral Torah, that are the [source of] vitality for man, as the breasts are the [source of] life for the infant."[13] These two passages relating scholars who study sacred text to children suckling from the breast demonstrate an internal Jewish suckling motif that does not rely on Christian influence.[14]

Looking closely at rabbinic and kabbalistic textual traditions illustrates the ways that Jewish communities used scriptural interpretation to address their distinctive cultural contexts and theological needs. By examining suckling imagery's emergence and development over time, it is possible to demonstrate that Jewish literature's characteristic intertextuality is present not only at the level of text and verse-based citations, but is also applicable to the images within Jewish texts.[15] When Ezra of Gerona presented a fully articulated image of God as a nursing mother in his *Commentary on the Song of Songs*, he invariably connected the image to a scriptural proof text from the Song. His commentary, composed in the 1220s, was widely read, and became an important source for the late thirteenth-century *Sefer ha-Zohar*. Yet when the Zohar described a breastfeeding divine, it often allowed the imagery to exist independent of such textual citation. While the Zohar's suckling images stand on their own, they are still engaged in conversation with Ezra's earlier verse-based imagery. Both Ezra and the Zohar's authors were aware of classical rabbinic texts such as *Genesis Rabbah* and the Babylonian Talmud, which contain narratives that employ the metaphor of breastfeeding as spiritual transmission. Medieval texts like the Zohar occasionally do cite the same breastfeeding proof texts as fifth-century rabbinic works. For example, both *Genesis Rabbah* 53:9 and Zohar 2:256b-257a present teachings that hinge on Genesis 21:7, "Who would have said to Abraham that Sarah would suckle children?" However, there is no reason to assume that texts containing similar imagery but lacking similar proof texts are unrelated. This intense intertextuality of both scriptural and image citation helped the kabbalists to naturalize their innovative ideas by drawing on the "public symbol system" that allows people to rediscover and transform their own cultures.[16]

Questioning the suckling metaphor's growth in relation to its Christian context also prompts inquiry into why the kabbalists, an exclusively masculine group, chose to develop feminine divine images and whether the use of such imagery should be read as sexual, nonsexual, or as something else entirely. Elliot Wolfson and Tova Rosen have recently characterized Kabbalah's general attitude toward women as negative; however, a feminine breastfeeding God suggests the possibility of rethinking these assertions.[17] The fact that formative kabbalistic texts contain positive feminine imagery directly applied to God suggests that such images fill a perceived gap in the kabbalists' ideal spectrum of divine and human relationships. Indeed, Melila Hellner-Eshed has suggested that the Zohar offers its readers the vision of a religious life lived in relation to "God the Mother," the aspect of divinity remaining in the world after the departure of "God the Father."[18] Understanding God as a mother indicates a positive view of certain female roles that were also valued in medieval Jewish society and provides a framework for an increasingly affective mode of spirituality that is particularly evident in *Sefer ha-Zohar*.[19] This movement toward affective spirituality was not confined to the Jewish community. European Christians also shifted toward a more affective spiritual stance during this period, and some scholars connect this shift to the feminine religious imagery associated with Marian theology.[20] Christians like the twelfth-century Adam of Perseigne, a member of the new Cistercian Order, also linked affective spirituality with suckling imagery.[21]

As in today's Western culture, medieval Jews perceived a mother's relationship to her children as special and unique. Breastfeeding and caring for infants was considered a natural female task, and a mother's care during her child's earliest years helped to determine its survival.[22] Nurture, love, and sustenance defined the mother-child relationship, which also incorporated a legal obligation to provide nourishment. Mothers had jurisdiction over their male children until the age at which it was considered appropriate to indoctrinate them into Torah study—thus, guiding their children's earliest and most formative interpretations of the world.[23] The kabbalists even used this mother-child relationship to define suckling as a form of spiritual transmission that surpassed the lifelong commitment to Torah and Talmud study so greatly valued in Jewish religiosity. The image of God as a nursing mother implied a divine-human relationship based in loving obligation that preceded and transcended intellectual attachment, just as a mother's early childcare preceded a father's authority over Jewish education. As the early kabbalist Isaac the Blind wrote of the *sefirot*, "They are interior and subtle beings that no creature is able to contemplate except he who suckles from it, for it is a way of contemplation by way of his suckling, and not by way of knowledge."[24]

Guiding Principles

Two central assumptions about Kabbalah and its rich image vocabulary guide my presentation of this subject. The first is that during its formative period, Kabbalah was a religious movement actively interested in relationality both within God (among the *sefirot*) and between God and humanity. As such, it attempted to redefine the spiritual experience in relational terms.[25] This concern is illustrated in Kabbalah's most basic tenets. For example, the *sefirot*—which are commonly referred to as *Keter* (Crown), *Hokhmah* (Wisdom), *Binah* (Understanding), *Hesed* (Love), *Din* (Judgment), *Rahamim* (Compassion), *Netzah* (Eternity), *Hod* (Majesty), *Yesod* (Foundation), and *Shekhinah* (Divine Presence)—are all considered interrelated aspects of the divine unity.[26] They represent internal divine characteristics that God chooses to reveal, essentially functioning as relational elements through which divinity engages the cosmos. God relates to human beings through these revealed *sefirot*, which are ultimately rooted within *Ein Sof* (Without End), the concealed divine aspect that exists beyond human understanding, and hence beyond accessible relationality.[27] The *sefirot* are generally described as emanating from *Ein Sof* in the order listed above, and relate to each other in a complex network described with nature imagery, anthropomorphic imagery, light imagery, and aquatic imagery.[28] The divine aspects closest to humanity, beginning with *Shekhinah*, are considered most accessible and relatable to human beings, while accessibility diminishes as the kabbalist makes his way further from humanity toward *Ein Sof*.

The kabbalists' nursing-mother image performed an important role in articulating human and divine relationships, because it provided a divine description rooted in relationality that served both to define and to construct kabbalistic perspectives on this topic. Kabbalah took divine imitation as a basic theological teaching, employing the model of macrocosm and microcosm to advance the idea that people's actions could have direct effects on divinity. For this reason, understanding the proper relationship between God and human beings was one of

these mystics' most essential concerns.[29] Rather than constructing relationality in a mechanical way, the kabbalists strove for a meaningful
presentation that resonated with human experience and allowed them
to interact with God on a number of different levels, including the
emotional, the intellectual, and the social.[30] The image of a motherly,
nursing God illustrates this paradigm and also allows exploration of the
emotions associated with kabbalistic relational models.

In the sense that it is concerned with redefining spiritual relationality, Kabbalah can be characterized as a religious revitalization movement "fundamentally interested in restoring the relatedness of things."[31]
Anthropologist James Fernandez has demonstrated that a theology comprised of varied, dynamically interacting metaphors gives its adherents
a sensation of cosmological coherence and effects a perceived "return to
the whole," a restoration of humanity's relative place within the ordering
of the universe.[32] Focus on understanding the human being's relationship to the greater cosmological structure manifests itself in Kabbalah's complex religious models, which are also grounded in dynamic
images.[33] This observation offers a model for understanding Jewish mystical writings. Kabbalistic texts actively create meaning in the minds
of their readers, and their use of vivid and unusual imagery fuels such
creation. For the kabbalists, who are primarily concerned with relating
themselves to a God who cannot be fully known, this process is critical;
their self-understanding is altered by their encounter with mystical text.
Perceiving God through objects of daily experience in turn allows these
objects to become lenses through which to perceive divinity. God, the
world, and the kabbalist's place within the world are mutually enlivened. When *Sefer ha-Zohar* 1:1a describes God's female Presence as a
rose that becomes a cup in the mystic's hand, his garden, his cup, and
his hand are all mutually transformed by divine connection.[34]

The second guiding principle of this book concerns religious imagery itself.[35] Throughout this work, I take as a given the idea that religious images—whether classified as metaphors, symbols, or mythic
figures—are cognitive tools that construct models for thinking about
religious and cultural topics.[36] James Fernandez defines the metaphoric
image as "a strategic predication upon an inchoate pronoun . . . which
makes a movement and leads to performance," while George Lakoff
and Mark Johnson explain, "The essence of metaphor is understanding
and experiencing one kind of thing in terms of another."[37] These images

are functional, and their usefulness extends beyond attractive poetics and scriptural hermeneutics. Religious images reorganize internal perceptions of the things they describe, leading to changes in behavior and experience. They are critical tools for defining models of religious relationality, because they reduce concepts to quickly understood experiential impressions while opening them to complex networks of connotations that stimulate thought in particular directions.[38] These images move the terms they describe (such as "God") through cultural space by embedding them in rich tapestries of existing associations, and authors deliberately select specific images to evoke such associative networks. A poet who describes love as a journey is intentionally making a different point than one that describes love as a battle, just as a kabbalist who describes God as a Father is seeking a different effect than one that describes God as a Mother.[39] Anthropomorphic images, such as the nursing mother, are especially powerful because they engage personal experience and self-perception.[40] Thinking of God in human terms reciprocally encourages a mentality that thinks of humans in godly terms, and this interactive property of religious imagery helps to provide a convincing internal logic for the kabbalistic principle of imitating God. It also underlies the kabbalistic idea that divinity and humanity act mutually upon each other, with the human being both reflecting and affecting the divine.[41]

Religious imagery's ability to affect experience is not confined to mystical literature. The traditional *Yom Kippur* prayer *Avinu Malkenu* (*Our Father, Our King*) combines two of Judaism's most familiar divine images to provide an exceptionally powerful religious experience during a peak moment of the yearly holiday cycle. In this prayer, fatherly connotations of love, family, and responsibility combine with kingly connotations of majesty, law, dominion, and power to provide a nuanced model for thinking about God. At the same time, the loving, respectful, familial emotions that nuance a child's relationship with his father interact with the servitude, awe, and obedience that characterize a king's subjects to direct the religious participant toward a particular understanding of his own relationship to divinity. None of these connotations need be stated in the prayer. They are implicit in the divine images themselves, which inspire a distinctive cosmological perspective based on contextual associations with Jewish culture, religion, family life, and governmental authority.[42] Furthermore, each person uttering the prayer will develop his own variation on these themes based on individual experience, personalizing his participation in this human and divine relationship. The prayer's images are more than poetic pictures. They actively construct the worshippers' experience as they approach and feel received by God.[43]

The kabbalistic texts explored in this book use divine imagery in deliberate, provocative, and insightful ways to achieve a similar effect to the *Avinu Malkenu* prayer, but on a much broader scale. Kabbalistic images construct elaborate symbolic networks that produce a contemplative, and eventually transformative, spirituality. They accomplish this by bringing metaphor's model-making qualities to bear upon their readers, reorganizing the ways in which readers experience and interact with the world around them.[44] When Zohar 3:65a-b describes divinity with the mixed metaphor of a pregnant river that is also a mother nursing children, it is not simply offering equivalent code words for the *sefirah Binah* or generating strange images in response to a transcendent nonverbal state experienced by its authors.[45] It is instead offering a startling juxtaposition specifically designed to promote contemplation and mental reordering for its reader, much as Victor Turner describes the function of strangely juxtaposed figures in liminal rituals.[46] Like Turner's ritual initiate, the Zohar's reader is provoked into a contemplative and transformative internal act that reorganizes his understanding of the universe and his place within it, ultimately affecting his interactions with the world around him. Through engaging with these images, the active reader begins a perceptual journey that may end in becoming a kabbalist himself.

Kabbalistic images are located at the intersection of exegesis, theology, culture, history, and self-understanding, and it is this unique intersection that allows them to become driving forces in religious transformation and revitalization. Progressing from masculine to feminine anthropomorphisms allows the kabbalists to explore new models for relationship between God and humanity. By looking at an individual image and the models it creates, it is possible to gain a more specific understanding of the kabbalists' desired modes of human and divine relationality. The following chapters will demonstrate how the image of God as a nursing mother developed over time, and how this development affected concepts of human and divine interaction by encouraging a holistically integrated understanding of self, God, and world.

Chapters and Topics

In the following pages, I will examine the image of God as a nursing mother from both textual and cultural perspectives. Chapter 1 explores rabbinic texts that include the metaphor of suckling as spiritual transmission, relating them to Jewish cultural innovations such as matrilineal religious transmission and ritual conversion. Although these works do not identify God as a nursing mother, they demonstrate two themes that are critical for the image's later development. The first theme, suckling as a metaphor for transmitting spiritual orientation, is found in stories of the matriarch Sarah, as well as in those surrounding other key Biblical figures such as Moses and Esther. The second theme, suckling mother's milk as a metaphor for experiencing Torah, anticipates converging ideas about spiritual transmission and Torah transmission in later mystical literature. Chronologically, the texts examined in this chapter represent a broad range, spanning the period from the fifth through the twelfth centuries. Reading these diverse works together demonstrates an ongoing fascination with the suckling-as-spiritual-transmission metaphor and a living cultural development of its associated imagery. All texts presented in this chapter are derived from sources known to the Zoharic authorship, anticipating this book's end point, *Sefer ha-Zohar.*[47]

Chapter 2 looks at three influential early kabbalistic works that develop and incorporate imagery associated with the nursing divine: *Sefer ha-Bahir* (*The Book of Brightness*), Isaac the Blind's *Commentary on Sefer Yetzirah* (*The Book of Formation*), and Ezra of Gerona's *Perush le-Shir ha-Shirim* (*Commentary on The Song of Songs*). As a group, these works represent a coherent sequence of kabbalistic development, since Ezra studied with Isaac and also drew upon the Bahir to develop his theological teachings. In addition, these writings contribute to *Sefer ha-Zohar*'s theology, since Ezra's commentary was influential for the Zohar's authors, who would have been familiar with Isaac's work and with the Bahir as well. All of these works were important to the Gerona School of Kabbalah, which emphasized literary production and receiving written knowledge, rather than focusing on the oral tradition of Naḥmanides' contemporary school.[48] This interest in written esoteric knowledge was also typical of Castilian Kabbalah and culminated in the Zohar, a Castilian work.[49] Chapter 2's texts demonstrate the critical process of transferring nursing imagery from the human world to the *sefirot*, where it is used to express both interior divine dynamics and the relationship between God and humanity. While Isaac presents divine suckling imagery in an abstract (though richly nuanced) manner and the Bahir draws connections between milk, spiritual transmission, and the emotions later associated with divine nursing, it is only with Ezra that the image of a breastfeeding divine mother emerges fully embedded in feminine connotations. These texts, while recording the suckling image's literary development, also open theological issues central to the Zohar's presentation of a nursing God by addressing divine interiority's relationship with itself and the application of this relationship to the connections between God and human beings.

Chapter 3 focuses exclusively on divine nursing imagery in the late thirteenth century classic *Sefer ha-Zohar*, exploring the suckling metaphor as it occurs among the *sefirot* and between God and humanity. I have selected this text as the focal point of my book because its group authorship allows it to represent a broad perspective on thirteenth-century kabbalistic thought.[50] In this voluminous work, the ideas and opinions of many different personalities are represented side by side, making the search for nursing images in other late thirteenth-century Spanish authors redundant.[51] The Zohar's role as Kabbalah's most influential text makes understanding its imagery relevant for studies of later kabbalists, while its connection to the Gerona School demonstrates the work's continuity with earlier kabbalistic formulations. However, unlike Kabbalah's earlier nursing images, the Zohar freely associates the breastfeeding divine with both feminine and affective language, weaving the image into a tapestry of clearly structured connotations that provides its reader with a richly textured and deeply coherent model for redefining his relationship with God. In doing so, the Zohar presents this image as a tool for religious revitalization, placing God and humanity in a relationship that allows for a "return to the Whole." This chapter also explores the unusual nursing father image and its connection to the rabbinic Sarah material, a relevant connection since the male in question is none other than Sarah's husband Abraham. Although suckling imagery remains important in later Lurianic Kabbalah, the Zohar marks the chronological stopping point for my presentation of this subject, as later innovations concerning this metaphor belong to their own distinct cultural and historical contexts in which the mothering imagery so richly depicted in the Zohar is no longer of primary importance.[52]

In chapter 4, I present some concluding thoughts about the nursing-mother image and reconsider the role of motherhood in medieval Jewish culture, relating the idea of a divine nursing mother to Jewish family life, perceptions of women as caregivers, and breastfeeding traditions. In connection with this discussion, I explore how divine mothering imagery fits into the context of sexualized kabbalistic images created by exclusively male mystics and engages with some contemporary evaluations of femininity and disempowerment in Kabbalah. This chapter also deals with the relationship between Jewish literature that incorporates the suckling image and Christian theology's presentation of similar motifs, addressing possible forums for interreligious influence and dialogue. Finally, the chapter offers some concluding words on the broad historical context from which early and classical Kabbalah emerge, suggesting reasons for developing a divine image focused so specifically upon relational themes.[53]

CHAPTER 1

BREASTFEEDING AND RELIGIOUS TRANSMISSION IN RABBINIC LITERATURE

> Sarah stood and uncovered herself, and her two breasts were pouring milk like two spouts of water. As it is written: "And she said, Who would have said to Abraham that Sarah would suckle children?" (Genesis 21:7).
> —Pesikta Rabbati 43:4

Introduction

This chapter explores rabbinic texts that use breastfeeding as a metaphor for spiritual transmission. While these works do not identify God as a nursing mother, they contain two themes that are central to the breastfeeding divine's development in later medieval mystical literature. The first theme presents nursing as a metaphor for transmitting spiritual orientation and is found in stories of prominent Biblical figures such as Sarah, Moses, and Esther. Although these texts address different ideological concerns, they are linked by the concept that suckling a mother's (or, as shall be seen, a father's) milk transmits a life-long spiritual disposition. The preferred disposition in these texts is an orientation toward Judaism, holiness, and performing good deeds. The second theme presents suckling mother's milk as a metaphor for learning and experiencing the Torah. This theme is related to the first, since Judaism understands Torah study as an important way to achieve positive and desirable spirituality. The second theme also incorporates descriptions of the Torah as a nursing mother. These feminine Torah associations anticipate the two themes' convergence in kabbalistic literature, where Torah becomes one of *Shekhinah*'s many signifiers.

In developing their suckling imagery, the rabbis present a metaphor comparing two complex actions: the physical act of breastfeeding and the psychological experience of spiritual transmission. Comparing these very different actions allows the rabbis to understand a mysterious interior experience by appealing to an observable, external one. Breastfeeding's characteristics and associations, as understood by the rabbis, provide structure for the inchoate, personalized experience of spirituality, bringing the abstract into relationship with the concrete.[1] The physical and emotional connections between a nursing mother and her child become tools for understanding how religiosity is passed from one person to another, and suckling's intimate, nourishing connotations are read onto spiritual transmission to provide structure for an experience whose motives and sensations would otherwise remain obscure.[2]

Each narrative that presents the suckling metaphor engages breastfeeding's basic associations with nurture and tenderness, while offering text-specific details that further texture the reader's understanding of spirituality.[3] These details begin, but do not end, with choices about who is suckling from whom, and why. A mother who suckles her own children evokes different associations than a wet nurse who suckles for money (or other reasons). A nursing mother has different connotations than a nursing father. A nameless baby directs a reader's attention differently than a young culture hero like Moses or Esther. In this way, both breastfeeding and spiritual transmission accommodate an almost unlimited number of variations on their central themes, fueling individual religious speculation as the reader interprets these variations for himself. Each permutation adds further nuance to the central idea of suckling as spiritual transmission, laying a firm foundation for the nursing mother image's incorporation into later kabbalistic theology.

The following textual excerpts represent a broad time period, ranging from the fifth century *Genesis Rabbah* through the twelfth century *Exodus Rabbah*. Several of the stories exist in variations that cover five hundred years or more. Although these selections are arranged thematically, their dates demonstrate an ongoing fascination with the metaphor of suckling as spiritual transmission and a living cultural interest in its related imagery. The texts included in this chapter do not represent all rabbinic works containing the suckling theme. Instead, they are restricted to works identified as "principal sources" for the Zohar's authors, connecting them to later kabbalistic suckling imagery.[4] All are fully integrated into the rabbinic canon of study and learning, demonstrating that the suckling metaphor is thoroughly embedded in Judaism's foundational literature.

Suckling as Spiritual Transmission of Jewish Identity

In the following texts, the rabbis explore the topic of conversion to Judaism by crafting a story that links converts to Judaism's founding couple, Abraham and Sarah. This story, repeated in several variations, uses the nursing-as-spiritual-transmission metaphor in three ways. It explores the motivations underlying conversion, suggests a "historical" cause for conversion and promotes a positive attitude toward converts. The first version presented, *Pesikta Rabbati* 43:4, is best dated to the sixth or seventh century CE and is the most expansive version of a story found in several parallel texts.[5] These include *Genesis Rabbah* 53:9 from the first half of the fifth century, Babylonian Talmud *Bava Metzia* 87a from the fifth or sixth century, *Pesikta de Rav Kahana* 22:1 (a fifth century text) and *Pirke de Rabbi Eliezer* 52, which dates from the eighth to the ninth centuries.[6] Of these texts, the *Genesis Rabbah* and Talmudic versions seem to provide the main source materials for *Pesikta Rabbati*, which combines and expands the two earlier narratives' themes.

Pesikta Rabbati 43:4:

> And what does it mean, "the happy mother of children" (Psalms 113:9). Rather, at the time that Sarah bore Isaac, the nations of the world were saying, He is the son of a maid-servant and she pretends as if she suckles (*meniqah*) him. At that time he [Abraham] said to her, Sarah, why are you [just] standing [there]?[7] This is not the time for modesty. Rather, stand and uncover (*hifri'ah*) yourself for the sake of sanctification of the name. Sarah stood and uncovered herself, and her two breasts were pouring (*moriqim*) milk like two spouts of water (*zinuqim shel mayim*). As it is written: "And she said, Who would have said (*millel*) to Abraham that Sarah would suckle (*heniqah*) children?" (Genesis 21:7). Rabbi Pinḥas

ha-Cohen ben Ḥama said in the name of Rabbi Ḥilkiah: The stalk of Abraham was dried up, and it was made as a stalk of standing corn (*melilot*)—"Who would have said to Abraham." And the nations of the world were bringing their children to Sarah so that she would suckle them. To fulfill what is said [in scripture]: "Sarah would suckle children." And there were some who were bringing their children in truth so that she would suckle them, and there were some who were bringing their children to investigate. Neither these nor those suffered loss. Rabbi Levi said: Those that came in truth became proselytes (*nitgayeru*).[8] This is as it is said: "Sarah would suckle children." What is "suckle children"? That they were adopted (*she-nitbanu*) into Israel. And those that came to investigate her? Our rabbis said: They were made great in this world by promotion. And all the proselytes in the world, and all the fearers of heaven that are in the world, are from those who suckled from the milk of Sarah. Therefore, "The happy mother of children"—this is Sarah.

Genesis Rabbah 53:9:

"And she said, Who would have said to Abraham that Sarah would suckle children?" (Genesis 21:7). *Would* suckle a child is not written here. Our mother Sarah was extremely modest. Our father Abraham said to her, This is not the time for modesty. Rather, reveal (*gali*) your breasts so that all will know that the Holy One, blessed be He, has begun to do miracles. She revealed her breasts, and they were flowing (*nov'ot*) milk like two springs (*ma'yanot*). And matrons were coming, and they were suckling (*menikot*) their children from her, and they were saying, We are not worthy to suckle our children from the milk of the righteous woman. The rabbis and Rabbi Aḥa [comment on this matter]. The rabbis said: All who came for the sake of heaven were made fearers of heaven. Rabbi Aḥa said: Even those who did not come for the sake of heaven were given power in this world. When they withdrew themselves at Sinai and did not receive the Torah, that power was removed from them.

Babylonian Talmud Bava Metzia 87a:

> "And she said, Who would have said to Abraham that Sarah would suckle children?" (Genesis 21:7). How many children did Sarah suckle? Rabbi Levi said: That day that Abraham weaned his son Isaac, he made a great feast, and all the nations of the world were muttering and saying, Do you see the old man and old woman that brought a foundling from the market and are saying, He is our son? And not only that, but they have made a great feast to uphold their words! What did our father Abraham do? He went and invited all the great people of the generation, and our mother Sarah invited their wives, and each and every one brought her child with her, but did not bring her wet nurse. And a miracle was done for our mother Sarah, and her breasts were opened (*niftehu*) like two springs (*ma'ayanot*) and she suckled (*heniqah*) all of them. And still they were muttering and saying, If Sarah, who is ninety years old, can bear, can Abraham, who is one hundred years old, beget a child? Immediately the countenance of Isaac was changed and he was made to resemble Abraham. They all opened (*pathu*) and said, Abraham begat Isaac.[9]

These stories are most obviously concerned with establishing the newborn Isaac's lineage as a direct descendant of Abraham and Sarah, and each makes its case with a story about miraculous breastfeeding. All three narratives respond to an unusual word choice in Genesis 21:7: "Who would have said to Abraham that Sarah would suckle children?" The word *children* seems inconsistent with Sarah's single son, and the rabbinic interpreters address this scriptural detail by placing her in a broader mothering role that allows her to nurse many children.[10] Although each narrative contains the same miracle, the three works assign different results to Sarah's superabundant milk. The oldest text, *Genesis Rabbah* 53:9, uses the suckling miracle to explain the origins of "fearers of heaven" and those with worldly power. The children Sarah breastfeeds build up fear of heaven in the world by becoming God-fearing people. The matriarch reveals her breasts, the physical miracle is revealed, and an interior miracle (the infants' orientation toward God) takes place. In BT *Bava Metzia* 87a, doubt about Isaac's real parents inspires the miracle, and Sarah's abundant milk resolves her status as a mother. Abraham's paternity is established by a second miraculous occurrence in which Isaac's face changes to resemble his father's more closely. The onlookers' spiritual transformation is reflected by the term *open*, used to describe both the manifestation of Sarah's milk and the former doubters' final, enlightened statement.

Pesikta Rabbati 43:4, the story's latest version, combines the earlier narratives' themes to construct a coherent myth about the origin of converts to Judaism. In this myth, the nations of the world (meaning non-Jews) express doubt about Isaac's lineage and God performs a milk-based miracle for Sarah, proving her fertility. The nations participate in this miracle, and the children of those who come to witness it are transformed into the ancestors of all future proselytes and God fearers, receiving Jewish religiosity through the medium of the matriarch's milk.[11] Not only does Sarah bear a child, she also becomes mother to a large adoptive family, a theme emphasized by Rabbi Levi's assertion that "suckling children" means adopting them into Israel.[12] This miraculous response to doubt engenders generations of belief in God, and spiritual orientation imparted through Sarah's milk does not end with the recipients' lifetimes, but continues for all time. It is as though the nursing children's ancestors bear within them the seeds of Jewish spirituality, which may emerge in their distant descendants.

In these texts, suckling milk serves as a powerful metaphor for transmitting Jewish spiritual lineage. This lineage includes an associative physicality, since all Jews are understood to be Abraham and Sarah's descendants. The conceptual claim underlying the metaphor is that proselytes are linked both spiritually *and* physically to the people of Israel through the medium of Sarah's milk. Rather than being strangers, they become adopted children, naturalized into the community. The term used for this process, *nitbanu*, is related to the verb *banah* (to build), a term included in the *Genesis Rabbah* variant recorded in Theodor and Albeck's critical edition.[13] There, the rabbis are inspired by the similarity between the word "children" (*banim*) and the word "builders" (*bana'in*), saying of Sarah, "she suckles children, she suckles builders." This theme is also found in Babylonian Talmud *Berakhot* 64a, where the sages' students are considered both children and builders of peace through their Torah.[14] Effectively, the children Sarah suckles are built up as her own children, causing them in turn to build up the people Israel. Through a mother's milk, interior religiosity is conveyed, and this religiosity is powerful enough to pass through innumerable generations of proselytes.

The suckling-as-spiritual-transmission metaphor found in these texts is not a purely rabbinic innovation. It can be traced to conceptual precedents in the Hebrew Bible, which contains its own group of metaphors linking life-giving liquid to faith and knowledge. The Bible's tales take place in an environment that is largely desert. In such a setting, water is a life-giving resource necessary to human survival, much as milk is necessary to an infant. Water imagery appears frequently in the Hebrew Bible, where it is often associated with divinity, salvation, and wisdom. Michael Fishbane notes, "open wells repeatedly serve in biblical texts as a metonymy for sustenance and life." His examples include Proverbs 18:4, "The words of a man's mouth are deep water, a flowing (*nove'a*) river, a fount (*meqor*) of wisdom," and Isaiah 12:3, which associates eschatological hope with drawing water "from the springs of salvation," (*mi-ma'ayney ha-yeshu'ah*). He also calls attention to Jeremiah 17:13, in which God is titled the "Hope (*miqveh*) of Israel," and the "Fount of Living Water (*meqor mayim-hayyim*)" pointing out that "The use of the epithet *miqveh* 'hope' adds a rich theological resonance . . . since the word can also mean 'pool of water.'"[15]

The language that Proverbs, Isaiah, and Jeremiah associate with the water-as-wisdom metaphor is strongly reflected in the Sarah story's multiple versions. *Genesis Rabbah* 53:9 explains that Sarah's breasts were flowing (*nov'ot*) milk like two springs (*ma'yanot*), and BT *Bava Metzia* 87a similarly states that Sarah's breasts were opened like two springs (*ma'ayanot*). Although the *Pesikta Rabbati* version employs different terms (spouts of water: *zinuqim shel mayim*), it is a later text, and the earlier linguistic connections are already clear. While none of the Biblical verses linking water with hope and wisdom appear quoted in the context of the Sarah story, linguistic clues and metaphoric similarities indicate an intellectual connection between the ideas. In both cases, spiritual orientation is transmitted through a liquid medium. The rabbinic texts about Sarah's miraculous suckling add definition and nuance to this basic metaphor by changing its medium from water to breast milk and restricting the type of spirituality being transmitted from generalized faith to motivation toward conversion.

In these miracle tales, Sarah represents a human well of living water as she literally flows with milk, her body becoming the locus of a divine event framed within the Biblical genre of the spring. The water-as-wisdom-and-salvation metaphor's expansion into the milk-as-spiritual-transmission metaphor demonstrates how religious imagery mediates the boundary between tradition and innovation, naturalizing new concepts by associating them with previously existing ones. In this case the associations surrounding the Bible's water-as-salvific-wisdom metaphor inspire a milk-as-spiritual-transmission metaphor that partakes of its antecedent while venturing forth in new directions. As water quenches thirst and sustains physical life, so does spiritual hope sustain interior life, an inchoate experience difficult to grasp without metaphor. In the Sarah stories, the psychological event of spiritual transmission is associated with the physical event of breastfeeding. The qualities associated with a mother suckling her child, such as emotional intimacy and physical sustenance, combine with other qualities of motherhood (such as the intimate life processes and early social lessons that a mother teaches her child) and become abstracted.[16] This experience is accessible not only to the mother and her child, but also to those who witness the intimacy and nurture of the suckling act (such as the male rabbis and later kabbalists).

The Sarah story represents a beautiful literary mode for conveying the passage of faith from mother to child, but clearly there are other concerns underlying the text. Clues about these texts' ideological purposes can be found by exploring the narratives' broad historical and cultural contexts. It is possible to suggest at least two motivations for Sarah's miraculous suckling and the proselytes' addition to the Israelite family. One motivation relates to the rabbis' legal innovation of matrilineal religious transmission, which asserts that when parents of differing religions produce offspring, Jewish religious and ethnic identity is transmitted from the mother. The other engages difficulties surrounding the conversion process. The Sarah stories reflect halakhic developments (and presumably social practices) surrounding Judaism's transmission by both birth and conversion, indicating a rabbinic concern with these topics and a concerted long-term effort to naturalize legal innovations about Jewish identity within the rabbinic community.[17] Presenting stories whose images provided holistic understanding of legal decisions was a valuable tool for encouraging the rabbinic community to accept and understand new laws.

Classical rabbinic literature was composed during the upheaval Judaism suffered after the Temple's destruction in 70 CE. In the wake of this loss and of failed rebellions against Rome, the rabbis worked to develop a Judaism that differed in many ways from the version that had dominated the Jewish world while the Temple stood. One of the rabbis' key concerns was self-definition, as they attempted to assert their theology and cultural messages within a particular community. Several scholars have observed that this formative period of Jewish development was spurred by the encounter with Hellenistic culture in the Roman world.[18] Hellenistic culture's broad appeal raised rabbinic concerns both about assimilation and about understanding the developing Jewish community's theological and cultural boundaries.[19] At the same time, emerging Roman legislation made it vitally important to understand who was Jewish and who was not. For example, the *fiscus Judaicus*, a Roman tax on Jews levied in the seventies CE and lasting until approximately the fourth century, made Jewish identity a financial concern, as well as an ideological one.[20]

Judaism's matrilineal transmission seems to have developed during this formative period, and it is an issue clearly addressed in the narratives that ground Isaac's and proselytes' religious identities in their contact with the matriarch Sarah. Shaye Cohen and Martin Goodman both date matrilineal transmission to the middle of the second century CE, while the principle appears for the first time in the *Mishna*, tractate *Qiddushin* 3:12.[21] (Before that time, women were naturalized into their husbands' families, and children followed the male's status.)[22] The reasons behind this development remain unclear.[23] Goodman suggests that it was spurred by the *fiscus Judaicus* requiring more rigorous forms of Jewish self-definition, while Cohen suggests it may have involved the dynamics of rabbinic logic or the developing idea that women could convert to Judaism officially.[24] In any case, the matrilineal principle was eventually embraced by the rabbinic community and is still applied by many Jewish groups today.

The Sarah story, particularly in the *Pesikta Rabbati* version, functions as a narrative explanation of how this matrilineal principle operates on physical and spiritual levels. Judaism is passed from mother to child in cases of mixed marriages, and the medium (at least in this rabbinic tale) is mother's milk. Although the story does not deal with a mixed marriage, it artificially creates a situation in which children have gentile fathers and a Jewish mother figure. The rabbis highlight the idea that spiritual stance is inherited from the mother by employing the metaphor of mother's milk as a medium of spiritual transmission. In *Genesis Rabbah* and *Pesikta Rabbati*, birth mothers' religious beliefs also affect their children, influencing the ultimate outcome of Sarah's spiritual contribution. The children of those women who come in truth become God fearers and proselytes, while the offspring of those who come to investigate receive only worldly good. By metaphorically becoming their spiritual mother through the physical act of nursing, Sarah enables these children to partake of the Israelite lineage, and the suckling metaphor provides a mythic prototype that promotes a recent halakhic ruling.[25]

The other issue addressed in the Sarah texts, and particularly in *Pesikta Rabbati*, is the status of proselytes. By providing an origin myth for converts to Judaism, the text asserts a particular ideological stance in relation to these ambiguous figures. Scholars maintain several different viewpoints about proselytes in the rabbinic period, with key debates centered on the rabbinic attitude toward converts' status and the extent to which an active proselytizing movement existed during the Hellenistic period. For example, Louis Feldman believes that the rabbinic attitude toward converts and proselytism was generally favorable, while incorporating some ambivalence.[26] He cites contrasting texts such as *Tanhuma Lekh Lekha* 6, which states that the proselyte is superior in status to the born Jew because he accepts the Torah without witnessing the revelation at Sinai—and BT *Qiddushin* 70b, in which Rabbi Helbo states that proselytes cause as much injury to the people of Israel as scabs.[27] Shaye Cohen concurs with this perspective, citing synagogue inscriptions that add "the proselyte" to people's names as evidence.[28] The topic's importance to the Jewish community is confirmed by evidence that converts' legal status remained problematic through the Middle Ages.[29]

Further complicating the conversion issue, some scholars believe that a substantial Jewish effort at proselytizing existed under Roman rule, peaking before the third century and continuing under later Christian dominion, while others argue that Jews accepted converts but did not make an active effort to gain them, except in a few cases influenced by contact with early Christian proselytizing.[30] Conversion rituals appear for the first time in rabbinic literature with BT *Yevamot* 47a-b, which gives the framework for a ceremony that was expanded in the post-Talmudic tractate *Gerim* 1:1.[31] Cohen dates this innovation to the second century CE, suggesting that before this turning point conversion was a private, personal, and unstructured matter—rather than a public, formal ritualized one.[32] Assessing an ancient conversion effort's existence is further complicated by a substantial body of Roman legislation against Jewish proselytizing passed during this period.[33] Interpreting this information with regard to rabbinic culture is clearly a difficult process. Yet these studies demonstrate that defining conversion and encouraging appropriate attitudes toward converts were topics of interest to both the Jewish and Roman communities during the Talmudic period—the formative period for the Sarah stories.

Of course, proselytes are not the only ambiguous characters in these stories. Fearers of heaven, known more commonly as God fearers, also bear a direct relationship to the Jewish community through their connection with Sarah.[34] Louis Feldman writes, "The term G-d fearers or sympathizers apparently refers to an 'umbrella group,' embracing many different levels of interest in and commitment to Judaism, ranging from people who supported synagogues financially . . . to people who accepted the Jewish view of G-d in pure or modified form to people who observed certain distinctively Jewish practices, notably the Sabbath."[35] Inscriptions that mention God fearers from Rome, Aphrodisias, Rhodes, Miletus, and Sardis show that the movement probably peaked in the third century CE.[36] This chronology coincides with the conversion ceremony's development and implies a period during which the rabbis were especially eager to distinguish Jews (and Jewish sympathizers) from gentiles.[37]

All of these cultural terms are evident in the *Pesikta Rabbati* text. Both proselytes and God fearers suckle religiosity from Sarah the matriarch, tying them to the Jewish people and integrating the conversion process with the matrilineal principle. This text shows the rabbis addressing cultural concerns by constructing narratives with metaphors that psychologically reinforce their ideologies, representing an attempt to affirm the ambiguous proselytes' and God fearers' religious validity by allowing them to participate in a divine event. The miracle's particular nature binds them to the wellspring of Jewish identity, creating a fictive lineage that allows them access to the Israelite group through adoptive naturalization, which Rabbi Levi describes as suckling's true definition.[38] In essence, this scriptural interpretation of Genesis 21:7 creates a mythological justification for those who otherwise inexplicably choose to become Jews, as well as advocating a particular attitude toward them. In explaining these converts' religious choice through a powerful, culturally relevant metaphor, the rabbis are strongly suggesting that "native" Jews treat proselytes as family.[39]

It is true that these cultural polemics are veiled in the text, and that it is not possible to draw concrete links between the rabbinic matrilineal ruling, the conversion process, and the miracle stories about Sarah. However, the Sarah texts do deal explicitly with issues of motherhood, Jewish lineage, God fearers, and the origin of proselytes in innovative ways, and it seems likely that contemporary cultural concerns helped to inspire the metaphor of mother's milk as a fountain of Jewish spirituality. These texts deal with identity issues that were being revised, defined, and explicated during the rabbinic period, particularly around the time of the second and third centuries CE, but extending to the fifth century and beyond. Such identity issues remained topics of comment and controversy through the Middle Ages, and continue to be debated topics within the Jewish community today. Although the *Pesikta Rabbati* text can be dated safely only to the sixth or seventh centuries, the *Genesis Rabbah* version from the fifth century and the Babylonian Talmud version from the fifth or sixth century indicate that this issue was being addressed at the height of the classical rabbinic period and suggests these texts likely had an earlier lineage. For example, the Rabbi Levi cited in the *Pesikta Rabbati* story was a Palestinian *Amora* from the third century CE, placing him squarely within these cultural concerns' most relevant time frame.[40]

Pesikta Rabbati 43:4 contains two further points of interest that strengthen the text's association with conversion issues. First, the ancient rabbis considered Abraham and Sarah to be prototypic proselytizers, bearing a special relationship to converts because of their own original "conversions" to Judaism. *Genesis Rabbah* 39:14, *Song of Songs Rabbah* 1:22, and *Numbers Rabbah* 14:11 all contain texts that describe the couple making proselytes. These texts are based on Genesis 12:5, in which Abraham and Sarah are said to have "made souls in Haran." The rabbis understand the term *souls* to mean "proselytes," perceiving the converts as somehow ensouled by the event.[41] Second, the text reflects the theory that women, more than men, were attracted to Judaism as converts and God fearers during the Roman period.[42] This cultural factor may be represented in the *Pesikta Rabbati* story, which features women acknowledging the Jewish God's holiness through a deferred relationship with Sarah.

Suckling as Spiritual Transmission of Holiness, Commandments, and Good Deeds

The following texts continue to develop the suckling-as-spiritual-transmission motif. While the Sarah stories present breastfeeding as a way to transmit spiritual identity at the community level, these works suggest that nursing shapes individual character, placing emphasis on breastfeeding's relationship to personal religious identity. Here, receiving physical nourishment from an appropriate source predisposes a child to be holy and to perform the commandments and good deeds. The identity of those who give and receive suckling becomes critically important, as a mother's social role in shaping her child's character is equated with the nursing act. These texts provide cultural context for the Sarah stories, since they imply a perceived rabbinic connection between a mother's physically nurturing role and her role as a child's earliest educator in spiritual behavior.

Exodus Rabbah 1:25:

> "And his sister said to Pharaoh's daughter, [Shall I go and call for you a wet-nurse woman of the Hebrews, and she will suckle the child for you?]" (Exodus 2:7). Why did Miriam say "of the Hebrews?" Is it [because] it was forbidden for Moses to suckle (*linoq*) from the milk of a gentile? Not so, for we have learned, "A daughter of Israel shall not suckle (*taniq*) the child of a gentile woman, but a gentile woman may suckle a child of Israel in her domain."[43] So, why did she say thusly? Because she took Moses around to all the Egyptian women to suckle him, and he rejected (*u-fasal*) all of them. And why did he reject them? The Holy One, blessed be He, said, The mouth that in the future shall speak with me, shall it suckle an unclean (*tame'*) thing? It corresponds to what is written: "To whom shall he teach knowledge, [and who shall he make understand tradition? Those who are weaned from milk, removed from the breasts"] (Isaiah 28:9). To whom shall one teach knowledge?

To "those who are weaned from milk," etc. Another thing: Why did he reject their breasts? The Holy One, blessed be He, said, This one, who in the future shall speak with me, shall the Egyptian women be saying in the future, This one who speaks with the *Shekhinah*—I suckled him![44]

This text tells a story in which a wet nurse is sought for the infant Moses after Pharaoh's daughter rescues him from the river. The tale intervenes in the Biblical narrative found in Exodus 2:6–9, which tells how Moses received his own Hebrew mother as a wet nurse. Although the Biblical text seems straightforward, the rabbinic interpreters assign additional significance to Moses' nursing from his own mother, depicting the infant actively rejecting Egyptian women available for the task. While *Exodus Rabbah* 1:25 is a medieval text that can be dated to the tenth or twelfth century, the story also exists in an earlier version. Babylonian Talmud *Sotah* 12b, a product of the late fifth or early sixth century, contains another presentation of the same narrative. The two texts are extremely similar, with most differences falling into the later text's elaboration on the former.[45] The story's presence in the Talmud locates it in close chronological proximity to the Sarah story's first written appearances, a connection that suggests the nursing-as-spiritual-transmission theme either remained compelling from the fifth century through the Middle Ages or reemerged into relevance during the time of the earliest kabbalists. While all the texts cited in this chapter provide source material for the Zohar, this work bears an especially close link to the kabbalists, since the first known quotations of *Exodus Rabbah* occur in writings by Azriel of Gerona and Naḥmanides, influential thirteenth-century kabbalists who preceded the Zohar's composition.[46]

Exodus Rabbah 1:25's terminology deserves some explanation. The term *u-fasal*, although translated as "and he rejected" for narrative integrity, connotes a declaration that something is ritually unfit. The infant Moses does not simply reject the Egyptians' breasts as an unknowing child. Instead, he makes a ritual judgment about these women that actually runs counter to an established halakhic ruling. As the passage notes, gentiles *are* allowed to nurse Israelite children under some circumstances. The passage's end discloses the source of young Moses' rejection. It seems that God has inspired the infant to reject the Egyptians' breasts because they threaten special ritual uncleanness for a special prophet. God Himself provides an explanation, asserting that a mouth that suckled from an unclean source should not speak with Him. God also curtails any opportunities for arrogance on the Egyptian women's part, reinforcing Moses' Israelite identity.

The implication here, as in the Sarah story, is that the milk an infant suckles transmits spiritual influence. In this case, milk metaphorically carries personal spiritual status and an individual orientation toward holiness. Suckling from an Egyptian woman would transmit uncleanness to the young prophet, rendering him unfit for his intimate future relationship with the divine. The text also emphasizes young Moses' relationship to his mother's personal spirituality, in which he participates through her milk. In doing so, it engages the matrilineal principle, because it accentuates the significance of Moses suckling his own Jewish mother's milk rather than that of non-Jewish women. Departing from the Sarah stories' halakhic connections, this work presents suckling appropriate spiritual transmission as a desirable end in itself, rather than as a narrative underpinning for a legal concept. While the Sarah story reinforces halakhic rulings on matrilineal Jewish transmission, the Moses narrative overrides a Mishnaic legal principle in its zeal for a suitable milk source. The next text makes a similar point.

Genesis Rabbah 30:8:

> It is curious, that Mordekhai fed and sustained (*zan u-mefarnes*)! Rabbi Yudan said: Once he went around to all of the wet nurses and did not find one for Esther. Forthwith, he suckled her [himself] (*meniqah ve-haya meniqah hu'*). Rabbi Berekhya and Rabbi Abbahu [said] in the name of Rabbi Eliezer: Milk came to him and he suckled her.[47]

In this text, the rabbis interpret the verb *haya* (literally, "he was") in Genesis 6:9 as an act of feeding and sustaining, extending this interpretation to several characters whose narratives include the verb. After discussing Noah, Joseph, and Job,—all of whose feeding and sustaining involve solid food—the text turns to Mordekhai and expresses surprise at his inclusion in the list. Rather than serving food, Mordekhai produces milk and breastfeeds the infant Esther after he fails to find an appropriate wet nurse. Although the narrative implies that women are available for this feminine task, none of them seem adequate for the young heroine. The story's masculine nursing is unusual, and in its continuation, the congregation ridicules Rabbi Abbahu for teaching this interpretation in public. He defends himself with BT *Shabbat* 53b, in which Rabbi Shimon ben Elazar rules, "The milk of a male is clean."[48]

The motivation for this story, which is not explicitly stated in the text, seems to be that Esther 2:7 reads, "And he [Mordekhai] was a nursing father (*omen*) to Hadassah." The curious term *omen* is also applied to Moses in Numbers 11:12, where the prophet complains to God about the Israelites' childish, petulant behavior, "Did I conceive all of this people, did I bear it, that you should say to me, carry it in your bosom as the nursing father (*ha-'omen*) carries the suckling child (*ha-yoneq*)?" To the rabbis, the term *omen* (nursing father) implies that Mordekhai actually did feed and sustain Esther from his own body. However, it is worth noting that not all midrashic texts make this gender-defying interpretive leap. *Midrash on Psalms* 22:23, a text of uncertain dating containing both early and late materials, interprets Esther 2:7 differently. In this work, Mordekhai's wife suckles Esther, allowing him the role of nursing father in a metonymic sense that reads his wife as an extension of himself.[49]

The rabbis in this text are making a point other than the congregational humor inspired by their unusual teaching.[50] Their reasoning runs roughly parallel to that of *Exodus Rabbah* 1:25 and chronologically parallels the version of that story found in BT *Sotah* 12b. Although the wet nurses to whom Mordekhai takes Esther are not specifically described as unclean, clearly they are unsuitable in some way. Mordekhai, an eminently righteous individual, is the only one whose spirituality is pure enough for the young Esther (a future religious heroine, as Moses is a future prophet), and so the only one whose milk is an acceptable source of nourishment for her. The matrilineal message is diverted to explain a confusing Biblical verse, but the principal metaphor of spiritual transmission via suckling remains securely in place. In fact, the strength of the underlying suckling-as-spiritual-transmission metaphor is maintained even in a case where the metaphor overrides normative rabbinic gender roles by positing a nursing father. This male suckling theme is also found in certain Zoharic passages and so is more significant than the bizarre aside it may seem at first glance.

Genesis Rabbah 39:3

"And the Lord said to Abram, [Go forth from your land, and from your kindred, and from the house of your father to the land that I will show you"] (Genesis 12:1). Rabbi Berekhya opened: "We have a little sister and she has no breasts. [What will we do for our sister on the day that she is spoken for?"] (Song 8:8). "We have a little sister,"—this is Abraham, who united all who came into the world.[51] Bar Kappara said: Like one who sews the tear. "Little,"—who while he was little was saving up commandments and good deeds. "And she has no breasts,"—no breasts suckled him in commandments or good deeds (*loʿ heniquhu loʿ l-mitzvot u-maʿasim tovim*).

This textual excerpt is embedded in a series of rabbinic interpretations that use Song of Songs 8 to enumerate Abraham's good deeds. The quoted portion comments on Abraham's greatness by explaining that even without suckling righteousness from a suitable source, he nonetheless achieved it. This interpretation alters Song 8:8's literal meaning; instead of a prepubescent girl who has not yet developed breasts, Abraham is compared to a girl-child with no righteous person to nurse her. Here, the suckling-as-spiritual-transmission metaphor is so deeply implicit that it is used as a counterexample, representing a benefit the young Abraham did not possess. The text is rooted in the idea that a mother transmits religious observance to her child by breastfeeding, implying an underlying cultural assumption about the close relationship between a mother's nurturing and teaching roles. This work is contemporary with one of the Sarah story's earliest versions, *Genesis Rabbah* 53:9, and seems to provide a cultural underpinning for the miraculous mothering in that story. If a mother regularly suckles her child in commandments and good deeds, it is not extravagant to assume that she suckles her child in Jewish status as well. The text does not say that Abraham lacked nourishment as a child, nor does it provide a story of his miraculous milk-free survival. Instead, it explains that he lacked a mother with proper spiritual orientation. As the first Jew (in the rabbis' understanding) it was impossible for him to receive the beneficial care of a Jewish mother.[52] This tale underscores his uniquely righteous character.

The expression "suckled in commandments and good deeds" is found in at least one other rabbinic passage from a relatively early source. *Song of Songs Rabbah* (mid-sixth century) also uses this terminology to explicate Song 8:8. In this work, Rabbi Yoḥanan associates

Song 8:8's little sister with the city of Sodom by connecting the verse with Ezekiel 16:46: "And your little sister who dwells at your right hand is Sodom and her daughters."

Song of Songs Rabbah on Song 8:8:

> Rabbi Yohanan interpreted the verse as [referring to] Sodom and Israel: "We have a little sister" (Song 8:8). As it is written: "And your big sister is Samaria [. . . and your little sister who dwells at your right hand is Sodom and her daughters"] (Ezekiel 16:46). "And she has no breasts" (Song 8:8). For she did not suckle commandments or good deeds (she-loʿ heniqah mitzvot u-maʿasim tovim).

These two texts demonstrate a rabbinic cultural assumption that mothers (and wet nurses) impart spiritual orientation to children during breastfeeding. This assumption arises because the rabbis associate breastfeeding with the cultural education a child receives during its formative years, placing great importance on the character of the woman entrusted with this early education. Rabbi Yohanan's teaching provides a cautionary statement about the wickedness that can intervene in people's developmental processes when they lack access to a proper caregiver, emphasizing the importance of a child's earliest spiritual influence. Connecting the physical act of suckling with the interior process of religious identity's formation inspires the suckling-as-spiritual-transmission metaphor.

Being suckled in commandments and good deeds may seem like an odd idea, but it is not really an alien concept for English speakers. Consider the expression, "It was mother's milk to me." There, mother's milk refers to an idea or activity that has been part of a person's life from an early age, eventually becoming second nature to that person and an important part of that individual's identity. The English language contains several expressions that associate knowledge and ideas with nourishment, giving rise to a metaphoric genre closely related to the rabbis' suckling image. English speakers refer to "swallowing" claims and "digesting" ideas, while describing puzzling matters as "food for thought."[53] These expressions illustrate that the ancient rabbis' suckling metaphor may be closer to modern thinking than it first appears.[54]

Suckling as Spiritual Transmission: Suckling Blessings

Pesikta Rabbati 7:9:

> [The verse], "All of you is beautiful, my beloved, [and there is no blemish in you"] (Song 4:7), speaks of the tribes. And if you will say: Behold, their father Jacob blessed the tribes, but chided Reuben and Shimon and Levi, and [so] how can you say [that this verse applies to them]? Rabbi Eleazar said: Although he blessed the latter tribes and chided the first, rather he returned and blessed them. As it is written: "All of these are the twelve tribes of Israel [and this is what their father spoke to them. And he blessed them. Each according to his blessing, he blessed them"] (Genesis 49:28). What is it: "And this is what their father spoke to them. And he blessed them?" Rabbi Eleazar said: He made them suckle one from another.

This interesting text, the final example for the suckling as spiritual transmission theme, exists in two forms. One is found in *Pesikta Rabbati* 7:9, dating to the sixth or seventh century and contemporary with the Sarah story found in that text, and the other occurs in *Numbers Rabbah* 13:8, placing it in the twelfth century.[55] The two versions are extremely similar, and do not contain variants on any of the story's core ideas. In both cases, the narrative provides evidence of a suckling-as-spiritual-transmission metaphor that is structured without feminine connotations. No mother figure is present here, and the passage also lacks reference to milk or breasts. Instead, suckling functions as a more generalized mode of spiritual transmission. Although the suckled spirituality transmitted in this text is a father's blessing, which hints at a connection to parental nurture, the tribal ancestors nurse spiritual inheritance from each other as a closed, organic system. Suckling, which has textual precedents associating it with religious transmission, is presented simply as the means by which spiritual flow is communicated from person to person. Blessings appear as religious forces transmitted via suckling, whether or not there is a mother figure present to provide milk.[56]

This text's use of suckling is particularly interesting because it anticipates kabbalistic literature's theology of suckling divine overflow, in which God's energy and blessings are passed among the divine aspects and between God and humanity in a similarly structured system. Furthermore, *Numbers Rabbah*, in which this narrative also appears, was a foundational source for early Kabbalah. Some of the first works to cite it were composed by mid-thirteenth-century Geronese kabbalists like Rabbi Ezra, whose theology will be further explored in the following chapter.[57] This passage implies that the Israelite tribal ancestors exist as an organic system in which each can derive blessings from the other. The *sefirot* are described similarly in kabbalistic writings, making this text an exciting link to mystical literature's suckling theology.

Suckling as Torah Transmission

Babylonian Talmud Eruvin 54b:

> Rabbi Samuel bar Naḥmani said: Why is it written, "A loving doe and a graceful mountain goat, [her breasts will satisfy you at all times, you will always be infatuated with her love" (Proverbs 5:19). Why are the words of Torah compared to a doe? To tell you that as a doe has a narrow womb and is loved by her lover each and every time as she was the first time, so the words of Torah are loved by those who study them each and every time as they were the first time. "And a graceful mountain goat?" Because She [the Torah] bestows grace on those who study Her. "Her breasts will satisfy you (*yeravukha*) at all times." Why are the words of Torah compared to a breast? As with this breast, that every time the child touches it he finds milk in it, so it is with the words of Torah. Every time that a man reasons in them, he finds pleasure (*t'am*) in them.

This text is part of a lengthier passage dealing with Torah transmission and interpretation. I would like to pass over this excerpt's very interesting erotic connotations and focus on its latter portion, in which the words of Torah are compared to a female breast. At first glance, the text appears to draw a simple analogy between the pleasurable physical nourishment a nursing infant receives from its mother and the pleasurable spiritual nourishment a person receives from the Torah. However, this analogy becomes more interesting when considering the suckling-as-spiritual-transmission metaphor's prevalence in other rabbinic teachings. Here, spiritual transmission occurs with the Torah standing in a mother's place and providing a direct link to religious values through the "milk" of its teachings. The Torah is presented as a metaphorical mother figure providing spiritual sustenance to the scholar.

In a male-centered culture such as the rabbis', there came a point at which a physical mother, who was generally excluded from Torah learning, could no longer remain the primary conveyor of her child's religious training.[58] To maintain the idea of spiritual nurturance, an alternate figure had to take her place, and the rabbis supplied the Torah as a metaphorical mother who filled this role.[59] The Torah's female characteristics, exemplified in this verse, associate it with a biological mother and contribute to the coexistent metaphor of suckling as religious transmission. Characteristics associated with the mother-child relationship, such as nurturance, nourishment, and pleasure in a mother's love are applied to the Torah. In that context, they restructure the idea of the Torah itself, transforming it into a loving, nurturing female figure that imparts knowledge via suckling.

A closer look at Proverbs 5:19's vocabulary can help to illuminate the reasoning underlying the rabbis' Torah transformation. The word *t'am* can mean pleasure, but it can also mean taste, examine, and experience, as well as reason, sense, and argument. By drawing on *t'am*'s connotations of eroticism, consumption, and intellectualism, the rabbinic interpreters construct a complex pun emphasizing the Torah as a source of intimate spiritual and intellectual nourishment. The term *yeravukha* derives from the verb *ravah* (to satisfy), and bears connotations of liquid satisfaction, such as drinking one's fill and being sated, drenched or drunk. The erotic verse Proverbs 5:19's powerful explication reflects the rabbis' nuanced understanding of Biblical vocabulary. The Torah-as-nursing-mother motif also becomes important in kabbalistic literature, where Torah is associated with the *Shekhinah* and incorporated into the system of divine life. In the mystical context, Torah functions both as an erotic figure and as a nurturing figure, a development this Talmudic teaching anticipates.[60]

Exodus Rabbah 30:9:

> Another thing: "He tells his words to Jacob, [his rules and laws to Israel. He did not do so for any other nation and they do not know laws– Halleluyah"] (Psalms 147:19–20). Rabbi

Abbahu said in the name of Rabbi Yosi bar Rabbi Ḥanina: A
parable– to what may the matter be compared? To a king who
had a garden, and he planted all kinds of trees in it. And none
entered into it except him who was its guard. When his sons
came to maturity, he said to them, My sons, I have guarded
this garden and have not allowed (*hinaḥti*) a man to enter into
it. You will guard it in the way that I have guarded it. Thus
said God to Israel: Before I created this world, I established
the Torah. As it is said: "And I was beside him [as a] suckling
child (*amon*)" (Proverbs 8:30). What is *amon*? [It is] *omen*. As
it is said, "As the nursing father (*ha-'omen*) carries the suckling
child (*ha-yoneq*)" (Numbers 11:12). I did not give it to one of
those who serve the stars, but rather to Israel. For when Israel
stood and said, "All that God has spoken we will do and we
will obey" (Exodus 24:7), immediately he gave it to them.[61]
Thus, "He tells his words to Jacob, his rules and laws to Israel.
He did not do so for any other nation" (Psalms 147:19–20).
But rather [He gave them] to Jacob, whom he chose from all
of those who serve the stars, to whom he gave only a few. He
gave Adam six commandments, He added one to Noah, to
Abraham eight, to Jacob nine, but to Israel he gave all.

This text, as mentioned above, dates to the tenth through the twelfth
centuries and has important connections to the kabbalistic circle at
Gerona. The critical portion is the Torah's characterization as either an
infant who suckles divine energy from God before the Creation or as
a nursing father breastfeeding divine knowledge and commandments
to the people of Israel. In this passage, the Torah is both a receiver of
divine immanence who suckles *from* God and a transmitter of divine
learning who nurses immanence *to* the people of Israel. The teaching's
ambiguity is the source of its powerful message. The terms *amon* and
omen play on each other, creating dual images based on the suckling
metaphor. God nurses an infant Torah, while the Torah nurses the people of Israel.[62] As the garden rewards the king's sons with fruit for the
care it is given, so the Torah rewards those who care for it, and are cared
for by it, with knowledge.

The text's imagery allows suckling's associations to restructure the
Torah as both nurtured and nurturer. This sophisticated use of the
suckling metaphor alters humanity's relationship with the transcendent—transforming an intellectual act into an emotionally charged

relationship based on loving, nurturing communication. Each idea augments the other, with the Torah presented as a locus both of intellect and of intimate spiritual nourishment. The ambiguity of who is suckling from whom in this text also anticipates a kabbalistic development on the suckling-as-spiritual-transmission metaphor, since the kabbalists use "suckling" to describe both the process by which the *sefirot* receive divine overflow from each other and humanity's reception of divine blessings. *Exodus Rabbah* 30:9 anticipates this kabbalistic innovation by showing how suckling imagery can apply to both intra-divine spiritual transmission and to spiritual transmission between God and human beings. Although the Torah is not considered part of the sefirotic system in this text, the idea of the Torah as a suckling entity deriving nourishment directly from God and relaying it to humanity anticipates kabbalistic theology.

Conclusion

This chapter has presented suckling imagery's association with religious transmission in a consistent stream of rabbinic literature. In these texts, religious transmission is presented as a communal reception of spiritual lineage, an individual reception of spiritual character, and an intellectual reception of Torah learning. By developing the suckling metaphor, rabbis of the fifth century and later were able to address cultural questions about Judaism's transmission and to include proselytes and God fearers into their communities. Gentle mothering imagery was particularly well suited to dealing with these social issues, since lack of a Jewish lineage for converts produced social ambiguities, and even antagonisms.

As time progressed, later kabbalistic theologians found the suckling metaphor and its web of connotations productive for expressing their own interests and intellectual priorities. By transforming the metaphor's central relationship from one that takes place on an earthly plane between two humans (or between a human and a sacred text) into one that takes place on a transcendent level, incorporating both divinity's *sefirot* and humanity, the kabbalists developed new tools for understanding their relationship with God.[63] The idea of suckling as a profoundly nurturing form of religious transmission is eloquently embellished in writings such as Ezra of Gerona's *Commentary on the Song of Songs* and *Sefer ha-Zohar*.[64]

CHAPTER 2

SUCKLING THE DIVINE OVERFLOW
IN EARLY KABBALAH

"Suckling at my mother's breasts" (Song of Songs 8:1). And you will receive suckling from the place of my suckling, [from this place] which is the spirit of the living God.
  —Rabbi Ezra of Gerona's Commentary on the Song of Songs 8:1[1]

This chapter looks at three kabbalistic texts from the late twelfth through the early thirteenth centuries. In these works, the image of God as a nursing mother takes shape as part of an emerging mystical theology. As in the previous chapter's rabbinic literature, the texts apply suckling imagery to the process of spiritual transmission. The early kabbalists, however, divert the metaphor from its human context and instead apply it to the *sefirot*, the kabbalistic divine gradations that express God's inner life. Rather than images of a child suckling spirituality from its mother or a man suckling knowledge from the Torah, in Kabbalah the suckling metaphor describes God's flow of life-giving energy through the sefirotic system and into the human world. In this context, the suckling-as-spiritual-transmission metaphor no longer emphasizes physical, spiritual, and intellectual lineage. Instead, breast-feeding's connotations of nurture, sustenance, and dependence express sefirotic intimacy and humanity's close connection to the divine.

The texts presented in this chapter—Isaac the Blind's *Commentary on Sefer Yetzirah*, the early kabbalistic volume *Sefer ha-Bahir*, and Ezra of Gerona's *Commentary on the Song of Songs*—reveal exegetical dynamics and theological concerns that prefigure *Sefer ha-Zohar*'s emotionally

39

rich breastfeeding imagery.[2] The nursing divine does not emerge fully in these texts. In fact, it is only with the latest work, Ezra of Gerona's kabbalistic Song of Songs interpretation, that feminine imagery is clearly linked to the suckling metaphor. Isaac the Blind, who taught Ezra, uses suckling in an abstract, though richly nuanced, manner. The earliest of these works, Sefer ha-Bahir, does not contain divine nursing imagery at all. Instead, it applies milk imagery to Torah transmission and emotions later associated with spiritual suckling. Despite the image's incomplete presentation in these texts, they bridge the gap between rabbinic literature's human suckling imagery and the Zohar's divine breastfeeding by opening thematic issues central to the nursing mother's later use as a relational model for thinking about God.

Two thematic developments set the stage for this transition. The first, evident in Isaac the Blind and Ezra of Gerona's work, reconfigures the suckling metaphor as a way of explaining the sefirotic system's complex, interdependent nature and its relationship to humanity. Connected by the divine overflow (often called shefa'), each sefirah receives God's energy from those above and all are bound together by partaking in this divine life process. Human beings are also connected to this system, receiving the overflow from God as it passes through the sefirot and into the human world. Nursing imagery helps to define the sefirotic and human relationships as nurturing, sustaining, and interdependent. The second thematic development is suckling's association with the affective language that provides nuance for this divine relational model. Suckling's positive emotional attributes are not fully developed in these works, but are clearly implied in both Sefer ha-Bahir and Ezra of Gerona's Commentary.

Although these writings allow an understanding of the exegetical and poetic processes that contribute to the Zohar's image of God as a nursing mother, a full discussion of the image's cultural context will be deferred to chapter 4, after the weight of textual evidence has been presented. Determining breastfeeding's social, intellectual, and emotional implications for twelfth and thirteenth-century Jews helps to further define the relationship between God and humanity that these texts encourage. The works in this chapter cannot be used to fill cultural space; they are obscure even to themselves. They can, however, provide a view of the thinking that underlies Kabbalah's nursing mother image, pointing toward its later development.

Isaac the Blind's Spiritual Suckling

Rabbi Isaac the Blind (ca 1165–ca 1235) was one of the most influential Provençal mystics, and his teachings provide some of the earliest kabbalistic sources available.[3] He was the first known kabbalist to use suckling imagery as a way to clarify the relationship between God and human beings. A powerfully innovative theologian, Isaac emerged in the context of a Provence that served as a focal point both for European cultural trends (including troubadour poetry, courtly love, philosophical speculation, and the Church's war against heresy) and for Jewish intellectual production.[4] His difficult writings are directed toward an esoteric audience, and his teachings influence one of the major kabbalistic groups of the mid-thirteenth century; the Geronese group centered around his students Ezra and Azriel.[5]

Commentary on Sefer Yetzirah is one of the few extant works attributed to Isaac himself, although his theology can also be inferred from his students' writings.[6] The Commentary interprets an esoteric work of uncertain provenance dating to some time between the first and the ninth centuries.[7] In spite of its obscure origins, *Sefer Yetzirah* (*The Book of Formation*) was enormously influential for the Jewish intellectual community. In commenting on this work, Isaac joined a group of prestigious Jewish literary figures that included Sa'adya Ga'on, Dunash ibn Tamim, Shabbetai ben Abraham Donnolo, Judah ben Barzillai, Yehudah Halevi, and Eleazar of Worms. *Sefer Yetzirah*'s focus on understanding God through the creative power of Hebrew letters and numbers made it an especially appealing text for the emerging kabbalistic community. It is also the source text for the kabbalistic term *sefirot*, although it applies the word to numerical qualities rather than to Kabbalah's divine aspects.[8]

Isaac's theology describes a holistic cosmology in which everything is essentially linked to everything else.[9] He is particularly concerned with understanding divine Wisdom as represented by the second *sefirah*, *Ḥokhmah*, and proposes that each of creation's various levels (including the sefirotic and the human worlds) are linked in communication with the "roots of all being," which he often locates within *Ḥokhmah*.[10] Connection between creation's levels depends upon a flowing divine substance, left largely undefined in Isaac's writing. This substance passes from the highest emanated beings (such as the *sefirot*) who continuously receive the divine flow, down to the lowest beings of the created world, who receive the enlivening substance discontinuously.[11] It is this aspect of Isaac's thinking that leads him to develop a unique reapplication of the earlier rabbis' suckling-as-spiritual-transmission metaphor. For Isaac, suckling becomes a way to describe all of creation's interdependence and unity. Although he avoids structuring the suckling metaphor with feminine and fluid imagery, his usage is a necessary predecessor to later Kabbalah's nursing divine. The following passages from Isaac's Commentary demonstrate how he applies the suckling metaphor to divine spiritual dynamics, shifting suckling imagery's focus from rabbinic literature's human context to the interactions between God's interior life processes and the created world. Doing so, he constructs a model of divine and human relationality that emphasizes humanity's utter dependence on God's continuing flow of life.

Commentary on Sefer Yetzirah, Chapter 1:

> And the paths, they are the Mothers (*imot*) of the ways, for the path is the mother of the way (*em ha-derekh*), and the way is a generality and a principle, for the ways disperse, and separate, and extend from there.[12] And the paths of the wonders are like cavities that are within the tree's core, and *Ḥokhmah* is the root. And they are interior and subtle beings (*havayot*) [that] no created being (*briyah*) is able to contemplate (*lehitbonen*), except he who suckles (*hayoneq*) from it. For it is a way of contemplation by way of his suckling (*yeniqto*), and not by way of knowledge (*yediy'ah*).[13]

In this passage, Isaac describes the sefirotic system's inner workings and the flow of divine life among God's aspects. He paints a literary picture of pathways along which divine energy streams, branching and extending from the sefirotic world until they come into contact with the created world beneath them. While the passage's imagery is effusive, mixed metaphors ensure that many of its details remain obscure upon first examination. Human mother imagery blurs into a topographical description of pathways, which then shifts into vegetative tree-imagery, closing with a created being that suckles from the entire system. The exegetical motive behind this teaching is a reinterpretation of *Sefer Yetzirah* 1:1's thirty-two paths of Wisdom. While Yetzirah's *Ḥokhmah* represents divine Wisdom's mysteries, Isaac updates the ancient text by associating the term with Kabbalah's second *sefirah* (also called *Ḥokhmah*). Divine Wisdom is given a meaning beyond its original sense and extended to include the *sefirah* that Isaac considers divine overflow's source. Wisdom's thirty-two paths, which in *Sefer Yetzirah* refer to the twenty-two letters of the Hebrew alphabet plus the first ten numbers, become the paths that the divine substance travels.[14] *Ḥokhmah* becomes a wellspring of divine life, which flows along "paths" and subdivides into "ways" that bear it throughout creation, linking the "interior and subtle beings," (presumably the *sefirot* or the even the paths themselves) to the created being who stands in a direct and receptive contemplative relationship with the flow of Wisdom. This relationship is characterized by suckling, rather than by knowledge.

However, Isaac's suckling is complex and ambiguous. Suckling's giver and receiver are not clearly identified, and suckling itself is defined as a contemplative act, functioning as an alternative to receiving knowledge. In order to understand Isaac's suckling theology, it is necessary to seek more specific definitions for his difficult terminology, particularly with regard to the Mothers, the created being, and the suckling experience. Although the phrase *mother of the way* can refer to a crossroads, providing an appropriate reference for Isaac's subdividing paths and ways, the term *mothers* is extremely important in *Sefer Yetzirah*, referring to the letters *alef, mem,* and *shin*; the "three Mothers" of the alphabet. These Mothers are complex figures, associated with the elements air, water, and fire—as well as with various human body parts and the seasons of the year.[15] Descriptions of the Mothers occur in Yetzirah 1:2, 2:1, 3:1–6, and 6:1–2, while terminology of Mothers, Fathers, and Generations is found throughout the text.[16] This focus on the word *mother* in Isaac's source text may have inspired the suckling imagery he develops for divine energy's flow into creation. Mothers, of course, are associated with life-giving nurture and breastfeeding, and these textual resonances would have been available to Isaac and his readers. While this passage's Mothers do not offer suckling directly to the created being, they create a context from which suckling imagery naturally flows.

The created being's origins and identity are more difficult to understand. Isaac seems to use "created being" to refer to an entity that participates in an order of existence distinct from the unified and interdependent sefirotic world. This reading is reinforced by Isaac's use of *havayot* (beings) for participants in the sefirotic world and *briyah* (created being) for the suckling entity who receives divine overflow from them. *Havayot* bears nuances of life and existence, emphasizing this term's attachment to the *sefirot*, which represent aspects and extensions of the living God. *Briyah*, on the other hand, implies a willful creative act, and this created being is further defined by the abilities Isaac grants it. It is capable of contemplation (*lehitbonen*), a term that kabbalistic texts frequently associate with meditative practices. The being is also able to acquire knowledge through its contemplation and furthermore to participate in contemplative options that include both a way of knowledge and a way of suckling. For these reasons, the created being can be identified as the human kabbalist who wishes to enter into a particular relationship with the sefirotic world and its divine overflow.

Isaac's text provides a guide for receiving this flow, explaining that such reception is connected to "suckling," rather than to intellection. Suckling's specific characteristics are not clearly explained or characterized in the passage, leaving the metaphor open to a wide variety of connotations and interpretations. As noted in the last chapter, suckling (*yeniqah*) can refer both to human breastfeeding and to plants drawing nourishment from the earth. Neither meaning is dominant, so context is the surest way to determine which application is meant.[17] Since Isaac's dense imagery incorporates both of these associations, it is difficult to determine which meaning is primary, just as it is difficult to determine whether the created being suckles from the *sefirot* or from the paths connecting them. Both meanings are brought into play for the reader, defining suckling as a wordless, hidden, and intuitive relationship that transcends knowledge, existing instead at a more essential level. This passage's obscure, shifting imagery—in which a mother may refer to a crossroads, a supernal letter, or a female parent, while suckling corresponds both to mother-child imagery and to tree imagery—creates a densely structured web of meaning in which all the images' connotations interact in the reader's mind.[18]

However, identifying the suckling being as the human kabbalist helps to foreground human mother-child connotations, and it is on this anthropomorphic aspect of Isaac's suckling that scholars have focused. Mark Sendor, Daniel Abrams, and Yechiel Goldberg all note Isaac's use of suckling to represent a particularly intimate and intuitive form of divine connection. Sendor and Abrams suggest that Isaac uses Hebrew's sexual and intellectual senses of "knowing" to imply that the suckling relationship between a mother and child is more intimate than the adult sexual relationship, while Goldberg suggests that suckling bypasses intellectual processes that might be dangerous for the kabbalist to explore via intellection.[19] These associations with intimate but nonsexual contact and with protection from danger are characteristics of the mother-child relationship. Furthermore, there are cultural reasons to associate nonlinguistic knowledge with the mother-child relationship. Medieval Jewish culture associated mothers with childcare prior to Torah learning, giving fathers and male teachers primacy only after a child reached an age appropriate for scholarship and "knowing."[20] Rabbinic literature read by medieval Jews also inspired a belief in the wordless transmission of spiritual qualities and characteristics between mother and child, as demonstrated in chapter 1. These factors, combined with *Sefer Yetzirah*'s language of "mothers," may have encouraged Isaac to categorize divine nursing as a nonverbal form of contemplation comparable to a mother's sphere of care for her child, which he would have associated with intimate and life-giving characteristics outside the category of "knowledge."[21]

Although Isaac may have been inspired by the previous chapter's rabbinic materials, he transfers the suckling metaphor from human relationships to those that exist between divinity and humanity. In doing so, he transforms the spirituality that suckling transmits, addressing Kabbalah's most central relational concerns: the processes of God's inner life as revealed in the sefirotic system and the kabbalist's role in relation to that system. For Isaac, the spirituality being suckled is no longer that of religious orientation, but is now the overflow of God's interior substance. Suckling becomes the means by which this life-giving flow is transmitted through sefirotic pathways and into the created world. This form of the suckling metaphor is considerably more abstract and complex than the one found in rabbinic literature, and its complexity is reflected in Isaac's ambiguous imagery. Isaac's broad metaphor of suckling as divine transmission provides an excellent example of metaphor's power to naturalize a concept, avoiding methodical explanation.[22] His assertion that it is impossible to receive this transmission through "knowing," and that it instead requires the intimate, wordless bond of "suckling," echoes metaphor's own capacity to subvert step-by-step argumentation, constructing an idea that is grasped wholly and intuitively through the metaphoric image itself.

This process may be precisely what Isaac intended for his readers. His work was composed within the context of a twelfth-century intellectual culture (both Jewish and Christian) that was deeply interested in sacred metaphor as a guide to divine reality.[23] Since Isaac himself acknowledged the phenomenal world as a guide to the noumenal and incorporated this principle into his writing, it is possible to understand him as a thinker who deliberately crafted poetic images rooted in experienced reality as a way of guiding qualified readers toward heavenly knowledge.[24]

Commentary on Sefer Yetzirah, Chapter 3:

> Three Mothers: things that emanate, and are emanated and received each from each. But when it arrives at the world of the separated entities, they are not called [Mothers], but rather Fathers, from whom are Offspring.[25] For at first [they are] Mothers, for the Fathers themselves are called thus, like flames from coals.[26] And when it arrives at the separated entities, it becomes the effect that goes forth from all the Mothers. And from all the connections that we have spoken of, Fathers are made, to make connections in the separating of all of the things that made Offspring. Although we speak of separated entities, it does not depart from the connections, for all suckles (*yoneq*) from there. And therefore these Fathers are sealed in every thing and it says how world, year, and soul are made from them.[27]

In this passage, Isaac obliquely asks and answers two theological questions rooted in relational issues: how do the *sefirot* relate to each other, and how are they connected (if at all) to the human world? He answers these questions by explaining that the *sefirot* maintain a mutualistic relationship with shared divine substance connecting them in a vast unity. Even created beings that live in the human, separated world are connected to God's inner unity, because the *sefirot* extend to provide a flow of divine life from which the separated beings suckle. Isaac explains that as interior divine gradations, the *sefirot* are called Mothers. These Mothers are unified within divinity, since they all emanate divine substance to each other. He then explains that when the *sefirot* produce outward effects in the separated world, they are called Fathers, although they remain the same entities. Their nomenclature is contingent upon whether they are acting internally or externally. The Fathers' external actions produce Offspring, a term that may refer to worldly effects or to actual created beings. These Offspring occupy a lower state of existence characterized by separation, just as the sefirotic world is characterized by unity. While the Offspring may appear to be cut off from their sefirotic parents and God's overflowing life energy, they remain connected to divine life by suckling.[28]

Although the mothers and fathers in *Sefer Yetzirah* refer to Hebrew letters, Isaac uses his source-text's anthropomorphic language and his own suckling-as-spiritual-transmission metaphor to teach a lesson about the sefirotic system's intimacy.[29] This intimacy extends throughout the divine world and into the world of human beings. *Sefer Yetzirah*'s mothers and fathers allow Isaac to present a very human breastfeeding analogy for describing the *sefirot* and the world. While the *sefirot* are all understood as coequal mothers who share a unifying divine flow, the human being is conceived as a child. A child is originally created from its parents' inner substance, but is then born, becoming separate from them while still maintaining kinship. A nursing child, however, remains connected to its mother's inner substance by suckling her flow of milk. This link between nursing mother and child is real in a very physical sense, and provides a strong model for the kabbalistic reader to understand his ongoing relationship to the divine. Although his soul originates with God, as a created being he becomes a separated entity. This separation is transcended when he receives the flow of divine life from the sefirotic world, a state he can encourage by practicing the contemplative "suckling" Isaac describes in his Commentary on *Sefer Yetzirah* 1:1.

Isaac's nursing metaphor creates a model for intimate relationship between God and humanity that defies human concerns about being disconnected from the divine. By shifting not just the image of a mother suckling a child, but also the entire associative landscape that surrounds breastfeeding onto divinity, he creates a theological model in which God and humanity take on roles of nurturer and nurtured as the *sefirot* and the human creature below suckle from supernal *Ḥokhmah*'s divine flow.[30] Isaac takes advantage of metaphor's mediating qualities by choosing a metaphor that is itself about mediation and applying it to interactions between the transcendent and the mundane. In this way, he creates a coherent cosmology that stresses not only sefirotic unity and interdependence, but also places humanity in a relationship of part to whole with divinity, since both beings incorporate a common substance. By introducing a cosmology in which divine spirituality suffuses all of creation, he reinvigorates the relationship between God and human beings and effects a conceptual "return to the whole"—a restoration of humanity's relative place within the ordering of the universe.[31] The suckling metaphor's application to kabbalistic theology allows divinity and humanity to interact within the common medium of suckling as divine life's transmission, ultimately constituting a new cosmological whole by becoming participants in the same ongoing spiritual process.

Deliberate as Isaac's presentation of divine suckling may be, it lacks two elements that become critical in later kabbalistic writings: direct connection to a breastfeeding feminine figure and explicit affective terminology. The terms *mother* and *suckling* are not directly related in Isaac's writing: in the first passage examined, Isaac ambiguously associates suckling with Mothers and trees, and in the second Fathers intervene in the suckling process. Indeed, in the second passage, suckling's source remains unclear. It may proceed from the Mothers, from the Fathers, or from the connections between them. While the Fathers can be read as Mothers ("they are not called [Mothers], but rather Fathers, from whom are Offspring"), and are thus capable of suckling, Isaac again leaves his metaphor ambiguous. Nursing's connotations of intimacy, nurture, and sustenance remain intact, but are not drawn out or detailed. Instead, all of this information is left implied, setting the stage for future elaboration.

Fluid Imagery in *Sefer ha-Bahir*

While Isaac the Blind provides a source for kabbalistic suckling imagery, it is helpful to look at other early kabbalistic texts that provide source material for the Zohar's image of a divine nursing mother. *Sefer ha-Bahir* (*The Book of Brightness*) does not include suckling imagery, but it does introduce affective terms later associated with divine breastfeeding. The Bahir presents its readers with an emotionally textured interpretive context for milk imagery, establishing relationships among the *sefirot* and conditioning them with a broad symbolic vocabulary that draws connections between milk, mercy, truth, and peace.

Before the Zohar was composed in the late thirteenth century, *Sefer ha-Bahir* was the most authoritative kabbalistic work. Its teachings helped to shape the thought of the thirteenth century Spanish kabbalists.[32] Appearing in Provence the second half of the twelfth century, the Bahir is a multilayered text of very obscure origins with possible roots in medieval Germany and Near Eastern late antiquity.[33] The work's authorship is also unknown.[34] The Bahir is most famous for being identified by scholars as kabbalistic theology's first coherent presentation, and it includes the concept of ten *sefirot* presented as divine gradations, the traditional sefirotic organization into three higher and seven lower gradations, and standard sefirotic terms.[35] The kabbalistic idea of divine femininity seems to appear for the first time in the Bahir, particularly with regard to the tenth *sefirah*, which is associated with images of mother, bride, and daughter, as well as with rabbinic concepts of *Shekhinah* (the divine Presence, depicted as masculine or genderless in earlier literature) and the Assembly of Israel.[36] This *sefirah*'s role as a mediating figure between the divine and human worlds appears to be the Bahir's innovation.[37] The *sefirah Binah* is also associated with femininity and represented as mother of the lower *sefirot* and the world.[38] In addition, the Bahir presents the idea of multidirectional influence between divinity and humanity so essential to Kabbalah's focus on relationality.[39]

Isaac the Blind may have been a key figure in transmitting and developing the Bahir's theology. Scholem notes, "In Isaac's writings, the esoteric tradition, which was still fluid in the Bahir, crystallized in fixed conceptions and continued its development in a manner peculiar to the author. He quotes the Bahir, though only infrequently, but also implicitly assumes his reader's acquaintance with it."[40] Daniel Abrams, on the other hand, denies that the kabbalists of twelfth-century Provence quoted the Bahir, claiming instead that the text was popularized by Isaac's students, Ezra and Azriel of Gerona.[41] It is therefore possible to suggest that this work, along with early rabbinic and late aggadic texts, provides inspiration for Isaac's suckling imagery and its implied connotations. It is also certain that passages from the Bahir, combined with Isaac's own writings, influenced Ezra's later suckling theology. Although Isaac consistently avoids milk imagery, Ezra's use of nursing imagery is more explicitly related to the human breast. Milk is the substance suckled in a human context, and passages like the one below may have helped to inspire the kabbalists' thoughts on divine nursing.

Sefer ha-Bahir 136–37:

[Bahir 136] And what is it: Mercy (*Ḥesed*)? It corresponds to the Torah, as it is written, "Ho! All who are thirsty—come to water. And he who has no silver . . . " (Isaiah 55:1). This is "silver," as it is written: "Come, buy grain and eat. And come, buy wine and milk without silver and without price" (Isaiah 55:1). He will feed you Torah and he will teach you for you are already meritorious with the merit of Abraham, who did deeds of mercy (*asher haya gomel ḥesed*). Without silver he used to feed, and give drink without price: wine and milk [Bahir 137]. What is it: "wine and milk?" And what is the relationship of one with the other? Rather, it teaches that the wine is Fear (*Paḥad*) and the milk is Mercy (*Ḥesed*). And why is wine cited first? Because it is closer to us. Wine and milk: Should it [i.e., literal wine and milk] arise in you mind, rather, say [that] it is the likeness (*demut*) of wine and milk. And by the merit of Abraham, who merited the attribute of Mercy, Isaac merited the attribute of Fear. And [as] Isaac accomplished and merited the attribute of Fear, Jacob merited the attribute of Truth (*Emet*), that is, the attribute of Peace (*Shalom*). And the Holy One, blessed be He, measured him according to his nature (*ke-midato*). As it is written: "And Jacob was a perfect (*tam*) man, dwelling in tents" (Genesis 25:27). And [do] not [read] "perfect" (*tam*), but rather "peace" (*shalom*). As it is written: "You will be perfect (*tamim*) with the Lord your God" (Deuteronomy 18:13). And the Targum translates [this]: "You will be complete (*shalem*)." And [do] not [read] perfect (*tam*), but rather Torah. As it is said: "A Torah of truth (*torat emet*) was in his mouth [and unrighteousness was not found in his lips. He walked with Me in peace (*be-shalom*) and in uprightness, and he brought back many from wrongdoing"] (Malachi 2:6). And what is written after it? "He walked with Me in peace (*be-shalom*) and in uprightness." And [do] not [read] "uprightness," but rather, "peace" (*shalom*). As it is written, "Perfection and uprightness" (Psalms 25:21). Therefore [it is written]: "[And] when Moses held up his hand, Israel prevailed" (Exodus

17:11).[42] It teaches that the attribute that is called Israel has a Torah of truth within it.[43]

These two passages introduce symbols and characteristics associated with the fourth, fifth and sixth *sefirot*. Bahir 136 deals with the fourth *sefirah*, *Ḥesed* (Mercy), using Isaiah 55:1 to establish an analogy between Mercy, the Torah, and human consumption on both physical and intellectual levels. Using milk imagery, divine Mercy and Torah are depicted as corresponding substances that both feed and teach their recipients. The connection between feeding and teaching implies the necessity of intellectual sustenance and asserts life's reliance upon the Torah. Both Mercy and Torah are then connected with the patriarch Abraham, who is consistently associated with merciful qualities in rabbinic and kabbalistic theology. According to this passage, the patriarch's merciful qualities continue to characterize his Jewish descendants.[44]

In Bahir 137, the association between Mercy and milk becomes explicit. Continuing interpretation of Isaiah 55:1's "wine and milk" associates wine with the fifth *sefirah*, Fear (*Paḥad*), more commonly known as Judgment (*Din*) or Might (*Gevurah*) in later kabbalistic literature. This *sefirah* is also linked to the patriarch Isaac. Milk is identified with the fourth sefirah, *Ḥesed* (Mercy), and again linked to the patriarch Abraham.[45] In kabbalistic symbolism, the color red is associated with Fear and Judgment, while the color white is associated with Mercy, a correspondence that helps the text to continue opening Isaiah 55:1 for further interpretation.[46] The Bahir urges its reader to understand, however, that actual milk is not the subject of its discourse; instead the text refers to milk's "likeness." In this way, the Bahir informs its reader that milk serves as a metaphoric image for Mercy. By the time the passage arrives at the patriarch Jacob's traditional association with the central (sixth) *sefirah*, here called Peace (*Shalom*), the text has set up a series of analogies between Torah, peace, and perfection.[47] These analogies compliment the ones established in Bahir 136 and the beginning of Bahir 137, creating a broad set of correspondences that include Mercy, Abraham, Milk, Torah, Perfection, Jacob, Israel, Truth, and Peace.

This associative series, which runs consistently through both passages, provides the Bahir's reader with a set of cognitive tools for thinking about God. While it elaborates on ideas found in earlier rabbinic literature, like the metaphor of suckling as Torah transmission, it also provides new affective models for understanding the divine. Mercy,

Fear, and Peace all represent *sefirot*, but they also describe relational attitudes that human beings can take toward each other. These divine qualities, whose names reflect emotional and intellectual stances, provide a guide for relating to God's inner life. The most desirable of these qualities, Mercy and Peace, are described with a milk metaphor, implying their ability to feed and sustain humanity. While the text declines an association with human milk and breastfeeding, milk's nurturing, sustaining qualities are inscribed onto the *sefirot* and become models for divine relationality both among God's aspects and with the human world. Although Fear is included in the emotions that structure divine life, it is quickly glossed over in the text, which explains that Fear is closer to humanity than Mercy. This teaching can be read as observant commentary on the human condition, but it is also a basic teaching about sefirotic order; proceeding upward from the tenth *sefirah*, the fifth *sefirah* (Fear) is closer to the human world than the fourth (Peace). The text implies that although Fear is closer to humanity's experience of divine relationship, it is necessary to strive for a higher connection with divine Mercy, Peace, and Torah. This lesson conditions the kabbalistic reader's perception of his relationship to divinity by stressing God's positive affective qualities, all of which are connected to milk. The Bahir's positive emotional associations with milk are not lost on later kabbalists, who integrate these qualities into their teachings on divine nursing.

Ezra of Gerona's Divine Breastfeeding

Rabbi Ezra ben Solomon of Gerona has been called "the first full-fledged literary figure among the kabbalists."[48] As a central figure of the kabbalistic community at Gerona and a disciple of Isaac the Blind, his writings constitute a valuable resource for understanding Jewish mystical theology's development.[49] In addition, his work includes some of the first kabbalistic documents intentionally made available to a public beyond the elite esoteric communities of southern France and northern Spain.[50] Ezra's *Commentary on the Song of Songs*, written in the 1220s, is no exception to this rule.[51] Kabbalah's first fully articulated image of a feminine, breastfeeding divine emerges in this work. Widely disseminated, the Commentary's ready availability drew criticism from rationalists and kabbalists alike. In the 1240s Meir of Narbonne, an opponent of kabbalistic theology, called for the work's destruction, fearing that simple folk would read and interpret it inappropriately.[52] Ezra's teacher, Isaac the Blind, also wrote a letter expressing his concern at this casual spread of mystical theology.[53]

Ezra's theology, as presented in the *Commentary on the Song of Songs*, often reflects that of Isaac the Blind, while including influence from textual sources like *Sefer ha-Bahir*.[54] R. Ezra describes a transmission of divine overflow that passes from *Hokhmah* throughout the divine and human worlds, infusing all existence with enlivening divine influence. "From that overflow (*shefaʿ*), all the causes suckle (*yonqot*)."[55] Describing the flow's cosmological effect, Ezra writes, "All is one within another, and one from another, and all is bound one in another and one with another."[56] However, the smooth and untroubled flow of divine energy between the divine and human worlds is not something Ezra takes for granted.[57] Human sin and insufficient religious practice can repel the *sefirot* from their relationship with the created world, causing them to retreat from the lower realm and flee toward divine energy's source. In his Commentary on Song 6:2, Ezra explains that during the Jewish exile and its consequent cessation of Temple ritual, "The spiritual things ascend and are drawn up to the place of their suckling (*yeniqtam*)." To counter this effect, human beings must "strive and cause to emanate and to draw the blessings to the Fathers, so that there be a drawing for the Children."[58] While this teaching borrows Isaac's familial terminology to explain sefirotic relations with the created world, Ezra grants human beings the power to draw divine flow (and the *sefirot* themselves) back toward the human world through righteous religious effort.

The suckling metaphor is a major theme in R. Ezra's Commentary, with appearances surpassing Isaac's use of the theme in both number and theological impact.[59] Ezra's nursing imagery helps to define his ideas about divine overflow and the relationships it establishes between different levels of being. He describes the *sefirot* themselves as suckling, reading this intimate communication onto the interior divine life-process. He also uses nursing to describe humanity's relationship to the divine aspects, promoting a cosmology in which all levels of being are bound together in divine nurture. For Ezra, divine and human nursing are also engaged with human spiritual disposition (since human sin can cause the *sefirot* to flee to their nursing place), highlighting Kabbalah's theurgic concerns about humanity and divinity's partnership in promoting positive world order.

Commentary on Song 7:9:

> "Let your breasts be like clusters of grapes and the scent of your breath [like apples]" (Song 7:9). The place of suckling (*meqom yeniqah*) is like clusters of grapes, for you receive splendor (*zohar*) and overflow (*ve-shefa'*) from the fountain (*mi-meqor*) of *Hokhmah*.[60]

This passage summarizes Ezra's sefirotic suckling theology by showing the *sefirot* nursing divine overflow from *Hokhmah's* breasts. Here, divinity's outpouring is clearly related to the female form as Ezra incorporates breastfeeding imagery, rather than abstract suckling language. Fountain imagery, reminiscent of the Sarah texts examined in the previous chapter, is also applied to *Hokhmah*. Just as the suckling metaphor transformed Sarah into a living fount of Jewish spiritual identity, *Hokhmah* becomes the wellspring of a divine overflow that spiritually sustains the entire cosmos. By combining breast imagery with references to fruit, light, and fountains, Ezra draws sefirotic suckling beyond human categories to emphasize divinity's multivocal transcendence. Even so, linking breasts and suckling in the same brief passage foregrounds breastfeeding's anthropomorphic connotations of nurture, reliance, and familial connection. By highlighting these connotations, Ezra extends his suckling theology beyond a teaching on divine overflow and into an explanation of relationality among God's aspects. As in Isaac's teaching on the relationship between the *sefirot* and the created being, this intra-sefirotic suckling implies a doubled intimacy in which divinity's various gradations are connected by shared inner substance. The suckling metaphor helps to communicate the essential kabbalistic point that although the *sefirot* may seem like separate aspects of God, or even like potencies separated from divinity, they are all bound together and unified within divine life by partaking of the shared divine spirit.

Commentary on Song 8:1:

> "If only you were as a brother to me, [suckling at my mother's breasts]" (Song 8:1). The Glory replied: If you desire and yearn

that I will unite with you, I shall also direct all of my desire to you, so that you will be as a brother to me and I will not be separated from you. "Suckling (*yoneq*) at my mother's breasts." And you will receive suckling (*yeniqah*) from the place of my suckling (*yeniqati*), [from this place] which is the spirit of the living God.'[61]

In this passage, the feminine imagery associated with intra-divine suckling becomes even more explicit, inspired by the Song of Songs' own breastfeeding language. Here, the *sefirot* are personified as the Song's lovers, resulting in a conversation between the Glory (the feminine tenth *sefirah*) and the masculine sixth *sefirah Tif'eret*. This beautiful passage provides further keys to understanding Ezra's sefirotic theology. According to Ezra's system, each *sefirah* (and humanity as well) desires what is above it. As it is joined and united with the object of its desire, it receives a flow of energy from the wellspring of divine life. This life source, as indicated by other text passages, is the fountain of *Ḥokhmah*. Ezra also clarifies the divine overflow's nature, identifying it with "the spirit of the living God."[62] This clarification makes the suckling-as-spiritual transmission metaphor's purpose in the Commentary even clearer, and helps to personalize divine overflow by relating it to God's life-giving spirit.

Drawing on Song 8:1's imagery, Ezra depicts God as a nurturing, sustaining, feminine figure, expressing divine life-energy from its supernal breasts. His interpretation draws not only on the Song of Song's language, but also on the rabbinic suckling-as-spiritual-transmission metaphor, whose nurture, intimacy and sustenance associations he adapts and applies to divinity. While the suckling metaphor's initial application to God is Isaac's innovation, Ezra builds on his teacher's work by structuring the metaphor with clear human imagery, highlighting its relational connotations. This passage presents the explicit literary image of God as a nursing mother, demonstrating the suckling metaphor's power for expressing divine relational dynamics. Ezra allows Song 8:1's strongly personal "my mother" to lend an additional spiritual intimacy to this passage, personalizing connection among the *sefirot* with motherhood's nurturing social connotations.

The male and female *sefirot* in this passage are brought together through their mutual desire, but Ezra's suckling metaphor also draws attention to the Song's description of the lovers' close kinship. He presents the *sefirot* as siblings, sharing a common divine substance whose flow prevents their separation both from each other and from their heavenly source. Just as this passage's breasted, nursing divine places emphasis on a mother's nurturing and sustaining characteristics, presenting the *sefirot* as suckling children underscores their utter dependence on God's flowing spirit. Their desire for divine suckling paints a picture of a sefirotic world structured by a deep longing for connection, providing the kabbalistic reader with a description of the emotional qualities displayed in the upper world. Given this model of an upper world longing for connection, the kabbalist can begin to model his own religious affectivity on that of the *sefirot*, experiencing spiritual connection to God through the paradoxical distance of longing and desire.

Commentary on Song 8:10:

> "I am a wall and my breasts are like towers. [Then I was in his eyes as one who finds peace]" (Song 8:10). She is proud that she will be like a fortified wall, to strengthen [herself] with her faith and with the two Torahs; the Written Torah and the Oral Torah, that are the [source of] vitality for man, as the breasts are the [source of] life for the infant. "Then," she said, I was in the eyes of the Holy One, blessed be He, "as one who finds peace."[63]

In this passage, Ezra begins to explain that human beings receive divine life energy by suckling, just as the *sefirot* do. He accomplishes this by joining the rabbinic Torah-as-nursing-mother metaphor with the tenth *sefirah*'s established feminine imagery.[64] Here, the Assembly of Israel (the tenth *sefirah*) prides herself on her ability to guard the Torah and transmit it to Israel. Her two breasts represent the two forms of Torah: Written and Oral.[65] This anthropomorphic wellspring of Torah is understood as the true source of human vitality and is likened to a human mother's breasts, which are an infant's lifesource. Ezra also incorporates some of the Bahir's imagery, linking the Torah with peace in a lovely interpretation of Song 8:10. Although milk is not mentioned in this passage, Ezra's suckling infant clearly implies a transmission of milk, and the Bahir's teaching on the close relationship between Torah, milk, and peace in the sefirotic realm becomes explicit through his skillful scriptural interpretation.[66]

Humanity, like a child, enters into an intimate relationship with divinity to receive the life-sustaining spiritual flow of Torah transmission. This intimate suckling relationship between humanity and divinity is very similar to the suckling relationship described among the *sefirot* in Ezra's Commentary on Song 8:1, encouraging the reader to understand that the upper and lower worlds are linked by a common relational structure, a point also made by the mother-child metaphor applied both to the relationships among the *sefirot* and to the relationship between the *sefirot* and human beings. The suckling metaphor applied to the upper and lower worlds encourages a cosmological model of universal kinship in which the *sefirot* and human beings are all bound together in a close, familial relationship. As with the *Avinu Malkenu* prayer, Ezra's text suggests to the kabbalist that he exists in a particular relationship with God—one in which divinity becomes a heavenly Mother, he himself takes an earthly infant's role, and he receives spiritually nourishing divine overflow (and Torah knowledge) directly from his Mother's breasts. The model is humbling, in that it discourages human power or independence, but it also conditions a direct bond with God that is both loving and sustaining, as humanity's vitality depends on its divine Mother's nurturing care.

Commentary on Song 8:8:

> "We have a little sister [and she has no breasts. What shall we do for our sister on the day that she is spoken for?]" (Song 8:8). This is a parable concerning [the people of] Israel, who are in exile, despised and lowly. "And she has no breasts." They do not have a nursing-place (*meqom heniqah*) because they have gone forth from the land of the living and are separated from the place of Torah (*mi-meqom ha-torah*). As it is written, "For Torah shall go forth from Zion" (Isaiah 2:3).[67] And concerning the exile it says, "For many days Israel has not had the God of truth . . . and the Torah" (2 Chronicles 15:3). "What shall we do for our sister on the day that she is spoken for?" What shall we do for them? With what shall we be able to sustain them, and give them a future and hope in their exile?[68]

As in the previous excerpt, this passage depicts God and humanity in a mother-child relationship. In an interpretive move similar to earlier rabbinic texts, Ezra understands the Song of Songs' bosomless little sister as a specific nation: the people of Israel.[69] The Israelite people's helplessness and lack of worldly power are reflected in their personification as a preadolescent girl. Ezra's reading also alludes to earlier Song interpretations in which Israel is understood as the bride of God (rather than as the feminized *Shekhinah*). Unlike the theme explored in chapter 1, which equates lack of breasts with lack of suckling in commandments and good deeds, Ezra's text suggests a far more distressing situation. If the people of Israel lack a nursing place, then according to Ezra's theology they are not just lacking in religious observance but are actually detached from the source of divine life, *Ḥokhmah's* spiritual overflow. As in his interpretation of Song 8:10, Ezra links Torah transmission to human vitality: the people of Israel cannot suckle because they have left the "land of the living." Ezra reinforces the cosmological breastfeeding link between Torah and the Assembly of Israel's breasts by repeating the word *place* (*meqom*) in connection with each. The tenth *sefirah's* breasts are both the "place" of suckling and the "place" of Torah. He explains Israel's separation from these loci by linking Song 8:8 with 2 Chronicles 15:3, from which he derives the Land of Israel and the Torah as nursing places. Joining this verse's lament over lack of God and Torah to lack of a nursing place, Ezra reinforces Israel's tragic dislocation.

Rather than presenting an idealized model for human and divine relationship, in this passage Ezra uses breastfeeding imagery to highlight a destructive cosmic disconnection. Israel's detachment from God's flowing life force is caused both by separation from the Holy Land and by consequent detachment from the Torah, which (as Ezra elegantly interprets Song 8:10) is transmitted from the breasts of the Assembly of Israel, the tenth *sefirah*. Israel, away from the Holy Land, is like a lost child separated from its mother's caring and nourishing presence. In this case, the nursing-mother image inspires a deep sense of loss. To further structure this model, Ezra grounds Israel's separation from divine nursing in emotional terms. The people of Israel need sustenance while separated from the divine breasts and spiritual nourishment they once suckled. They lack hope, implying depression; a way must be found to improve their situation. In the passage, Ezra identifies a problem with the relationship between divinity and humanity while crying out for a solution.[70]

Although this passage begins to imply emotional context for its reader, there is little affective language present in Ezra's suckling theology. Yet because such language is present in the Zohar, it is interesting to look for it in Ezra's work, which was an important source text for the Zoharic authorship.[71] I would like to present a final passage from Ezra's Commentary, in which he uses emotional terms to great effect. This passage does not contain the suckling metaphor, but because Ezra often uses the terms drawing (*hamshakhah*) and suckling (*yeniqah*) for similar purposes in describing divine overflow, it is helpful to look at this passage in conjunction with ones that do contain the suckling image and make some observations. Although drawing and suckling have different metaphoric connotations, later kabbalists would have felt free to recombine Ezra's powerful metaphors to convey their own ideas.

Commentary on Song 1:7:

> "[Tell me, whom my soul loves,] where do you graze (*tir'eh*)?" (Song 1:7). The satiation (*ha-histapqut*) from the pleasure (*mi-ta'anug*) of the drawing (*ha-hamshakhah*) and the increase (*ve-ha-tosefet*) is called grazing, and thus our rabbis, may their memory be for a blessing, called it "eating." As it is said in *Midrash Exodus Rabbah*: "And they saw God [and they ate and drank]" (Exodus 24:11).[72] For their eyes were nourished (*she-zanu*) from the *Shekhinah*. Rabbi Yoḥanan said [that this was] true eating. As it is said: "In the light of the king's face [there] is life" (Proverbs 16:15).[73]

In this passage, the sefirotic Assembly of Israel (also called *Shekhinah*) asks *Tif'eret*, her beloved, to identify the source of his spiritual sustenance. Although a more literal translation of Song 1:7 might use "pasture," rather than "graze" for *tir'eh*, it is clear from context that Ezra's grazing applies not to the beloved's flocks, but rather to the beloved himself as he consumes the divine overflow. In its original context, Exodus 24:11 refers to the Sinaitic revelation beheld by Moses, Aaron, Aaron's sons, and the seventy elders of Israel. Although the *Shekhinah* is understood neither as feminine nor as a kabbalistic *sefirah* in the rabbinic interpretation Ezra cites, he himself interprets the *Shekhinah* as the tenth *sefirah*, from whom the Israelites draw divine overflow. The Biblical passage's eating and drinking seem to indicate that all of these people were especially blessed because they were not struck down for beholding the divine Presence. Ezra, however, reads eating and drinking as metaphors for taking in the divine overflow, an action he calls "drawing."[74] He also collapses Exodus' eating and drinking into a more generalized term for receiving nourishment, *zan*, emphasizing that spiritual sustenance is gained from divine encounter.[75] This energy is metaphorically expressed as light from the face of God, using Proverbs 16:15 as a reference. The light, which represents divine spiritual energy, is understood as the essence of life itself.[76] Through this series of interpretations, Ezra suggests that drawing involves an ecstatic consumption of divine energy. In the rest of the passage, he continues describing this consumption, indicating its nature and grounding it in an affective context.

In his Commentary on Song 1:7, Ezra depicts divine overflow's passage linking both the *sefirot* and humanity by moving the passage from an intra-sefirotic conversation to a kabbalistic interpretation of the revelation at Mount Sinai.[77] This common process in which all levels of being participate generates a sense of kinship between divinity and humanity, stressing that the lower world is modeled on the upper world. However, the passage's most distinctive feature is the way Ezra emotionally structures divine overflow's transmission through the sefirotic world and into humanity. Rather than relying on the Song's own language of desire, longing, and satisfaction, he provides additional terms to associate divine influx with positive sensation and pleasurable increase. Increasing pleasure brings satiation (*histapqut*), a key term in the Commentary. *Histapqut* is a noun deriving from the reflexive verb *lehistapeq* (to supply one's self), which bears connotations of contentment, nourishment, filling, and sustaining. The most effective way to translate these nuances into English is the term *satiation*. Ezra uses variations on *histapqut* ten times in his Commentary, and although the term does not appear in conjunction with suckling, it consistently represents the sensation derived from receiving *Ḥokhmah's* divine overflow.[78] In this sense, it can be read at a broad textual level as a term related to suckling, which is also a mode of receiving divine energy associated with nourishment, filling, sustenance, and contentment.

Although Ezra does not add his own affective terminology to the Commentary's suckling imagery, he seems more comfortable applying terms like *pleasure* and *satiation* to the metaphor of drawing divine energy.[79] Reasons for the difference remain unclear. It is possible that Ezra found the image of God as a nursing mother radical enough without added emotional context, and that abstract drawing terminology lent itself more readily to positive emotional terms. Ezra carefully grounds each reference to God as a nursing mother in direct Song citation, using the Biblical text's own authority to assert his innovative divine imagery. The breastfeeding God image emerges as a side effect of reading the Song's female lover as *Shekhinah*. On the other hand, "drawing" acts as a freestanding theme in the Commentary and is not bound so concretely to the Song's verses, allowing more creative freedom. The idea of drawing divine energy was much less radical than that of a breasted God, requiring less caution on Ezra's part. Furthermore, suckling's parental associations grant it inherent emotional texture, making elaboration on divine tenderness, nurture, and caring unnecessary. A generalized drawing metaphor requires elaboration to convey a similar idea. In any case, the combination of emotional terminology with suckling imagery divorced from scriptural citation is often present in *Sefer ha-Zohar*, a text that is rarely shy about employing human imagery (whether anthropomorphic, anthropopathic, or both).[80]

From these examples of Ezra's work, it is clear that divine energy's flow through the sefirotic realm and into the human world can be described in terms of nurturing, relational imagery. The *sefirot* suckle their life energy from supernal *Ḥokhmah*, which provides a divine overflow that Ezra describes with liquid images, pouring from *sefirah* to *sefirah* and infusing the divine being's entire structure. This flow of divine energy ultimately continues into the human world, where the people of Israel suckle divine overflow from the final *sefirah*, *Shekhinah*. Ezra links both *Ḥokhmah* and *Shekhinah* to feminine breast imagery found in The Song of Songs. The suckling imagery in which this theology is expressed conveys the intimate connection and absolute interdependence of the *sefirot*, as well as the intimate bond between divinity and humanity. Supernal suckling's nature is profoundly rarified, yet Ezra clarifies that it transmits the spirit of the living God. This spirit, as it moves through the worlds, produces the sensation of utter contentment associated with infants drawing pure nourishment from their mothers. Although the *sefirot* receive continuous suckling, humanity's divine nursing may be interrupted by sin, lack of ritual practice, or dislocation from the Holy Land.[81] Ezra's text introduces his reader to a subtle, yet all-encompassing universal life process that links God and humanity in its ebb and flow.

It is reasonable to assume that the unique character of the Song of Songs itself, beautifully voluptuous while wholly sacred, inspired Ezra's elaborations on divine nursing. Beyond the Song, Ezra clearly drew on the suckling theology that Isaac the Blind developed in his *Commentary on Sefer Yetzirah*, on the Bahir's fluid imagery, and on earlier rabbinic writings to express his own unique theology. The resulting work is an intertextual masterpiece that references previous Jewish writings both textually and through preexisting religious imagery. However, it is the Song's lush language that permeates Ezra's writing, allowing him to venture into a realm of vivid, richly structured imagery that his predecessors seem to have felt was best left implied. This is particularly true of Ezra's breast imagery and affective overtones, inspired by the Song's descriptions of the female lover and the emotional bond between the poem's male and female voices. By drawing on a text with a rich image vocabulary directly related to human experience (however the Song of Songs has been interpreted over time), Ezra provides himself and his readers with direct access to experiential theological understanding. This experiential lexicon emerges from Jewish tradition's deepest authority, the Bible itself.

Ezra's references to mothers, children, and breastfeeding allow the divine and human roles of nurturer and nurtured to be more deeply explored, structuring the suckling metaphor with connotations of dependence, sustenance, and intimacy that are clearly stated, rather than merely suggested. Since the kabbalists were religiously required to maintain a family life alongside their spiritual pursuits and to marry and conceive children, they would have been familiar with breastfeeding and the connections (both physical and emotional) it creates between mother and child.[82] As with the modern Jew reciting the *Avinu Malkenu* prayer, when reading Ezra's text each kabbalist would have been aware of the connotations surrounding the mother-child relationship and reapplied these ideas to the divine and human relationships described in the Commentary. By combining ideas about physical, emotional, social, and cosmological relationships in readily accessible images, Ezra helps his readers to discover an interdependency of mind, body, and world.[83] This interaction of Jewish text and physical context provides coherence for the kabbalistic universe by allowing readers to model their relationships to God on an observable and fulfilling relationship between human beings.

Conclusion

Considering Isaac the Blind's *Commentary on Sefer Yetzirah*, *Sefer ha-Bahir*, and Ezra of Gerona's *Commentary on the Song of Songs* side by side, it is possible to see the image of God as a nursing mother emerging from early kabbalistic theology and exegesis. The transition from rabbinic suckling to kabbalistic suckling was achieved by reinterpreting both scriptural imagery and earlier Jewish exegetical images. Both Isaac and Ezra would have been familiar with the rabbinic texts on suckling presented in the previous chapter, and at least Ezra (and possibly Isaac as well) would have known the Bahir. Each man combined these traditional texts with his own innovations, recasting earlier material into forms that are strange, powerful, and profound, sowing the seeds of a new theology centered on divine and human relationship. These early kabbalists' writings use metaphor to present models for thinking about God that make the divine more accessible and understandable to humanity. Since the suckling metaphor deals primarily with relationality in the social and emotional contexts of mother and child, it helps to create a familiar, familial relationship between God and human beings. The Zohar takes this process further, establishing an enhanced pattern of intimate reliance between humanity and divinity.

CHAPTER 3

GOD AS A NURSING MOTHER
IN *SEFER HA-ZOHAR*

A place to draw from that river, to bathe in the whiteness of *Atika*,
in the milk that flows from the Mother.
—Sefer ha-Zohar 2:122b[1]

This chapter examines the image of God as a nursing mother in *Sefer ha-Zohar* (*The Book of Splendor*), the quintessential work of kabbalistic literature. As in the previous chapter's early kabbalistic writings, the Zohar applies the suckling-as-spiritual-transmission metaphor to divinity, using it to define spiritual overflow's passage among the *sefirot* and between the divine and human worlds. While early kabbalists often avoid feminine imagery and affective language in conjunction with suckling, the Zohar builds up the nursing divine with feminine language, milk imagery, and emotional terms. Providing this structured network of connotations emphasizes the relational roles that nursing imagery engages. This emphasis encourages the kabbalist toward self-transformation by restructuring his ideas about the relationships between humanity and divinity, and by providing models for understanding both God's inner life processes and the human being's role within the kabbalistic cosmology. These new models for understanding God and human beings emphasize divine abundance, nurture, love, and duty, while highlighting human dependence, intimacy, and familial inclusion in the divine life processes.

Sefer ha-Zohar is a lengthy work that includes many literary strata and stylistic genres. It appeared in Castile during the last quarter of

the thirteenth century as a pseudepigraphic body of work attributed
to the second century sage Rabbi Shimon bar Yoḥai and written in a
distinctive form of Aramaic.[2] While much of the work presents itself
as an esoteric Torah commentary, the Zohar also includes sections that
resemble a mystical novel whose central characters are the kabbalis-
tically inclined sages surrounding R. Shimon. The work synthesizes
earlier rabbinic and kabbalistic literature, while introducing critical elaborations of kabbalistic theology. It also reworks historic forms
of Jewish mysticism. For example, a substantial section of the Zohar
describes the *sefirot* according to the divine palaces of *hekhalot* (palaces)
mysticism, an earlier branch of Jewish esotericism.[3]

The Zohar includes elaborate feminine divine imagery, which
emerges from its tendency to openly embrace strong anthropomorphic
and anthropopathic descriptions of God. Its pages dwell on the feminine tenth *sefirah*'s (*Shekhinah*'s) imagery in an unprecedented way,
while also providing detailed descriptions of the feminine third *sefirah*
(*Binah*). The text often refers to these *sefirot* as the Lower Mother and
the Upper Mother: "Two females: One above and one below, and each
one is called World."[4] While these divine aspects' feminization is rooted
in Kabbalah's late twelfth-century beginnings, the Zohar contains some
of divine femininity's most daring articulations, which include breastfeeding imagery.

Historically, the Zohar occupied a position of authority and popularity unparalleled in kabbalistic literature. During the centuries following its composition, it became the only post-Talmudic literary
work to achieve nearly canonical status within the Jewish community
at large.[5] After the Jewish expulsion from Spain in 1492, the Zohar's
teachings spread throughout Europe and into the Near East, exerting
enormous influence on the sixteenth-century kabbalistic community at
Safed.[6] Toward the latter part of that century, printing made the Zohar
more widely available, and it was adopted by a more diverse reader-
ship, including Christian Renaissance theologians. The first printed
editions of this text were produced in Mantua between 1558 and 1560
and in Cremona between 1559 and 1560. Printing helped to solidify
the previously nebulous body of Zoharic literature, which existed in
many different versions and forms prior to its printed editions.[7] In the
early twentieth century, Gershom Scholem identified the Zohar as the
work of Moses de León (1240–1305), a prominent Castilian kabbalist and head of a mystical group. Scholem based this conclusion on an

elaborate study of the text's language, vocabulary, writing style, and historic inconsistencies.[8] More recently, Yehuda Liebes suggested that the Zohar resulted from a collaborative effort among kabbalists closely associated with Moses de León, and many modern scholars have come to share his perspective.[9] Some scholars have even suggested that the group of texts comprising the Zohar originated in multiple kabbalistic circles with multiple leaders.[10]

Each text presented in this chapter contains divine nursing imagery, and all are arranged according to the image's placement within the sefirotic structure. The first group, associated with the feminine *sefirah Shekhinah*, includes passages that show divine breastfeeding in direct relation to the human world. The next group of texts addresses nursing imagery related to the *sefirah Binah*. The final set of texts explores breastfeeding language attached to masculine *sefirot* structurally located between these two feminine divine aspects. These texts do not represent the entire range of Zoharic passages that include the nursing divine, nor do they represent even a small portion of passages that employ suckling terminology without mother imagery. Instead, they offer a representative sampling of excerpts relevant to understanding the Zohar's divine nursing-mother metaphor and are intended to demonstrate the text's main elaborations on this concept.[11]

Suckling from *Shekhinah*

Sefer ha-Zohar 1:203a:

> But come and see: "Valley of Vision," (Isaiah 22:1) this is the *Shekhinah* who was in the Temple and all the children of the world used to suckle (*yanqin*) from her; they suckled (*yeniqu*) of prophecy. For although all the prophets surely used to prophecy from another place, they used to suckle (*yanqin*) their prophecy from within her.[12] And for this reason she is called "Valley of Vision." . . . For when the Temple used to stand, Israel used to perform services and offer offerings and sacrifices. And the Shekhinah rested upon them in the Temple, like a mother covering over her children. And all the faces used to shine, while blessings were found above and below. And there was not a day on which blessings and rejoicings were not

found. And Israel rested in safety in the land, and all the world was nourished (*itzan*) because of them.

In this passage, The Zohar offers its reader an idealized kabbalistic cosmology in which correct universal order is experienced as a mother-child relationship between God and human beings. Radically reinterpreting Isaiah 22:1's Valley of Vision as a name for *Shekhinah*, rather than a physical location, the text contends that this *sefirah* was the source of ancient prophecy.[13] When the Temple stood in Jerusalem and its cult was properly maintained, the Israelite prophets suckled their revelations from the *Shekhinah*'s inner substance, receiving a divine overflow that blessed the people of Israel. The Israelites in turn brought blessings to the world at large by extending the *Shekhinah*'s nourishing flow. The Zohar expresses this beneficial cosmic alignment with literary parallelism; the *Shekhinah* rested upon Israel, and Israel rested within the holy land, enabling blessings to flow out from divinity and into the world.[14] In fact, "all the world" was spiritually nourished through Israel's ideal alignment with the *Shekhinah*. Nourishment language is often linked to mothering imagery in the Zohar, helping to develop the idea of a divine mother's nurturing role toward her child.[15]

With its clear feminine and affective language, this text shows just how far Kabbalah's nursing divine has come from its tentative early kabbalistic formulations. *Shekhinah*'s role as a mother is clearly defined and linked to nursing imagery, establishing a mother-child relationship between divinity and humanity that the text reinforces with repeated references to humanity as children. God as a nursing mother also exhibits caring and protective qualities by covering Her children to preserve them from harm. These images stand freely; they do not receive support from Biblical verses about motherhood, breasts, or nursing. Such verse-independent mothering imagery marks a significant departure from feminine divine language found in earlier texts like Ezra of Gerona's Song Commentary, which takes care always to root divine motherhood in established Biblical context. The Zohar often refers to *Shekhinah* as a mother, and its authorship has no need to cite scriptural proof texts to reinforce what, by the late thirteenth century, has become a standard theological model.

While the Zohar explores suckling imagery as a way to structure relationships between God and human beings, it also informs its reader how this relationship should be emotionally experienced. The prophecy and blessings that pass between divinity and humanity are clearly associated with "rejoicings," rather than leaving their character implied by the nursing mother image alone. The identity of the being who experiences these rejoicings remains unstated. Since the text locates blessings and rejoicings both above (in the divine realm) and below (in the human realm), it appears that both humanity and divinity experience joy from the divine overflow's transmission, much as human nursing is a source of pleasure for both mother and child. The suckling that occurs when human and divine relationships are properly enacted is also associated with safety, nourishment, and the shining of faces—an indication of spiritual fulfillment.[16] This fulfillment is reinforced by nourishment terminology found in the text. The Zoharic authorship, like Ezra of Gerona, uses the root *z.v.n.* to indicate spiritual nourishment received from the divine overflow.[17] All of these terms add to suckling's positive emotional context.

Although this text uses the suckling-as-spiritual-transmission metaphor to depict divine overflow, its nursing imagery is grounded in a series of accessory descriptions that help to define divine overflow's nature, God's mothering qualities, and the emotions associated with nursing divine blessings in the upper and lower worlds. Unlike Isaac the Blind or Ezra of Gerona's use of the suckling image, the Zohar is unhesitatingly explicit about the image's positive emotional connotations, highlighting not only the nursing divine's anthropomorphic nuances, but its anthropopathic ones as well. It is in passages such as this that the full impact of suckling imagery is brought to bear upon the reader, restructuring his ideas about the relationships between God and self. This imagery's fullness, with its clearly depicted, idealized human and divine relationships, serves as a model for the kabbalists' desired and ideal connection with divinity. It also depicts an illustrious Israelite past that the medieval kabbalist hopes to rediscover in his present. In this way, the text draws on human experiences of nursing and childhood combined with longing for a bygone era to characterize the relationship between God and human beings as an intimate, positive, and joyous connection.

Sefer ha-Zohar 2:65b-66a:

Rabbi Shimon said: And if this battle with Amalek is inconsequential in your eyes, come and see: From the day that the world was created until that time, and from that time until the king Messiah comes, and even in the days of Gog and Magog, one like it will not be found. Not because of the mighty and vast armies, but rather because it was on all sides of the Holy One, blessed be He. "And Moses said to Joshua, [Choose men for us, and go out: battle with Amalek. Tomorrow I will stand at the top of the hill with the staff of God in my hand"] (Exodus 17:9). Why "to Joshua" and not to another? For behold, at that time he was a youth. As it is written: "And Joshua son of Nun, a youth [did not depart from within the Tent"] (Exodus 33:11).[18] . . . At that time, Joshua was found at a very high level. If you will say that he was found with *Shekhinah* at that time, [this is] not so. For behold, She was married and united with Moses. Joshua was found united below him. . . . And this is the secret, as it is written: "And Joshua son of Nun, a youth." Truly, a youth. "Did not depart from within the Tent," that is called "a tent that will not wander" (Isaiah 33:20).[19] This teaches that on each and every day he was suckling (*yaneq*) from the *Shekhinah*, like that upper youth who does not depart from within the Tent and suckles (*ve-yaneq*) from her continuously.[20] Likewise, this youth below does not depart from within the Tent, and he suckles (*ve-yaneq*) from her continuously. . . . Rabbi Shimon said: At the time that the youth Joshua went out, the youth above was stirred, and was prepared with many preparations, with many weapons that his Mother prepared for him for this battle to take vengeance for the covenant. This is the secret, as it is written: "A sword taking vengeance for the covenant" (Lev. 26:25). And this is the secret, as it is written: "And Joshua weakened Amalek and his people with the sword."[21]

These excerpts are found in a passage that mystically interprets Exodus 17's clash between Israel and Amalek as a cosmic battle taking place both on earth and in heaven, "on all sides of the Holy One, blessed be He." Each earthly combatant is linked to a heavenly combatant. The demonic prince Samael fights on Amalek's behalf, representing evil forces that the Zohar refers to as the "Other Side."[22] The angel Metatron, an important figure in pre-kabbalistic Jewish mysticism, fights on Israel's behalf and is represented on earth by Joshua son of Nun. In *hekhalot* mysticism, Metatron is often equated with the transformed patriarch Enoch of Genesis 5:21–24 and associated with the divine name and the heavenly throne.[23] He is also found in medieval Ashkenazic literature as the angel of the Torah, the crown of God, and the divine presence, as well as in the writings of the thirteenth-century ecstatic kabbalist Abraham Abulafia.[24] In the Zohar, a text that makes frequent and creative use of earlier Jewish material, Metatron occupies a prominent position as leader of the angelic hosts. He is closely associated with *Shekhinah* and is frequently depicted as her heavenly minister, warrior, and son.[25] It is in his capacity as *Shekhinah's* son that he is known as "youth."[26] In the passage, Metatron fulfills his Zoharic role as the Lower Mother's warrior son. As Samael and Metatron battle in heaven, representing the forces of evil and good, Amalek and Israel (led by Joshua) battle on earth. The conflict's dramatic conclusion represents a cosmic triumph over evil.

In the full Zoharic passage excerpted here, Moses perceives the battle's heavenly roots and summons Joshua as the divine warrior's earthly representative. The passage explains the reason for his choice. Although only Moses is mystically married to the *Shekhinah*, Joshua also has a relationship to this feminine aspect of divinity, occupying the role of a child in relation to a heavenly Mother.[27] This Mother, *Shekhinah*, is often described with both feminine and domestic imagery. Here, She is depicted as the Tent of Meeting, a metaphor that expresses her mediating role between the divine and human worlds. The Zohar joins Exodus 33:11 (which tells that Joshua did not depart from the Tent of Meeting where he supplicated God on a regular basis) with Isaiah 33:20's vision of Jerusalem as a stable tent that does not move, in order to explain Joshua's relationship to this divine aspect. Their relationship draws on suckling imagery and models itself on the connection between a mother and her child.

In this passage, *Shekhinah* nurses both Joshua and Metatron, extending the cosmic connections inspired by divine energy's flow from the heavens, to the angelic realm, to the earth. The suckling process creates a sense of kinship and connection between three different levels of being, all of which are enlivened by the same divine substance. Unlike Moses' marital relationship to *Shekhinah*, Joshua and Metatron's suckling places them in the role of children to a heavenly parent. Both figures suckle "continuously," ensuring their enduring connection to divinity's powerful overflow and emphasizing their holiness.[28] While motherhood's associations with love and nurture are still present in the passage, the *Shekhinah* also appears as a powerful protective figure preparing heavenly armaments for her children. Rather than covering Israel as in the previous passage, She sends her children into battle, armed with protections She has devised. These armaments are presumably benefits derived from suckling the divine overflow. The passage's image of *Shekhinah* as a mother arming Metatron recalls an earthly queen sending her princely son into battle.

This passage's characterization of divine overflow as armaments, rather than as prophecy and blessings, is linked to Kabbalah's association of femininity with Judgment and other divine aspects of containment. In the sefirotic structure, *Shekhinah* is equidistant from the *sefirot* located on the right side (which are associated with Mercy and expansion) and from those on the left (which are associated with Judgment and containment).[29] Therefore, according to the Zohar, the *Shekhinah* may channel Mercy, Judgment or a mixture of the two into the world, depending largely on humanity's correct or incorrect actions.[30] In this case, channeling spiritual armaments to Israel can be understood as a form of nurture and support, leading to the victory of a beloved child. Again, the Zohar cultivates a mother-child relationship between God and human beings. Here, the child is grown and able to defend himself, but he still requires his mother's care. A kabbalist reading the passage might be encouraged to aspire to this divine relationship. Although Moses' level is not readily available to him, the kabbalist can still strive to suckle blessings and strength from his heavenly Mother.[31] The Zohar implies that such divine connection strengthens a person's ability to perform and defend the divine commandments.

Sefer ha-Zohar 3:150b:

And it [*Tzaddiq*] gathers all those rivers and streams that flow from the flowing of that holy river that does not cease from its day until eternity, that flows and goes out from Eden above, and goes forth continually from inside and fills the lake.[32] And from there all the worlds inherit blessings in all. Come and see: At the time that the Assembly of Israel is blessed, all the worlds are blessed, and Israel below suckle (*yanqin*), and are blessed in the garden. And have we not established that she is a basin upon they that are Israel, as we have said?[33]

This passage appears close to the end of a much longer discourse describing the tenth *sefirah* (here called the Assembly of Israel rather than *Shekhinah*) as both well and sea. This passage presents a case in which juxtaposing plant-suckling imagery with subtle divine nursing language (a combination also found in early Kabbalah) produces interesting results, demonstrating how the Zohar uses mixed and multivocal metaphors to great effect. The passage begins with an aquatic metaphor for the transmission of divine spiritual energy. However, once the "waters" are gathered within the Assembly of Israel, the metaphor undergoes a subtle transformation. The people of Israel, poised below in the proper relation to the sefirotic structure and awaiting the divine overflow, do not simply drink from a lake. Rather, they suckle from on high, inheriting blessings in the "garden."[34] These are no longer strictly natural images, but instead indicate cultural associations by referencing the people of Israel, the garden (a landscape transformed by human labor or divine action), and the term *inherit*.[35] The suckling metaphor mediates the passage's natural and cultural images for transmitting divine energy, and in doing so highlights suckling's maternal connotations, which are also cultural associations. While the passage's suckling language describes Israel as young saplings drawing water in an earthly garden, it simultaneously evokes a human people of Israel nursing divine overflow from their supernal Mother.

This metaphoric juxtaposition is representative of the Zohar's versatility, and is far from a random linguistic choice. The shift from natural to cultural imagery highlights a shift in divine representation and conveys new ideas about the divine and human relationship. Natural metaphors, such as rivers and lakes, imply forces that are beyond human understanding or ability to affect. This imagery is beautiful, but impersonal, indicating divinity's vast and awe-inspiring power. On the other hand, at the point in this passage where the feminine Assembly of Israel encounters humanity, cultural metaphors and anthropomorphic implications are drawn into play, as the people of Israel are located in a parent-child relationship with divinity. This parental relationship is reinforced by the text's assertion that Israel inherits divine blessings, since an inheritance is precisely what a child receives from his parent.

Likewise, blessings help to indicate an affective spiritual stance of joyful reception. By using this metaphoric juxtaposition to describe the divine blessings' flow into humanity, the Zohar transforms the divine overflow from an impersonal natural phenomenon beyond human

culture and understanding into a comprehensible, anthropomorphic-
ally structured interaction. Divine blessings are gentled and tenderly
suckled to the people of Israel, who are portrayed as ultimately dependent upon God for their spiritual nourishment. These mixed metaphors draw freely on a broad network of connotations that highlight
the point at which divinity ceases to be understood in terms of nature
and begins to be understood in terms of nurture.[36] In this way, the
Zohar encourages its reader to realize divinity's fullness, which exists
simultaneously beyond comprehension and engaged in an intimate
relationship with the Israelite who suckles from the Assembly of Israel.
Again, the suckling mother image is used to define the relationship
between God and Israel, transforming distance and awe-inspiring vast-
ness into an all-encompassing relationship of nurture, intimacy and
dependence.

A Breastfeeding *Binah*

Sefer ha-Zohar 3:65a-b:

[Rabbi Shimon] said to him: Eleazar, my son, behold, the
companions have established it. And now, everything is bound
in one matter, and the secret of the matter is this: *Ehyeh*. This
is the sum of all. For when the paths are concealed and not
separated and are gathered in one place, then it is called *Ehyeh*,
the sum.[37] All is concealed and not revealed (*itgalyya'*). After
the beginning went forth from it and that river became pregnant to produce all, then it was called *Asher Ehyeh*. That is to
say: Therefore I will be. I will be prepared to produce and to
beget all. *Ehyeh*: That is to say: Now I am the sum of all, the
generality of every particular. *Asher Ehyeh*: The mother that
became pregnant and prepared to bring forth all of the partic-
ulars, and to reveal (*u-le-itgalyya'*) the upper name.[38]. . . Come
and see: *Yud* in the beginning is the sum of all, concealed from
all sides. The paths are not open: the sum of male and female.
The stroke of the *Yud* that is above hints toward Nothing.[39]
Afterwards, *Yud*: That brought forth that river that flows and
goes forth from it and becomes pregnant by it: *He'*. Of this it

is written: "And a river goes forth from Eden [to give drink to the garden. And from there it separates and becomes four channels]" (Genesis 2:10). "Goes forth (*yotze*)," and not "went forth (*yatza*)."[40] Therefore, it does not desire to be separated from it. And therefore it is written: "My love (*ra'yati*)"[41] (Song 1:9 ff). And if you will say "river" is written, meaning one, but behold, here are three—this is actually so.[42] *Yud* brought forth three—and in the three all is included. *Yud* brought forth before itself that river and two children whom the Mother suckles (*de-yanqa*), and she became pregnant with them and brought them forth. Afterwards: *He'*, in this manner: *He'* and those children that are below the Father and the Mother.

This description of *Binah* as a pregnant and birthing mother who nurses sefirotic children is part of a discussion about divine names that takes place between the Zohar's Rabbi Eleazar and his father Rabbi Shimon bar Yoḥai. Eleazar wants his father to clarify Exodus 3:14's revelation of the divine name *Ehyeh Asher Ehyeh* (I Will Be What I Will Be). The passage is excerpted from a lengthy discussion about divine dynamics that stresses unity among the seemingly diverse *sefirot*. To explain the close-knit relationships within the sefirotic structure, Rabbi Shimon invokes the third *sefirah Binah*, presenting Her as a nursing mother who is also a river.[43] Like divinity Itself, *Binah* is both included in everything and the summation of all. *Binah's* motherhood helps to explain her role as source and origin point for all the lower *sefirot*, while her pregnancy and nursing help to define divinity's revelation through the Tetragrammaton.

Rabbi Shimon explains emanation by identifying *Binah* as the womb in which the lower *sefirot* are formed and from which they emerge, correlating each of the Tetragrammaton's letters to the *sefirot*. The paths that represent the sefirotic potencies begin in a concealed state. *Binah's* pregnancy and childbearing then signify revelation being birthed into the world, as the Upper Mother mediates the point at which concealment becomes revealment. The Tetragrammaton's first letter, *Yud*, gestures toward the first *sefirah Keter* and beyond to intimate God's unknowable existence as *Ein Sof* (here represented as the divine Nothing).[44] As a masculine gradation, *Keter* impregnates *Binah*, who signifies the Tetragrammaton's second letter, *He'*. The third letter,

Vav, is represented by the six masculine *sefirot* from *Ḥesed* to *Yesod*, understood as a group. The Tetragrammaton's final letter *He*ʿ is associated with the feminine *Shekhinah*.

According to this teaching, both the *sefirot* and the divine name are arranged in a familial structure, with the Tetragrammaton's initial *Yud* and *He*ʾ representing divine parents and its final *Vav* and *He*ʿ signifying nursing children birthed from the supernal Mother. This esoteric social imagery is complicated by aquatic images that are also attached to the sefirotic structure. Using a river metaphor to describe divine emanation and overflow helps to teach that God's aspects are perpetually engaged in emergence. This teaching is facilitated by Rabbi Shimon's interpretation of Genesis 2:10, which uses the present tense ("goes forth") to describe the Edenic river's continuous flow. Rabbi Shimon then links this continuous divine outpouring to potentiality's transformation into existence by drawing on the divine name *Ehyeh*'s literal translation: "I will be." Yet it is only when the river, representing *Binah*, takes on anthropomorphic qualities by becoming pregnant that the *sefirot* and the divine name are revealed. The confused chronology at the passage's end, in which the two children suckle from the Mother before her impregnation by the supernal *Yud* is recapitulated, emphasizes the lesson about ongoing divine overflow and sefirotic interdependence.

While this text's nature and nurture connotations are similar to Zohar 3:150b's, stressing an all-powerful God's choice to reveal itself to humanity in comprehensible fashion, here mother-imagery plays a dominant role. This authorial choice is emphasized by the text's affective language of desire and love; the supernal river that is also the Mother desires to remain with her beloved. The Zohar draws on the Song of Songs to develop this emotional context, applying the female beloved's role to *Binah*, rather than *Shekhinah*. The loving relationship between the supernal Mother and the supernal *Yud* implies that the relationships among the *sefirot* are structured by a similar love and desire, layering this text with affective connotations generally absent from earlier works. All of these textual elements condition the reader's understanding of the divine world with which he stands in relationship, urging him to envision a loving, nurturing God whose enlivening life energy flows like an unceasing river.[45]

As in the writings of Isaac the Blind and Ezra of Gerona, the Zohar uses the suckling metaphor to depict divine overflow's transmission. Yet while these early kabbalists source suckling and overflow in the masculine *sefirah Ḥokhmah*, the Zohar shifts divine nursing from *Ḥokhmah* to the feminine *Binah*.[46] This change grants the suckling image additional coherence as a model for thinking about God. By freely using the language of desire, pregnancy, childbirth, mother-hood, and suckling with reference to the Upper Mother, the Zohar firmly links the suckling-as-spiritual-transmission metaphor to a feminized sefirotic gradation. These associations add cognitive structure, as well as affective texture, to the basic suckling metaphor. In this text, the image of God as a breastfeeding mother exists in a fully realized form, providing a structured series of divine interrelationships that in turn inspire a particular perception of divinity—one of nurture, interdependence, and intimacy. Although femininity is often associated with Judgment in the Zohar, this passage's female images are structured only with nurturing connotations. The Zohar's enthusiasm for anthropomorphic imagery, which sets it apart from many earlier kabbalistic texts, allows access to unprecedented metaphoric structures that in turn encourage new ways to understand humanity's relationship with the divine.

Sefer ha-Zohar 2:122b:

> The brows of the eyes are called "Place," for they give watching to all the colors, the Lords of Watching. These brows, with regard to [that which is] below, are brows of watching from that river that flows and goes forth: a place to draw from that river, to bathe in the whiteness of *Atika'*, in the milk that flows from the Mother. So that when Might is stretched forth and the eyes glow with a red (*sumqa'*) color, *Atika' Kadisha'* shines his whiteness and glows in the Mother, and she is filled with milk and she suckles (*ve-yanqa'*) these.[47] And all the eyes bathe in that milk of the Mother that flows and goes forth continuously. As it is written: "Bathed in milk" (Song 5:12). In the milk of the Mother that flows continuously and does not cease. . . . The ears of the King: When pleasure is found and the Mother suckles (*yanqa'*) and the shining of *Atika' Kadisha'* is brightened, the light of the two brains is aroused and the shining of the Father and the Mother. All of these are called the brains of the King, and they glow as one. And when they glow as one, they are called the ears of the Lord, because they receive the prayers of Israel.

This passage is excerpted from a Zoharic teaching on the divine coun-tenance and the uppermost *sefirot*. The text uses the nursing mother image extensively, specifically describing the divine overflow as milk nursed from *Binah*.[48] *Atika' Kadisha'* (The Holy Ancient One) repre-sents the masculine *sefirot Keter* and *Hokhmah*, although it may also bear implications of *Ein Sof*. *Atika'* is also the Father, while *Binah* is the Mother whose sexual stimulation inspires her to express milk. This flowing milk pours throughout the divine world, bringing heal-ing and unity in its wake.[49] In kabbalistic symbolism, white represents Mercy while red represents Judgment.[50] The Mother's white milk rem-edies Judgment's potentially destructive power as it flows through the sefirotic structure and heals by eradicating redness.[51] Melila Hellner-Eshed has linked white light in the Zohar to the face of *Atika'* and the fullest expression of *Hesed* (divine love).[52] She has also correlated this whiteness with the Zohar's highest level of mystical consciousness.[53] This color symbolism makes milk directly relevant to the passage, con-tributing further structure to the image of God as a nursing Mother and its associated experience of suckling.

While the text relies on feminine imagery to convey its theology, it also draws motherhood beyond human proportions and invests it with cosmic significance. This cosmological aspect is emphasized by the pas-sage's implication that milk is not just a suckling medium, but is also a substance in which total immersion can be achieved. The *sefirot* (and possibly the angelic potencies as well) receive divine milk both inter-nally, via suckling, and externally, by bathing. This startling image of complete inundation in the divine overflow is achieved by referencing Song 5:12, allowing the Zohar to depict a divine world washed fully and completely in an ongoing flow of milk. It is even possible to read this immersion as a reference to mystical experience. Melila Hellner-Eshed has demonstrated a strong correspondence between mystical consciousness and white light in the Zohar, connecting this light to the desire for ascent beyond the realm of differentiation.[54] She writes, "Above and beyond all the colors and forms experienced by the mystic, the kabbalist seeks the whitest light of all, the light of *Atika' Kadisha'* (The Holy Ancient One), the light of the sefirah *Keter*."[55]

The text does express humanity's engagement with this divine flow of whiteness. When Judgment and Mercy are balanced and the Mother's milk flows freely, Israel's prayers are received, reasserting the kabbalistic idea that when *sefirot* and human beings maintain proper relationships with each other, divine overflow pours into the world and in turn allows human prayer and blessings to ascend to God. Divine overflow is given in pleasure and mercy, structured by positive emotional connotations and feminine suckling language. When Israel's prayers ascend, they are received at divinity's highest levels amid such pleasurable emotions. Using this text as a model, the kabbalistic reader is able to locate himself in relation to this structure and participate in it through prayer. He is encouraged to do so by the text's description of the joyous atmosphere into which his prayers ascend.

This passage, like Zohar 3:150b, presents a case in which mixed metaphors and images highlight both divinity's concealed strangeness and its revealed familiarity. Breasts are located on the divine countenance; figures bathe in milky rivers; and milky flow gives way to shining light that admits human prayer. Juxtaposing familiar images in unfamiliar configurations, the Zohar provokes thought that approaches the borders of human understanding. It expresses God's complexity through mixed metaphors in which concrete terms blur together to extend the reader's perceptions. The divine countenance cannot be reduced to anything so normative as a human face. It must encompass the divine being, incorporating a multiplicity of metaphors in an attempt to express divinity's ultimate mystery.[56] There is little difference in the conceptual process of understanding this Zoharic passage and the process of understanding *Avinu Malkenu's* model of a God who is both Father and King in relation to a self who is both child and subject. The difference is one of degree rather than one of kind: it is significantly more complicated to understand the self's relationship to a God who is both a Father and a nursing Mother—both a river and a flow of milk, and whose face contains both breasts and eyes. Striving to understand such complex theological models to their fullest capacity is an exercise central to the kabbalistic endeavor of drawing ever closer to God.[57]

Nursing Between *Binah* and *Shekhinah*

Sefer ha-Zohar 3:17a:

In the book of Rav Hamnuna Sava, it says: Every time that the Assembly of Israel is found with the Holy One, blessed be He, it is as though (*kivyakhol*) the Holy One, blessed be He, is in his perfection, and he takes delight (*re'ey*) in the pleasure (*be-re'uta'*) that is caused for him from his suckling (*yeniqo*) of the milk of the Upper Mother.[58] And from that suckling (*yeniqo*) of his that he suckles (*yaneq*), he gives all the rest of the others to drink, and he suckles (*ve-yaneq*) them. And we have learned that Rabbi Shimon bar Yoḥai said: Every time that the Assembly of Israel is found with the Holy One, blessed be He, the Holy One, blessed be He, is in his perfection, in joy (*be-ḥedvvah*). Blessings rest upon him and go out from him to all the rest of the others. And every time that the Assembly of Israel is not found with the Holy One, blessed be He, it is as though (*kivyakhol*) blessings are withheld from him, and from all the rest of the others. And the secret of the matter is that in every place that male and female are not found, blessings do not dwell upon it. And because of this the Holy One, blessed be He, roars and weeps, as it is said, "Surely He roars over his dwelling" (Jeremiah 25:30).

This passage is taken from a Zoharic interpretation of Song of Songs 1:7, "Tell me, you whom my soul loves, where do you pasture (*tir'eh*), where do you lie down at noon?" It presents two different models for relationships among the *sefirot*: one positive and one negative. Connection, perfection, blessings, and pleasure characterize the positive model, while disconnection, weeping, and withheld blessings are associated with the negative model.[59] The difference between the two intra-divine states is defined by suckling's presence or absence. In the ideal sefirotic configuration, the Upper Mother's milk is suckled by the Holy One (the masculine *sefirah Tif'eret*), who in turn nurses the rest of the divine aspects. This positive situation depends upon the masculine *sefirah*'s interdependent relationship with the feminine Assembly of Israel. Divine overflow passes steadily among the *sefirot*, uniting them in a perfected state and enabling blessings to pass through the system. Suckling's absence creates a stoppage in the blessings' flow, causing distress within divinity (and by implication the lower world as well). Divine breastfeeding, stimulated by correct relationships among masculine and feminine *sefirot*, becomes the medium by which God and the world achieve harmony and perfection.

Divine suckling is unambiguous in this passage. Structured by both feminine imagery and affective language, the text clearly directs its reader toward understandings of the divine overflow as *Binah*'s milk, nursing as this milk's method of transmission, and *Binah* Herself as a mother. The suckling relationship is attached to emotions of plea-sure and delight. These terms are exegetically derived from the Song of Songs through a play on words between the Song's term pasture (*tir'eh*) and the Zohar's terms "taking delight" (*re'ey*) and "pleasure" (*re'uta'*), which all share a common root (*r.'.y.*). Suckling relationships among the *sefirot* also involve joyous emotion (*ḥedvvah*). Here, the pleasure (*ta'anug*) that Ezra of Gerona associates with drawing (*hamshakhah*) from the divine overflow in his Commentary on the same Song verse is attached to suckling imagery.[60] In both interpretations, love between the male and female speakers from the Song of Songs, understood as male and female *sefirot*, grounds divine spiritual transmission in posi-tive, tender nuance. However, only the Zohar overtly encourages its reader to associate these emotions with divine nursing.[61]

The text's affective terminology also evokes passionate, erotic qualities. The *sefirot* are understood as the Song's lovers, and integra-tion among the masculine and feminine divine aspects is accompanied by pleasure and joy in divine energy's flow—a flow made possible by correct sefirotic interrelationships. The passage also cautions its reader about the dire possibilities that derive from misalignment and plea-sure's absence, during which suckling ceases. The Holy One is depicted as anguished and angered when deprived of His intimate relationship with the Assembly of Israel. Jeremiah 25:30, in which God roars with anger against Jerusalem and the nations, highlights this undesirable state. However, the Zohar interprets the verse as God's anguished cry over his own disunity and separation from *Shekhinah*, rather than as anger against earthly beings. Since a dominant metaphor for the femi-nine tenth *sefirah* is that of a dwelling place, when the Holy One roars over his dwelling he is actually protesting separation from the Assembly of Israel and His own interrupted relationality.[62]

Although the people of Israel are not mentioned in this passage, the kabbalistic reader would understand union between the Holy One, blessed be He, and the Assembly of Israel to be partially con-sequent upon his own actions and relationship to divinity. A strong reader would understand both this passage's positive model for divine relationality and the corollary that by aligning his own relationship with divinity through proper prayer, deeds, and intentionality, he helps to inspire divine suckling and perfection. Furthermore, this description of joyous pleasure among the *sefirot* teaches him about the environment into which his prayers ascend. While the text deals exclusively with relationships among the *sefirot*, the kabbalistic reader's role in the divine drama is clear from other Zoharic teachings. Like the divine aspects themselves, the kabbalist's ideal relationship to divinity is defined by nursing divine overflow from God, and thus receiving blessings, pleasure, and nurturing contentment.

Obviously, there is an unusual element to this passage's suckling imagery. It is not only feminine *sefirot* that act as suckling's sources, but also the Holy One, blessed be He, who represents the *sefirah Tiferet*. This masculine gradation nurses the rest of the divine aspects with milk he receives from *Binah*, creating a suckling system that carries divine overflow throughout the *sefirot*. Such male nursing recalls both early kabbalistic writings that name the masculine *sefirah Hokhmah* as suckling's source and rabbinic texts about men who miraculously suckle children, such as *Bereshit Rabbah* 30:8's Mordekhai and the unfortunate widower of BT *Shabbat* 53b.[63] Finally, this masculine suckling alludes to the *Bahir*'s link between milk and the masculine *sefirah Hesed* (Mercy).

In *Zohar* 3:17a, these themes converge to express the kabbalistic theology of divine overflow and its role in positive sefirotic interrelationships. Through intertextually associating all of these elements (which can be assumed to have been present in Zoharic authors' and readers' minds), the masculine *sefirah*'s suckling act becomes surprisingly natural. Caroline Walker Bynum notes that the medievals had a far more fluid notion of gender than modern people, based partially in the medieval medical understanding of women as men whose physiology has been turned "outside-in." She suggests that medieval people perceived the body as generative rather than sexual and that these ideas allowed medieval thinkers to use gendered imagery more fluidly than do moderns. The Zoharic passages in which masculine *sefirot* suckle divine overflow to the rest of the sefirotic structure would tend to indicate that Bynum's assessment is correct.[64]

Extending nursing imagery beyond feminine *sefirot* also helps to emphasize one of the suckling metaphor's most important themes—that all *sefirot* are part of the greater divine whole. This theology, which appears in Isaac the Blind's work without overtly gendered connotations and is associated with femininity in Ezra of Gerona's Song of Songs Commentary, becomes a normative mode for expressing divine energy's transmission in the Zohar. The most important aspect of the suckling mother image is not, after all, the image itself, but rather the concept that the image presents and the relationships it seeks to structure and define. In this case, the text stresses that proper cosmic order is established by maintaining intimate, positive divine relationships that create unity in the sefirotic world and allow blessings to flow into the human world.

Sefer ha-Zohar 2:256b-257a:

Here it is spirit within spirit, cleaving as one. From here dwells Abraham who is the right that is called Love (*Ahavah*).[65] (There are many who say: and he took the place that is called Love.)[66] And then: "breasts (*shadayim*) formed" (Ezekiel 16:7). And they were filled with all good to satiate (*le-safqa'*) and to nourish (*le-'itzana'*) all from here. And when those breasts formed and they were filled from amidst his supernal compassion (*rehimo*), then this palace was called *El Shaddai*, as we have said. And in this all the world was satiated (*istapaq*) when it was created, because when the world was created it was not able to exist in being, and it did not exist, until this palace which Abraham took was revealed (*de-itgeley*), and when Abraham was revealed (*itgeley*) in this place.[67] And then he said to the world: This is enough (*day*) satiation (*sipuqa'*) for the world to be nourished (*le-'itzana'*) from it, and for it to exist. And in addition *El Shaddai* was called *El Shaddai* to all in it. And the Holy One, blessed be He, prepared to fill it and to prepare it for the time to come, as it is written: "So that you will suckle (*tinqu*) and be satisfied (*u-seva'tem*) from the breast of consolation, so that you will suck (*tamotzu*) and have pleasure (*ve-hit'anagtem*) from the teat of glory" (Isaiah 66:11). The breast of consolation and the teat of Glory: both of these are in this palace. And in that time, it is written: "Who would have said to Abraham that Sarah would suckle (*heniqah*) children?" (Genesis 21:7). Because this suckling (*yeniqa'*) depends on Abraham.

This passage is found in a Zoharic sequence that connects the sefirotic and angelic worlds to *hekhalot* mysticism's heavenly palaces. The text uses the suckling-as-spiritual-transmission metaphor to describe divine overflow's role in creating and sustaining the entire world. Emerging from the fourth *sefirah*, *Ḥesed* (Mercy), the overflow is described as an outpouring of Love emerging from the divine breasts, which are revealed in conjunction with the compassionate patriarch Abraham and the divine name *El Shaddai*.[68] The divine breasts' world-sustaining flow is tied to experiencing love, compassion, consolation and pleasure, embedding the suckling metaphor in joyous emotions. Combining these emotional terms with references to satiation and nourishment characterizes the divine overflow as an overwhelmingly positive force from which creation emerges and with which it is continuously enlivened and renewed.[69] In this passage, absolute love between parent and child characterizes the relationships among the *sefirot* and between these divine aspects and the world. Divine breastfeeding, with all of its experiential connotations, is presented as a cosmological foundation.

The divine name *El Shaddai*, found throughout this passage, ties together all of the text's major concepts and images in a series of linguistic allusions. Although the Biblical name *El Shaddai* is an ambiguous term that has little (if anything) to do with breast imagery, the sound and spelling of *Shaddai* recall the sound and spelling of *shadayim*, the Hebrew term for "breasts," which is also found in the passage.[70] In addition, the name *El Shaddai* emphasizes the Zohar's teaching on fulfillment and satiation by recalling the word *day*, which means "enough" (and is also found in this passage). In fact, *she-day*, an expression that uses the same letters as *Shaddai*, means "that is enough." This is a classical pun, since the name *El Shaddai* is also associated with *day* in rabbinic literature. Both *Bereshit Rabbah* 5:8 and BT *Ḥagiga* 12a associate this divine name with the world's creation, explaining that God is called *El Shaddai* because he orders the heavens and earth (in the Midrash) and the sea (in the Talmud) to cease expanding by telling them, "Enough!" Zohar 2:256b-257a plays on these words' similar sounds, drawing a punning link between the divine name, the breasts of Abraham, and the satiation derived from suckling divine love's overflow. In this way, the Zohar uses allusion to draw the physical aspects of suckling implied by the word *breasts* together with the satiation aspects of suckling (both physical and emotional) implied by the word *enough*.

The Zohar is not the only kabbalistic text to incorporate a similar play on the name *El Shaddai*. Rabbi Joseph ben Abraham Gikatilla, a late thirteenth century kabbalist who was known to Moses de León and may have been a member of the Zoharic authorship, cites BT *Ḥagiga* 12a in his kabbalistic work *Sha'arey Tzedeq* (*Gates of Righteousness*).[71] Describing the *Shekhinah*, he writes, "Know that this attribute is also called *Shaddai*. And the reason is that from Her divine overflow (*shefa'*) comes to all that are found in the world, and She sustains all created beings. . . . [She] is the place of divine overflow and emanation and nursing. . . . Every one receives joy and existence and life from Her, each according to his food and to his type. Therefore this attribute is called *Shaddai*, because there is in Her enough (*day*) sustenance and life and existence and placement for all who are found in the world. And there is no lack in Her, and all suckles from Her. And this is as it says in *Ḥagiga* of the name *Shaddai*: Who said to the world enough! . . . And the matter is likened to the breasts from which an infant suckles."[72]

In this passage, Gikatilla links the name *El Shaddai* to existence, nourishment, and divine overflow's transmission, while also incorporating feminine breastfeeding imagery.[73] Both Gikatilla's work and Zohar 2:256b-257a connect *El Shaddai* to spiritual satiation's source, and in both passages breast and suckling imagery further enhance this concept, providing it with additional structure that creates a strong cognitive model for the reader. The Zohar, however, brings in additional emotional language to depict a cosmos driven by divine love and flowing with compassion; one in which divine breasts both reveal the time for the world's birth and are present to console the world at its ending. Here, God's love and nurture extend beyond individuals and become essential for universal continuation. The kabbalist, by implication, participates in this system as a child of God who is united with all creation by suckling from his divine parent's breasts.

Three proof texts contribute to the Zoharic text's suckling imagery, while also driving its theological message: Ezekiel 16:7, Isaiah 66:11, and Genesis 21:7. In their Biblical context, the Ezekiel and Isaiah verses both refer to a personified, feminine Jerusalem, expressing love between God and Israel. Although the phrase from Ezekiel is found in a tender Biblical scene that leads to Israel's eventual transgression (Ezekiel 16:15–34), the Zoharic passage includes only the story's positive side, allowing the Biblical breast reference to introduce God's breasts to the reader.

The Isaiah verse is drawn from an eschatological vision of ultimate reconciliation between God and the Israelite people. This proof text drives the passage toward its theological climax. According to the Zohar, divine breasts formed prior to creation, and suckling the divine overflow is presented as a precondition for existence, as the world is nourished from God's overflowing love. Isaiah 66:11 presents these same divine breasts as components of the "time to come" (the *eschaton*), when they will offer consolation, pleasure, and glory to the world as part of a final cosmic reconciliation. By incorporating both the eschaton and the creation, the Zohar portrays the Abrahamic palace and the divine breasts as embracing the created world's entire duration. This chronological embrace emphasizes the passage's main theological point—that the world is dependent on divine love at every moment of its existence. The suckling image not only describes how divine overflow is necessary to link and sustain the upper and lower worlds, but also presents a universe built on a loving, nurturing foundation. Suckling's associations with the parent-child relationship provide context for existence's ultimate divine homecoming.

Genesis 21:7 ties the other Biblical texts (and their breast imagery) to the patriarch Abraham, whose revelation as the breasted palace of Love is also a necessary precondition for divine energy's outpouring. In kabbalistic thought, masculinity is often associated with Mercy and femininity with Judgment, due to the locations of masculine and feminine gradations within the sefirotic structure.[74] Bahir 136–37 provides a precedent for linking Abraham, Mercy, and milk, allowing the Zohar to include the patriarch in its suckling imagery. That this breasted mother is actually a father fades in importance next to the full theological expression of a universe sustained by suckling love and Mercy's infinite overflow. Referring to the patriarch Isaac's miraculous birth sustains the text's atmosphere of love and wonder while also referencing rabbinic suckling stories. It can be no accident that this Zoharic text, with its elaborate divine suckling and its accompanying feminine elements, presents as its climax the very proof text that established Abraham's wife Sarah as a superabundant suckling figure. Although the passage locates Sarah's plentiful breasts on Abraham, it seems to understand the two as a marital unit, reading husband and wife as a single entity. Reading Abraham metonymically for Sarah in this way allows the Zohar to draw on kabbalistic associations between Abraham and Mercy, while still developing the suckling-as-spiritual transmission metaphor.[75]

As in the previous passage, suckling's importance as a cognitive model for understanding divine overflow's cosmic role overrides normative biological associations. Thus, the Zohar is able to cite a proof text that is actually about Sarah and apply its accompanying imagery to the patriarch, displacing Sarah's superabundant breasts onto her husband Abraham. In fact, the Zohar's term for revealing Abraham and the divine palace is closely related to the term for Sarah's breasts' revealment in rabbinic literature.[76] In *Bereshit Rabbah* 53:9, Abraham tells Sarah, "Reveal (*gali*) your breasts so that all will know that the Holy One, blessed be He, has begun to do miracles." Zohar 2:256b-257a teaches its reader, "When the world was created it was not able to exist in being, and it did not exist, until this palace which Abraham took was revealed (*de-itgeley*), and when Abraham was revealed (*itgeley*) in this place." In both texts, revealing abundant, flowing breasts signifies the revelation of God's abundant power. Furthermore, revelation and divine suckling are often linked in the Zohar. Consider Zohar 1:203a, in which the prophets suckle their revelations from *Shekhinah*, and Zohar 3:65a-b, in which *Binah* reveals the divine name through processes of pregnancy and nursing. It is this type of complex intertextuality, which includes both words and images, that contributes to the Zohar's character as an effective theological masterpiece.

Conclusion

In these Zoharic texts, the image of God as a nursing mother reaches its fullest expression. As in the writings of Isaac the Blind and Ezra of Gerona, suckling imagery serves as a metaphor for divine energy's spiritual transmission, both among the *sefirot* and between divinity and humanity. However, in *Sefer ha-Zohar* the image takes on immediate and experiential qualities absent from earlier literature because it is thoroughly embedded in a stated network of connotations that provide anthropomorphic and anthropopathic structure for the reader. Embracing the kabbalistic characterization of *Shekhinah* and *Binah* as divine mother figures, the Zohar uses vivid breast imagery, milk imagery, and parent-child imagery to further develop the suckling metaphor, making it accessible through the lens of personal experience. Affective language adds emotional texture to this imagery, encouraging the reader to understand that divine overflow is transmitted in love, nurture, and pleasure, and that it inspires a satiation that is emotional, as well as a physical.[77] Divine suckling imagery and its connotations encourage the Zohar's kabbalistic reader to re-envision his own relationship with God through this tender, familial lens.

CHAPTER 4

Concluding Thoughts on the Nursing Divine

Why a Breastfeeding God?

Kabbalah's divine nursing imagery encourages an interactive relationship between God and human beings by modeling divine character and humanity's relationship to that character along the lines of a tender family interaction. This model, which draws on all the positive emotional qualities of a mother suckling her newborn child, creates an intimate social bond that complements and corrects other divine descriptions such as King, Judge, Light, and Intellect.[1] It also destabilizes kabbalistic theology's association of masculinity with divine Mercy and femininity with divine Judgment, correcting a potential over-reliance on these abstract gender formulas by drawing on observations rooted in the dynamics of family life. According to kabbalistic theology, the sefirotic tree's right side is associated with Mercy, expansion, and masculinity—while its left side (on which the feminine *sefirah Binah* is situated) is associated with Judgment, containment, and femininity. *Shekhinah* occupies the center point between the two sides, directing divine energy into the world in a mixture of these qualities that is determined by humanity's adherence (or lack thereof) to the divine commandments.[2] For this reason, *Shekhinah* is frequently associated with a mediated form of Judgment that can be understood as a negative aspect of divine femininity, since the thought of punitive action by

God often evokes emotions of guilt, anxiety, and fear.[3] Breastfeeding and nurturing imagery attached to this same *sefirah* offer important correctives that prevent Kabbalah's connections between Judgment and the feminine from becoming overdetermined. Indeed, the fluidity of Kabbalah's divine images seems in part designed to prevent such symbolic overdetermination, which has the potential to diminish the kabbalists' understanding of divinity's omnisignificant nature.

Personal experience allows most people to understand the relationship between a nursing mother and her child as a connection involving nurture, love, and reliance. However, the relationship between mother and child was not a generic one for medieval Jews. Jewish focus on family and procreation remained intact even in the kabbalistic community, along with distinct laws and cultural assumptions concerning breastfeeding. Kabbalists such as Ezra of Gerona and the Zohar's authors lived within the context of these associations that inspired and affected their choice to apply suckling imagery to God. Although there are not many sources that deal directly with Jewish women's daily lives in the kabbalists' cultural milieu, thanks to recent scholarship some tentative statements can be made.[4]

The following information has been construed from sources that, like all the texts investigated in this study, were written by men for theological, legal, or literary purposes.[5] Such works often express cultural ideals without informing their readers whether or not these ideals existed as lived realities. However, lack of knowledge about medieval Jewish women's lives is not necessarily a disadvantage when investigating Kabbalah's nursing divine images. For example, the absence of such data helps to resist reading these sources from a positivist perspective that could eclipse the imagery's role within the mystical tradition. Kabbalah's breastfeeding divine relies upon an idealized literary representation of femininity that was understood and produced by men, based on their cultural associations regarding motherhood and breastfeeding. These associations relate more directly to the nursing divine than do the actual lives of medieval women.

Elisheva Baumgarten has demonstrated that motherhood was the premier social role for Jewish women in medieval family life.[6] Bearing and caring for children were understood (at least by men) as ideals toward which all women aspired, a conviction rooted partially in the Biblical narrative's concern with reproduction.[7] Men also believed that women naturally loved their children.[8] This love was considered to be reciprocal and was thought to inspire children to honor their mothers. In the thirteenth century, the French scholar Moses of Couçy explained that a mother's gentle manner with her children naturally inspired less fear than did a father's sterner approach to parenting.[9] Breastfeeding was an important activity, since infants were dependent on breast milk for survival.[10] Medieval Jewish men believed that women wanted to breastfeed, an idea based partially in traditional Jewish texts like BT *Pesaḥim* 112a: "More than the calf wants to suckle, the cow wants to nurse."[11] Families were encouraged to perceive nursing as a natural and positive womanly function, while breastfeeding was also written into marriage contracts as a wifely obligation.[12] Although a woman could fulfill this obligation by hiring a wet nurse, in Spain where the kabbalists lived maternal nursing was considered more desirable.[13] This opinion seems to derive from the idea that religiosity and character traits are transmitted via breast milk, a concept amply attested in chapter 1's rabbinic texts.

Nursing's duration could last anywhere between twenty-four months and six years of age, ending when a child could speak and was considered old enough to begin his formal religious education.[14] At that time, a child's father took over much of his son's instruction.[15] In his study of Ashkenazic rituals associated with religious instruction, Ivan Marcus notes that many foods connected with preliminary educational rituals symbolically represent milk, emphasizing a shift from maternal feeding to the "milk" of Torah.[16] This Torah-as-milk/nursing mother theme is represented both in aggadic literature and in Ezra's Song Commentary, in which Torah is suckled from *Shekhinah*'s divine breasts.[17]

These cultural associations with motherhood and nursing provide insight into the kabbalists' intentions in emphasizing the image of a breastfeeding God.[18] The kabbalists did not need to refer explicitly to these associations for their readers to understand breastfeeding's cultural connotations. Instead, personal experience structured the metaphor for its readers as they sought to understand the kabbalistic teachings. For a medieval kabbalist, identifying God as a nursing mother and himself as God's suckling child encouraged the model of a divinity whose relationship to humanity was rooted in natural love and beneficence, but also in duty and an obligation to care for the creatures It created. This imagery also encouraged the kabbalist to understand his own relational role as that of an utterly dependent child who was reliant upon divinity for spiritual nurture and sustenance. This dependence defined a relationship distinct from that modeled by masculine divine imagery, particularly because the relationship between nursing mother and suckling child was associated with developmental stages prior to both speech and formal education.

The nursing divine image offered a relational model based in emotion and experience, rather than scholarship and ritual. It emphasized a less intimidating aspect of divinity to which the kabbalists could attach their affection, just as an earthly mother offered a less intimidating version of medieval parental love than did a father. Although the nursing mother metaphor did not replace masculine divine imagery, it complemented divine and human relational models based on masculine imagery by bringing God into all areas of the mystic's life, rather than confining his interactions to scholarship, ritual, and authority. By developing an anthropomorphic divine image focused on the quality of relation, the kabbalist recreated himself as a being capable of standing in such a relation. As Roy Rappaport explains, "Every term that participates in a metaphor is transformed into more than itself."[19] Divine nursing imagery inspired a "return to the whole" by presenting a new and alternative cosmology whose structure was based on motherly love and nurture.[20]

Reasons for Relationality

It is possible to suggest (though difficult to prove) some underlying sociocultural reasons for Kabbalah's focus on relationality and its interest in structuring human and divine interaction to encourage intimacy and familiarity. In twelfth-century France and thirteenth-century Spain where classical Kabbalah developed, Judaism faced challenges directly associated with religious relationality. Scholars of Jewish mysticism generally understand Kabbalah's development in part as a response to Jewish philosophy, which promoted the idea of a divine accessible solely through intellectual communion.[21] For example, Moshe Idel has suggested that classical Kabbalah's development in the twelfth and thirteenth centuries was fueled by a desire to define the kabbalistic version of Jewish esotericism over and against philosophy's rationalistic esotericism.[22] However, kabbalistic responses to philosophy were by no means unified. While Naḥmanides and his school were strongly anti-Maimonidean, the Geronese school of kabbalists often incorporated Neoplatonic ideas and language into their literature.[23] Charles Mopsik and Daniel Abrams have suggested that the Zohar was composed in Aramaic as a means of disengaging with medieval Hebrew literature's growing philosophical focus, granting the work an appearance of ancient authority that superseded philosophy's more recent innovations.[24]

While Kabbalah's response to philosophy was complex, many kabbalists appear to have found its extreme reliance on intellect and rationalism an inadequate model for developing a fully nuanced relationship with God. Classical kabbalists were deeply engaged in the controversies surrounding Maimonides' *Guide of the Perplexed*, which presented a divinity describable through negative theology rather than through human or natural images, discouraging models of divine and human relationality based on social values.[25] In Guide 3:51, the philosopher writes, "If, however, you have apprehended God and His acts in accordance with what is required by the intellect, you should afterwards engage in totally devoting yourself to Him, endeavor to come closer to Him, and strengthen the bond between you and Him—that is, the intellect."[26] In Guide 3:51 and 3:54, Maimonides implies that achieving love of God and performing loving kindness come only *after* intellectual apprehension of the divine.[27] This perspective stands in marked contrast with that of Isaac the Blind, who suggests that a more intimate relationship with God is possible. Notably, Isaac characterizes this relationship as one of suckling *rather than* one of knowledge (as discussed in chapter 2). His description of the suckling relationship is particularly intriguing in light of Haviva Pedaya's study demonstrating his group's involvement with various types of mystical experience, including automatic speech.[28] Isaac's refusal to rely exclusively on intellection continues with Ezra of Gerona, who fleshes out the suckling relationship by using the Song of Songs' sacred language to clothe it in terms of femininity, intimacy, longing, and hope.

Although both Isaac and his student Ezra incorporate Neoplatonic ideas into their thought, both also insist that there is a relationship between divinity and humanity that stands alongside intellectual connection and transcends it—a view elaborated in the Zohar, with its emphasis on affective spirituality.[29] Melila Hellner-Eshed has suggested that the Zohar's mystical foundations are rooted in love rather than knowledge, and in this text the very act of expounding on scripture is framed in emotional terms that involve both weeping and wild displays of joy.[30] It seems that one strategy by which Kabbalah responds to philosophy's challenge is by redefining the Jewish relationship with God in new and compelling ways, many of which rely on the very anthropomorphic and emotional models that medieval philosophy disdains.[31] The kabbalists encourage modes of relationship with divinity that include intellectual communion but also extend beyond it. The image of a motherly, breastfeeding God, with its emphasis on relationality, affectivity, and spiritual connection that transcends both speech and knowledge serves as a distinct alternative to philosophy's intellectual divine model.

Kabbalistic interest in relationality may also respond to external challenges from the Christian Church. During the thirteenth century, increased missionizing activities were forcibly directed toward the Spanish Jewish community. With the growth of the missionizing Dominican and Franciscan orders and the 1215 Fourth Lateran Council's attempts to regulate Christian society, public religious disputations, enforced Jewish attendance at Christian sermons, and trials and censorship of Jewish religious texts became new means by which the Church attempted to consolidate and grow its faith community.[32] Some of the most notable episodes in these Christian efforts took place in Spain. For example, after the famous 1263 Barcelona disputation between the kabbalist Naḥmanides and the convert Paulus Christiani, King James I of Aragon appointed Raymond Martini, author of the famous anti-Jewish treatise *Pugio fidei*, to censor Jewish books and remove blasphemous passages.[33] New polemic and missionizing strategies also emerged in the thirteenth century, such as the use of rabbinic literature to support Christian truth claims.[34] Central to the Christian community's polemical efforts were the ideas that God had rejected Jews, that Jews were deliberately misinterpreting their own scriptures, and that the Jewish commandment-oriented relationship to God had been invalidated by the new relationship established through Jesus as Christ.[35] Two of these accusations, divine rejection and the Christ-based supercessionist argument, deliberately attacked the Jewish relationship with God.

The thirteenth-century kabbalists were aware of these activities and of the Christian source texts in which they were rooted. Kabbalistic fascination with Christian texts, polemic, and practices has been demonstrated by Yehuda Liebes, Elliot Wolfson, and Daniel Abrams, who show that the kabbalists had an intimate familiarity with the gospels of John and Luke and the Book of Acts, as well as broader aspects of Christian theology.[36] Liebes suggests that these mystical authors may even have known of Raymond Martini's *Pugio fidei*.[37] Ḥananel Mack has identified a long-standing tradition of anti-Christian polemic among Jewish writers in southern France, demonstrating that this polemic literature was known by the thirteenth-century Geronese kabbalists Ezra and Azriel, who studied with the French Rabbi Isaac the Blind.[38]

It is possible to read several kabbalistic innovations, including the image of God as a nursing mother, as responses to Christian polemic attacks on Jewish divine relationality. For example, the overflow that is so central to divine nursing theology acts as a vital and necessary connection between God and the Jewish people, sustaining not only the Jewish community but the rest of the world as well (as seen in chapter 3). Such theology makes a strong argument for positive relationality between God and the Jewish community. Kabbalah also affirms the commandments' intrinsic value by reading ritual performance as a way to encourage the divine overflow's transmission.[39] The nursing divine fits into this cultural context as an effective counterargument to key Christian claims of Jewish separation from God by emphasizing the intimate relationship between Jews and divinity. This relationship—which is based on divine mercy, love, and nurture—offers a vivid alternative to claims of divine abandonment. However, neither this suggestion nor the connection to philosophy can be proven in the current state of research, so the kabbalists' precise historical reasons for developing a breastfeeding divine must remain obscure.[40]

The Nursing Divine and the Question of Religious Influence

Negative response was not the kabbalists' only reaction to Christian ideas. Emphasis on divine femininity was one of Kabbalah's greatest innovations, yet kabbalistic images like the divine nursing mother were developed in the context of similar Christian theological trends. Both Peter Schäfer and Arthur Green have suggested a direct influence between Kabbalah's late-twelfth-century female divine imagery and the cult of Mary's rise in Western Europe.[41] During the twelfth century, Christian theologians increased their use of feminine religious language, producing texts that included images of the Virgin similar to Kabbalah's descriptions of *Shekhinah*.[42] Feminine religious imagery was invoked not only in Marian theology, but also in depictions of Jesus as mother, Ecclesia as mother, and male clerical authority figures as mothers.[43] All of these representations could appear in conjunction with suckling imagery.[44]

As in Jewish theology, Christian breastfeeding metaphors provided models for understanding the relationships between divinity and humanity. Bernard of Clairvaux (1091–1153), founder of the Cistercian Order (who, according to a popular medieval legend, suckled from the breasts of the Virgin herself) developed a theology in which Jesus nursed the Ecclesia, who then breastfed Christians with religious influence. Bernard's suckling represented a flow of instruction or affectivity, invoking a metaphor for spiritual transmission similar to Kabbalah's nursing divine.[45] Other Christian theologians such as William of St. Thierry (ca 1085–1148) also used suckling imagery to express religious knowledge's transmission between the Church and humanity.[46] The twelfth century Cistercian Adam of Perseigne maintained that when human souls suckled at the Virgin's breasts they became Jesus' spiritual siblings, an idea paralleled in chapter 1's rabbinic texts about Sarah.[47] By the thirteenth century, images of the lactating Virgin began to grow popular in Christian art, and Marian theology had become a focal point for Christian lay leaders.[48] Corresponding to its appearance among the exclusively masculine kabbalists, Christian suckling imagery was associated primarily with male clergy members rather than with female mystics or cloistered women.[49]

Within this context, Ezra of Gerona's *Commentary on the Song of Songs* is of particular interest. Ezra's was the first kabbalistic commentary on the Song, and his excursion into Song exegesis paralleled Christian exegetical developments.[50] As focus on feminine imagery grew in the twelfth century, Christian writers began to interpret the Song of Songs from a Marian perspective, understanding it as a loving dialogue between Jesus and his holy mother. Until that point, the Song had been interpreted as a conversation between Jesus and the human soul or between Jesus and the Church, ideas roughly parallel to Jewish readings of the Song as a dialogue between God and the Israelite people.[51] Christian Song interpretations that encouraged reverence of Jesus and Mary continued to be composed throughout the thirteenth century, gradually disappearing between the fourteenth and fifteenth centuries. Jewish Song interpretation paralleled its Christian counterpart both chronologically and thematically.[52] Both groups' literature made notable use of feminine figures and female breast imagery.[53]

Along with Marian devotion's emergence in twelfth century Europe, an increased emphasis on affective spirituality also occupied Christian exegetes. This engagement with spirituality's emotional side allowed Christian theologians to focus on particular aspects of their relationships with God.[54] According to Rachel Fulton, "praying to the Virgin and her crucified Son forced medieval Christians to forge new tools with which to *feel*," allowing them to develop "potentialities of emotion, specifically love, for transcending the physical, experiential distance between individual bodies."[55] Fulton suggests that Christian Song interpretation developed an increasing interest in compassionate mimesis that involved altering the relationship between Jesus and Mary, transforming the Virgin from a stately queen into a compassionate mother removed from common humanity.[56] Similarly, Caroline Bynum ties the mothering and suckling imagery associated with Marian devotion to affective spirituality, reading this emotional emphasis as a counterpoint and complement to religious authority.[57] She asserts that such images made divinity more approachable, explaining that emphasis on humanity created in the image of divinity allowed an increased sense of relationship between the two.[58] Miri Rubin also associates the growth in affective and empathetic spirituality with increased interest in Marian theology.[59]

Clearly, this Christian focus on transforming relationality both among divine figures and between the divine and human worlds is similar to that of Kabbalah, while Jewish mystical literature also exhibits a parallel interest in emotion and affectivity. Eitan Fishbane has demonstrated close ties between emotional display, mystical interpretation, and exposure of divine secrets in the Zohar, while Joel Hecker has shown the importance of "affective performance" among the Zohar's mystical brotherhood.[60] Melila Hellner-Eshed has emphasized the Zoharic group's technique of generating mystical experience by building "religious-emotional energy."[61] In both Christian and Jewish literature, nursing imagery applies this interest in affectivity by helping to increase the sense of emotional intimacy between God and human beings. Sometimes these parallel literatures come surprisingly close to each other, both conceptually and in their choice of Biblical proof texts. Bernard of Clairvaux's famous sermons on the Song of Songs state, "There is no pretence about a true mother, the breasts that she displays are full for the taking. She knows how to rejoice with those who rejoice, and to be sad with those who sorrow, pressing the milk of encouragement without intermission from the breast of joyful sympathy, the milk of consolation from the breast of compassion."[62] Bernard's citation of Isaiah 66:11 ("So that you will suckle and be satisfied from the breast of consolation, so that you will suck and have pleasure from the teat of glory") to emphasize heavenly compassion is very close to Zohar 2:256b-257a's use of this same text, as shown in chapter 3. Of course, positive theological ideas about femininity and motherhood do not guarantee increased status or rights for real women in either religious group. Whether or not the nursing divine had a beneficial effect on women's lives is impossible to say given scholarship's current state.[63] Medieval men certainly were capable of maintaining different attitudes toward abstract femininity and actual women, and women need not have occupied a high place in society in order to metaphorically represent the divine.

The question of mutual influence implied by these similarities is a difficult one.[64] There are several contexts in which encounters between Jews and Christians occurred, some of which may have been directly influential upon divine nursing imagery's development. The medieval Jews of southern France and northern Spain were not a ghettoized people, and they often interacted with their Christian neighbors. Spanish Jews also served in high positions at royal courts during times that they enjoyed political favor. In these situations, Jews had the opportunity to encounter Christian religious observances that included Marian processions, devotional shrines, and art on the outside of churches.[65] Jews observing these phenomena may have experienced a complex mixture of attraction and denial.[66] It is possible to understand the kabbalists' female divine imagery *partially* as a way of dealing with external influences by internalizing, transforming, and abstracting ideas that appealed while rejecting Christian thought's more alienating aspects.[67]

In addition to these daily encounters, medieval Jews were exposed to broad European theological developments by traveling Christian preachers, who became more numerous in the twelfth and thirteenth centuries. The Cistercians, Dominicans, and Franciscans all rejected earlier cloistered monastic models and instead focused on itinerant preaching and pastoral care.[68] For example, Bernard of Clairvaux preached in southern France in 1145, during the lifetime of Isaac the

Blind's father, the kabbalist Rabbi Abraham ben David.[69] Many of these orders were eager to extend the Church's authority over heretics to an authority over Jews.[70] In some cases, they were partially successful: Spanish clergymen secured legislation requiring Jewish attendance at Christian sermons and religious disputations, the most famous of which engaged the kabbalist Naḥmanides and the Dominican Paulus Christiani in Barcelona in 1263. Such efforts at missionizing Jews presented further opportunities for dialogue and mutual influence.[71] While it is difficult to know what individual Jews and Christians took from these encounters, it is undoubtedly true that each group considered the other's theological claims to some extent, even as they disagreed.

More prolonged religious conversations regarding Marian and Incarnational theology also occurred. One critical moment for such dialogue took place soon after the Crusaders' massacres of the Rhineland Jews in 1096. These massacres were accompanied by widespread Jewish suicide and the additional horror of Jews slaying their own children to prevent forced baptisms. This extreme Jewish response to potential conversion deeply dismayed Christian theologians and so became an active discussion topic in early twelfth century Christian communities—the same communities in which Marian theology was developing. Christians and Jews may have discussed these events at Rouen in France, where the early Marian Song commentator Honorius lived.[72] Interreligious discussion on the same topic did happen at Westminster in England. There, a learned Jew from Mainz entered into dialogue with Gilbert Crispin, a Christian interested in proselytizing Jews.[73] In Spain, Incarnational theology, which necessarily involved discussion of Mary, became a key item of public religious debate and Jewish conversion efforts.[74] Mary's role in Christianity was a central feature of such discussions, because much of the Jewish resistance to conversion apparently stemmed from an abhorrence of the claim that a human woman could become the mother of God.[75] Unhappy with Jewish responses to the new theology, Christian literature increasingly framed Jews as Mary's particular adversaries—as in the writings of the twelfth-century authors Odo of Tournais, Guibert of Nogent, and Honorius of Autun.[76] As Miri Rubin has shown, Marian theology was bound up with the desire for Jewish conversion and the public debates associated with this conversion effort.[77] When Christian conversion efforts grew and Jewish conversions did not, Jews became figured as Mary's enemies,

who "openly injured her in word, thought and gesture."[78] Peter Schäfer
has chronicled several examples of Jewish and Christian polemical texts
concerning the Virgin that circulated during this period.[79]

It is reasonable to suggest that early Jewish challenges and responses
to Marian theology helped to motivate Christian clergymen to clarify
the Virgin's role in heaven and on earth. As Rachel Fulton notes, "Jews
insisted that the doctrine of the Incarnation was nothing short of an
insult to God and that the height of the insult was the suggestion that
God had not only confined himself within a woman's womb but also
(horrible for them to think!) come forth through her 'shameful exit.'
. . . The more disgusting the Jews found this idea, the more Christians
found themselves forced to defend it."[80] It is also reasonable to suggest,
given Jewish familiarity with Christian scripture and theology, that the
early kabbalists were aware of such dialogues and inspired by them to
develop their own responses to Marian theology, as well as their own
subversions of it.

While kabbalistic feminine imagery and Christian Marian imagery
share a common chronology, as well as common focus on relationality,
affective language, Song Commentary, and motherhood and breastfeeding imagery, important divergences do exist. Mary and the feminine *sefirot* relate to God and human beings in strikingly different ways.
While *Binah* and *Shekhinah* are internal aspects of God, Christianity's
Mary is a human being who can never be part of the Trinity, even
though she occupies a distinctive spiritual location between the godhead and ordinary human beings. In addition, Mary's great affective
potential is rooted partially in her status as a real person and mother.[81]
A Song commentary that presents a dialogue between Christ and his
once-human mother is not the same as a kabbalistic Song commentary
configured as a conversation *within* God that occasionally references
humanity. In addition, Christianity and Judaism have very different
ideas about motherhood and breastfeeding's appropriate religious connotations. Kabbalah's divine mothering language does not shy away
from sexual symbolism, and sefirotic eroticism often precedes breastfeeding language in the Zohar just as sexual activity precedes conception, childbirth, and breastfeeding among human beings.[82] Kabbalah's
nursing divine imagery remains firmly rooted in human family life,
reflecting Judaism's continuing emphasis on obeying the command-
ment to procreate. Christianity's Virgin Mother occupies a very different sexual and family status, since her paradoxical virginity and

fecundity remove her from lived experience.[83] Instead of reflecting daily life, she provides a unique counterpoint to it. There are also divergences between Jews and Christians regarding lactation itself. Christian theologians drew on medieval medicine's conflation of bodily fluids, which encouraged their readers to associate milk with blood and allowed the Christian suckling metaphor to take on Eucharistic implications.[84] Such implications were alien to Jewish theology and ritual practice.

Influence alone is not sufficient to explain the vivid feminine imagery found in kabbalistic texts. As Daniel Abrams states, the *Shekhinah* is not "a Christian idea in Jewish garb."[85] Earlier Jewish suckling imagery—traditional associations that linked Torah, femininity, and breastfeeding—and medieval cultural norms all contributed to *Sefer ha-Zohar*'s presentation of the nursing divine. As I have demonstrated, the suckling-as-spiritual-transmission metaphor is found in Jewish texts ranging from the fifth through the thirteenth centuries. There is not much point debating (since there is no possibility of proof) whether the kabbalists were following in the footsteps of Christian thinkers, while adapting their ideas, or whether kabbalistic interest in divine nursing sprang purely from internal desire and closely reading earlier Jewish texts. Christian images can provide only limited information about the idea of a breastfeeding God in Judaism. The debate about whether Christian exegesis influenced Jewish exegesis (and vice versa), or whether some overarching cultural element spurred both medieval Christians and medieval Jews to turn to feminine religious imagery and relational, affective religiosity must necessarily be circular and difficult. What can be said with certainty is that both groups' work arose from a broad cultural context in which feminine religious language and its emotional connotations were growing both more desirable and more acceptable.

The Kabbalists on Breastfeeding, Womanhood, and Family Life

Having explored Kabbalah's breastfeeding divine in relation to medieval cultural associations and Christian imagery, I would like to offer a few comments for consideration. Throughout this study, I have taken the nursing divine as a positive feminine image, in that I consider it a purposefully chosen divine representation intended to bring the kabbalists into an intimate relationship with God textured by a positive emotional spectrum. I also consider divine femininity essential to this imagery's theological effectiveness. The mother-child model for divine and human relationality is nuanced by a tender closeness different from masculine divine imagery's connotations, since medieval Jewish men occupied social and family roles that encouraged associating masculinity with authority. Bringing mother imagery to bear on the divine allowed the kabbalists to explore God's nurturing, caring, and sustaining roles alongside God's more rigorous aspects, while grounding the divine and human relationship in a sense of God's loving duty to humanity. I do not, however, take this perspective for granted, since diverging scholarly opinions about kabbalistic motherhood and breastfeeding do exist.

One of the most interesting of these opinions is found in Elliot Wolfson's work. Wolfson asserts that kabbalistic theology devalued women to the extent that it masculinized both motherhood and breastfeeding, viewing as suspect the idea that the kabbalists would generate positive feminine images at all.[86] He suggests that the kabbalists internalized the philosophical tradition's negative attitude toward sensuality, causing them to devalue femininity and reinforcing negative social stereotypes about women.[87] Wolfson writes, "the symbol of the mother as employed by kabbalists in no way celebrated the feminine or even challenged the devaluation of the female and the corporeal . . . when the images of motherhood utilized by medieval kabbalists are considered culturally as opposed to anatomically, it becomes clear that they relate to the masculine aspect of the feminine, the quality of the female that is linked to . . . the urge of judgment to extend limitation beyond its limits and thereby emulate the phallic potency of the male to bestow on the other."[88] Regarding Kabbalah's divine breastfeeding, he asserts, "It must be concluded, therefore, that the breast that gives milk is functionally equivalent to the penis that ejaculates. If that is the case, then the righteous described as suckling from the splendor of the breasts of the *Shekhinah* are, in fact, cleaving to and drawing from the corona of the divine phallus."[89]

These statements are rooted in Wolfson's perspective on kabbalistic sexuality, in which eros is transferred, by means of ascetic practice (though not through complete celibacy) from carnal relations with a physical wife to spiritual intercourse with God.[90] For Wolfson, this spiritual intercourse is defined by homoerotic longing that has been covered in a thin veneer of feminine language, sometimes relating to a masculinized female and sometimes to a reconstituted divine andro-gyne in which femininity has been incorporated as the corona of the phallus.[91] From this perspective, there can be no positively constructed divine image that is also feminine, because such an image would always already have been masculinized in one way or another.[92]

Daniel Abrams, another scholar who works extensively with Kab-balah's gendered imagery, contends that the *Shekhinah* should be understood as a sexualized aspect of divinity, rather than as a feminized aspect.[93] He denies that the kabbalists' divine images valorize feminin-ity and suggests instead that such readings are mistakes deriving from misapplying modern feminist thought to Kabbalah.[94] From his per-spective, the *Shekhinah*'s femininity is the direct result of Kabbalah's focus on divine sexual union. Abrams has conducted his own detailed study of divine nursing, and while he considers the breast image impor-tant, signifying a divine need to nourish the world, from his perspec-tive nursing functions mainly an addendum to the sexual imagery that ultimately eclipses it. For him, the nursing divine provides a tempo-rary disengagement from sexual imagery by allowing an expression of intimacy that does not elicit homosexual implications.[95] He thus reads divine nursing as a way for the kabbalists to imbibe divine seed in the form of milk from God's breasts, rather than in the form of semen from the divine phallus. Abrams regards the *Shekhinah*'s breasts as intervening between the kabbalists and the phallic divine, represented by the *sefirah Yesod*. He also suggests that the two feminine breasts may symbolically parallel descriptions of the *sefirot Netzaḥ* and *Hod* as two testicles.[96] Much of Abrams' reading stems from his methodological reliance on the works of Freud and Lacan, whose psychoanalytic per-spectives are also framed in sexual terms.[97]

Although Wolfson's and Abrams' conclusions are drawn from their own sensitive and thorough textual analyses, as well as a concern with debunking unexamined feminist readings of kabbalistic theology, their conclusions need not hold true for every kabbalistic text and every appearance of the nursing divine.[98] Wolfson's and Abrams' perspectives hold in common a reliance on sexuality as the ultimate arbiter of gen-dered kabbalistic imagery. This view is not uncommon among scholars of Kabbalah.[99] Despite framing Zoharic theology as a religious life lived in relation to "God the Mother" and noting that in this literature, "the feminine and femininity is much more complex, diverse and nuanced," than Wolfson is willing to concede, Melila Hellner-Eshed also frames

Zoharic spirituality in largely erotic terms.[100] She writes, "I do not find here lack and absence, ruthless penetration, negation, and submersion in the masculine, but rather—on the contrary—a total language of feminine erotics, which surprisingly was formulated so poetically and with such nuance by men."[101] For her, the Zohar's entire reality is erotic, and the mystic's discipline involves training himself to recognize this reality and inhabit it.[102] While Hellner-Eshed does note and analyze breastfeeding and mothering imagery in the Zohar, such imagery often seems a footnote to her engagement with a thoroughly eroticized discourse.[103]

While I find great value in these scholars' works, I question their reliance upon sexuality as the premier underlying symbolism of all kabbalistic imagery. Although sacred eroticism is an important part of kabbalistic theology, it need not eclipse all other components of the kabbalists' complex imagery. The kabbalists were fully capable of presenting sexually explicit imagery in their literature, and the Zohar contains many passages whose sexuality is clear and obvious, even when cloaked in allusive language.[104] Kabbalistic sexuality is a fascinating and complex topic, exhibiting an intriguing gender fluidity in which the kabbalists sometimes imagine themselves as constituting the feminine *Shekhinah* and incorporating feminine traits (or as Wolfson would have it, masculinizing the feminine divine), and sometimes imagine themselves as *Shekhinah*'s masculine lovers.[105] This gender fluidity, which exists both among the kabbalists and among the *sefirot*, has inspired much speculation about Kabbalah's presentation of eros.[106] While some scholars, like Arthur Green, see the feminine *Shekhinah* as a way for non-celibate male mystics to relate erotically to God, others, like Elliot Wolfson, see the kabbalists' relationship to God as a homoerotic bond that is expressed in heterosexual images.[107] Although Abrams does not assert this point as dramatically as Wolfson, it is difficult to read his analysis of the kabbalists filling themselves with divine seed in the deferred form of milk without seeing strong similarities to Wolfson's perspective.[108] Meanwhile, Hellner-Eshed's suggestion that Wolfson's reconstituted divine androgyne may really be a feminine figure that is *perceived* by the male kabbalists as a phallicized yet feminine aspect of God takes the discussion in still more interesting directions.[109]

However, just because the kabbalists deliberately selected some sexual imagery does not mean that all their diverse divine imagery was selected with strong sexual connotations in mind. Breastfeeding

imagery need not be sexualized in order to be profound to its readers—the associated emotions and understandings it evokes are not
without inherent depth simply because they are neither overtly sexual nor covertly masculine. George Lakoff and Mark Johnson write,
"symbolic metonymies that are grounded in our physical experience
provide an essential means of comprehending religious and cultural
concepts"—while Victor Turner, James Fernandez, and Mary Douglas
all observe that some of the most important metaphors for understanding complex ideas are based on the human body, which allows these
metaphors to communicate messages about emotion, action, and social
integration.[110] Sexual imagery is only one form of anthropomorphism,
and it nuances everything it describes with its distinctive connotations.
Sometimes erotic connotations simply do not provide the right group
of associations to communicate a specific idea.

Divine breastfeeding provided kabbalistic writers and readers with
a forum that could shift associative focus away from sexuality by focusing instead on the mother-child relationship.[111] Although modern
Westerners are engaged in a debate about breastfeeding's sexual connotations that presents widely disparate opinions about public breastfeeding's appropriateness, medievals tended to associate breastfeeding with
food, rather than with eroticism.[112] For example, Bernard of Clairvaux
writes, "Once before when she sighed for the Bridegroom's kisses and
embraces she was told: 'Your breasts are better than wine,' to make her
realize that she was a mother, that her duty was to suckle her babes,
to provide food for her children."[113] Here, breastfeeding is defined as
a non-erotic, or even anti-erotic, activity. One of the main benefits of
suckling, mothering imagery is its provision for such an alternative
relational model.[114] This model is distinctive in part because it avoids
the dangers and tensions that sexuality presents in adult relationships.
Between the nursing mother and her child, there is no threat of incest,
lust, or impurity, but rather an essential flow of life-giving nourishment
dissociated from these concerns.[115]

While it is interesting to speculate on whether kabbalists who
thought of themselves as nursing from the divine breasts simultaneously maintained that they were imbibing divine seed, I do not think
such speculation is necessary to understand the nursing mother image.
Imagining the nursing divine's abundant breasts as an overflowing
phallus from which the kabbalists figuratively suck (as Wolfson suggests and Abrams implies) presents a metaphor with its own field of

distinctive connotations that in turn suggest a very different relational model.[116] Over emphasis of Kabbalah's erotic aspects and its supposed antifeminine perspective can generate a reductive viewpoint that is not always helpful when approaching this theology's complex and deliberate image use. Sometimes a breast is just a breast and milk is just milk. In the case of the breastfeeding divine, that imagery's own associations with nurture, intimacy, love and prelinguistic parental connection are sufficient to convey a coherent concept of divine and human relationality. There is no reason to assume that such breastfeeding imagery is not symbolically and cognitively potent in and of itself.

There are also several good reasons to read a motherly, breastfeeding God as a powerful religious image that is both positive and innately feminine. Divine nursing imagery arises from rabbinic literature that equates women's breastfeeding with transmitting positive spiritual qualities and religious lineage, and kabbalistic literature continues to equate divine breastfeeding with many beneficial results.[117] These beneficial results are linked to the nursing mother metaphor's social and religious connotations, and a breastfeeding divine who nurtures and sustains the world while relating to the kabbalist with tenderness and intimacy coheres with motherhood's associations in the kabbalists' cultural milieu. As I have demonstrated above, this positive, feminine reading of the nursing divine is consistent with medieval Jews' ideas about family life, motherhood, breastfeeding, and the religious educational process. Breastfeeding's earthly connotations give this divine image coherent structure, allowing it to serve as a useful cognitive model for reconfiguring the relationship between God and human beings, encouraging a "return to the Whole." While it would be incorrect and anachronistic to read the kabbalists as proto-feminists, Judaism traditionally valorizes motherhood and childcare as ideal female roles, and the kabbalists regarded these ideal images as fitting for divine application. The nurture, tenderness, duty, and dependence associated with the mother-child metaphor do an admirable job of expressing the interdependent relationship between divinity and humanity that kabbalistic theology embraces. Although the kabbalists also connect divine femininity with Judgment, that attribute's imagery and associations are not designed to construct the same human and divine relationship as the one explored in this book. The kabbalists investigate many kinds of relationality (including nurture, loving, judging, and eros) in order to

experience the full spectrum of possible relationships between humanity and divinity.[118]

Breastfeeding imagery allowed the male kabbalists to explore
women's symbolic potential for developing their own masculine relationships with God beyond erotic intimacy, extending these relationships into many different areas of their lives. To read the breastfeeding
divine's breast as anything other than what it seems to be (even when
it is located on a masculine *sefirah*) is to disassemble this divine image's
coherence, and thus to spoil its effectiveness as a cognitive model. If
God as a nursing Mother is cognitively equivalent to God as an ejac-
ulating Lover, then the breastfeeding divine cannot offer a relational
alternative, let alone a complement or corrective, to masculine religious
imagery.[119] The kabbalists wish to relate to God's divine plenitude, as
their shifting, diverse, and detailed imagery demonstrates. Restricting
divinity to masculinity creates the opposite effect, reducing kabbalistic
options for relating to and experiencing the divine. It leaves the kabbalist in the realm of language, scholarship, and authority, eliminating the
vital pre-linguistic, pre-scholastic mother-child relationship to which
Isaac the Blind seems to allude when he describes, "a way of contemplation by way of his suckling, and not by way of knowledge."[120]

It is also consistent with existing scholarship to expect that the
kabbalists would valorize motherhood, breastfeeding, nurture, and
these qualities' roles in family life. During the late twelfth through the
late thirteenth century in France and Spain, marriage, sexuality, and
femininity were becoming topics of great ambivalence, which resulted
in women being increasingly viewed as Other and opposed to men.[121]
In the twelfth century, the Church officially enforced the doctrine of
clerical celibacy, while the Albigensian heresy combated by the Church
practiced celibacy even within marriage as the correct way to lead a
holy life.[122] During the same period, the integration of philosophical
(and particularly Aristotelian) ideas into Judaism presented medieval
Jews with negative views of femininity, linking women to matter and
its corollaries: sensuality and eroticism.[123] In the thirteenth century, the
Galenic "two-seed" theory of reproductive sexuality was increasingly
challenged by the Aristotelian "one-seed" theory, which diminished the
woman's role in conception.[124] David Nirenberg notes that during this
period in Spain, Jews, Christians, and Muslims produced laws to prevent interfaith sexuality, identifying a collective miscegenation anxiety

that focused on women's bodies as sites of social rupture.[125] In short, a debate on the virtues of marriage and women in general raged throughout European culture.[126] This debate was especially virulent in Spain, where there was no firm Jewish position on practicing monogamy versus polygamy, and concubinage (often employing non-Jewish concubines) was a common practice among the upper classes.[127]

Within this debate's context, the kabbalists generally opted for the pro-marriage stance, defending Jewish family life, marriage, and procreation even when they were concerned it might put strain on their relationships with God.[128] Kabbalists as early as Isaac the Blind's father, Abraham ben David of Posquières (d1198), defended marriage from its detractors in a work titled *Ba'aley ha-Nefesh* (*Masters of the Soul*). Thirteenth-century Spanish kabbalists like Todros ben Joseph Abulafia and Jonah Gerondi continued to defend marriage as part of their concern with religious and ethical reformation.[129] As necessary participants in traditional marriage, mothers were honored for their role in nursing and childcare.[130] These ideas did not emerge from an impulse that embraced what moderns would call feminism, but rather from a religious and familial traditionalism that the kabbalists favored. Attaching positive feminine imagery to the divine allowed the kabbalists to develop an alternative to the growing cultural trends that defamed women and threatened Jewish family life, while also providing innovative models for framing divine relationality.[131] Among the kabbalists' many innovations, the nursing divine image responded in a unique way to a broad group of cultural, historical, and theological concerns, providing a coherent link between kabbalistic thought and its context.

Final Remarks

The conclusion of any project involves reflection on roads not taken and avenues of inquiry left unexplored. In this study, one of my main goals was to avoid injecting modern categories into the kabbalists' cultural environment. Instead, I hoped to disclose the kabbalists' own system of affect as it is revealed in these texts. Investigating medieval Jewish attitudes regarding motherhood and breastfeeding helped me to approach divine nursing imagery without relying heavily on gender philosophy, critical-theoretical literature, or psychoanalytic interpretations of kabbalistic materials. In my opinion, this type of contextual reading is an important tool for understanding premodern sources composed by authors whose world views and self-understandings may have been quite different than those of the great modern thinkers who produced these bodies of work. While perspectives drawn from their insights are valuable, when dealing with medieval sources they also can act as distorting lenses that obscure the truths they seek to expose. For similar reasons, I chose not to consider the kabbalists' works as representative of ideas that twenty-first-century readers would call feminist or misogynist. These categories were unknown to them, as was the abstract concept of gender equality, and expecting them to conform to modern ideals (or blaming them for failing to do so) is unrealistic.

However, having situated the classical kabbalists' breastfeeding imagery within its context, it is intriguing to speculate on what future scholars might do with this material. Applying the insights of gender philosophy, critical-theoretical literature, and psychoanalysis to a feminine, nursing divine that is neither overtly sexualized nor covertly masculinized could yield very interesting results—complementing existing studies that interpret Kabbalah from these perspectives. Feminist readings of the breastfeeding divine could also yield fruitful results, particularly if they move beyond the old goal of exposing misogyny toward an informed, constructive reading of how the kabbalists' feminine divine images might translate from a medieval context into a modern one.[132]

Finally, it is my hope that this work will encourage further scholarship investigating categories of kabbalistic imagery that are not reliant on sexuality for their conceptual impact. The kabbalists' fluid, shifting language for divinity's revelation is as diverse as it is beautiful. Each image, and each combination of images, yields a new model for thinking about God that acts in harmony with all the others. This dynamic conception of the divine offers scholars an intriguing puzzle. It will disclose its secrets only when each piece is considered in relation to the others and gently laid in place.

Notes

Notes to the Introduction

1. The edition of *Sefer ha-Zohar* used in this study is Reuven Moshe Margaliot, ed., *Sefer ha-Zohar al Ḥamishah Ḥumshei Torah*, 3 vols. (Jerusalem: Mosad ha-Rav Kook, 1999). All text translations from Hebrew and Aramaic are my own, unless otherwise stated.
2. Georges Bataille describes this process beautifully. "The poetic is the familiar dissolving into the strange, and ourselves with it. It never dispossesses us entirely, for the words, the images (once dissolved) are charged with emotions already experienced, attached to objects which link them to the unknown." Georges Bataille, *Inner Experience*, trans. and with an introduction by Leslie Ann Boldt (Albany, NY: SUNY Press, 1988), 5.
3. Melila Hellner-Eshed identifies "flow" as one of *Sefer ha-Zohar*'s most central metaphors, noting that it relates to divine overflow, universal structure, erotic dynamics and the workings of human consciousness. Melila Hellner-Eshed, *A River Flows from Eden: The Language of Mystical Experience in the Zohar* (Stanford, CA: Stanford University Press, 2005), 230.
4. For example, in this work the term *suckling mother* indicates a mother who breastfeeds, not a mother who is the recipient of breastfeeding.
5. Elisheva Baumgarten, *Mothers and Children: Jewish Family Life in Medieval Europe* (Princeton, NJ: Princeton University Press, 2004), 120–23, 133.

6. By rabbinic literature, I mean both aggadic and halakhic texts from the time of the earliest rabbis through the Middle Ages. Works that I group under this term do not fall into other literary categories composed by rabbinic authors—such as philosophical, ethical, and kabbalistic writings.

7. Arthur Green, "Shekhinah, the Virgin Mary, and the Song of Songs: Reflections on a Kabbalistic Symbol in Its Historical Context," *AJS Review* 26, no. 1 (2002); Peter Schäfer, *Mirror of His Beauty: Feminine Images of God from the Bible to the Early Kabbalah* (Princeton, NJ: Princeton University Press, 2002); Rachel Fulton, *From Judgment to Passion: Devotion to Christ and the Virgin Mary, 800–1200* (New York: Columbia University Press, 2002); Miri Rubin, *Mother of God: A History of the Virgin Mary* (New Haven, CT: Yale University Press, 2009), 159–65. Also see Peter Schäfer, "Daughter, Sister, Bride, and Mother: Images of the Femininity of God in the Early Kabbala," *Journal of the American Academy of Religion* 68, no. 2 (2000): 221–42.

8. Rachel Fulton, *From Judgment to Passion*, 249.

9. Hereafter, I will shorten the title rabbi with the commonly used abbreviation, R.

10. Caroline Walker Bynum, *Jesus as Mother: Studies in the Spirituality of the High Middle Ages* (Berkeley, CA: University of California Press, 1982), 117–19.

11. Babylonian Talmud will be abbreviated BT.

12. Brackets in translated texts contain words that are implied by the text or are necessary for grammatical clarification, but are not actually present in the text itself. In this instance, they contain both grammatical clarifications and the next phrase of the Song of Songs, which Ezra's readers would have known without seeing the words written.

13. Charles Chavel, ed., *"Perush le-Shir ha-Shirim,"* in *Kitve Rabenu Moshe ben Naḥman*, vol. 2 (Jerusalem: Mosad ha-Rav Kook, 2002), 473–518.

14. Daniel Abrams also stresses the need to evaluate how kabbalistic ideas arise from within rabbinic culture before seeking to explain them through outside influence. Although I do not share his ideological emphasis on preserving Jewish thought's inherent Jewishness or his position on American universities (which he perceives as undermining Jewish thought's independent character), I agree

with him that it is important to understand how internal trends in Jewish thought give rise to innovations. Tracing these internal trends allows for a fuller evaluation of Jewish thought's character as *both* proactive and reactive. Daniel Abrams, "The Virgin Mary as the Moon That Lacks the Sun: A Zoharic Polemic Against the Veneration of Mary," *Kabbalah: Journal for the Study of Jewish Mystical Texts* 21 (2010): 15–16.

15. For a helpful resource on intertextuality in Jewish texts, see Daniel Boyarin, *Intertextuality and the Reading of Midrash* (np Bloomington, IN: Indiana University Press, 1990; reprint, Eugene, OR: Wipf and Stock Publishers, 2001).

16. Sherry Ortner, "On Key Symbols." *American Anthropologist* 75 (1973): 1339.

17. Elliot Wolfson, *Language, Eros, Being: Kabbalistic Hermeneutics and the Poetic Imagination* (New York: Fordham University Press, 2005), 49; Elliot Wolfson, "Occultation of the Feminine and the Body of Secrecy in Medieval Kabbalah" in *Luminal Darkness: Imaginal Gleanings from Zoharic Literature* (Oxford: Oneworld Publications, 2007), 276; Tova Rosen, *Unveiling Eve: Reading Gender in Medieval Hebrew Literature* (Philadelphia, PA: University of Pennsylvania Press, 2003), 23, 103–14.

18. Hellner-Eshed, *A River Flows from Eden*, 71–74.

19. Joel Hecker, Eitan Fishbane, Melila Hellner-Eshed and Ronit Meroz have written on *Sefer ha-Zohar*'s emphasis on emotional performance and display, both as acts of *imitatio dei* and as signifiers of revelation and anxiety about revelation. Joel Hecker, *Mystical Bodies, Mystical Meals: Eating and Embodiment in Medieval Kabbalah*, Raphael Patai Series in Jewish Folklore and Anthropology, ed. Dan Ben-Amos (Detroit, MI: Wayne State University Press, 2005), 130–6; Eitan Fishbane, "Tears of Disclosure: The Role of Weeping in Zoharic Narrative," *The Journal of Jewish Thought and Philosophy* 11, no. 1 (2002): 29–39; Hellner-Eshed, *A River Flows from Eden*, 189, 279–85; Ronit Meroz, "Zoharic Narratives and Their Adaptations," *Hispania Judaica* 3 (2000): 12.

20. Fulton, *From Judgment to Passion*, 197, 397, 462; Caroline Walker Bynum, *Fragmentation and Redemption: Essays on Gender and the Human Body in Medieval Religion* (New York: Zone Books, 1992), 158; Bynum, *Jesus as Mother*, 115, 160.

21. Bynum, *Jesus as Mother*, 124.

22. Baumgarten, *Mothers and Children*, 119–20.

23. Ivan Marcus, *Rituals of Childhood: Jewish Acculturation in Medieval Europe* (New Haven, CA: Yale University Press, 1996), 43, 75–76; Baumgarten, *Mothers and Children*, 126–27.

24. Gershom Scholem, ed., "Perush Sefer Yetzirah," in *Ha-Kabbalah bi-Provans: Ḥug ha-Rabad u-Veno R. Yitzḥak Sagi Nahor*, appendix 1: 1–18 (Jerusalem: Akademon, 1969). The reference is from chapter 1 of the Commentary. I will return to the idea of a divine relationship that transcends knowledge in the following chapters.

25. This project deals specifically with Kabbalah's formative period, which occurred between the late twelfth and the late thirteenth centuries.

26. The sixth *sefirah* (*Raḥamim*) is also commonly called *Tif'eret* (Splendor), while the tenth *sefirah* (*Shekhinah*) is also called *Malkhut* (Kingdom). The divine aspects have many other cognomens as well. I have listed these two because they are particularly common.

27. It is difficult to generalize about Kabbalah, since the term represents a broad theological trend rather than a unified body of teachings. For example, while many kabbalists understood the *sefirot* and God to be the same entity and of the same essence, other kabbalists preferred to think of the *sefirot* as emanated instruments through which God relates to the created world, implying a further degree of separation. According to Daniel Abrams, very early kabbalists like Isaac the Blind held an essentialist perspective regarding the *sefirot*, while the instrumentalist view gained in popularity during the fourteenth and fifteenth centuries. Much of Kabbalah's conceptual power lies in its ability to hold such ideas in tension without fully resolving them. In general, the kabbalistic texts and authors presented in this book maintain an essentialist perspective on the *sefirot*. See Daniel Abrams, *R. Asher ben David: His Complete Works and Studies in His Kabbalistic Thought* (Los Angeles, CA: Cherub Press, 1996), 14.

28. These are just a few of the image categories used to describe the *sefirot*.

29. Moshe Idel characterizes one of Kabbalah's most important trends as a "correlative approach" based on "active interaction" between the human and divine worlds. Moshe Idel, *Ascensions on High in Jewish Mysticism: Pillars, Lines, Ladders*, Pasts Incorporated, vol. 2, (New York: Central European University Press, 2005), 104. Also,

see Hellner-Eshed, *A River Flows from Eden*, 19.

30. "Theosophical-theurgical kabbalists, despite the baroque theosophy they generated, apparently tried to portray a divine sphere which was familiar, isomorphic, and sensitive to the most widespread human needs." Moshe Idel, *Kabbalah and Eros* (New Haven, CA: Yale University Press, 2005), 149. Idel goes on to note that this concern diminished over time, and that a gap eventually widened between the internal world of the *sefirot* and the external world of human religious expression.

31. James Fernandez, *Persuasions and Performances: The Play of Tropes in Culture* (Bloomington, IN: Indiana University Press, 1986), 191.

32. Ibid., 191–208.

33. Bizarre human imagery was also employed during the medieval period in mnemotechnic techniques related to monastic spiritual contemplation. Mary Carruthers, *The Craft of Thought: Meditation, Rhetoric, and the Making of Images, 400–1200*, (New York: Cambridge University Press, 1998), 118; Frances Yates, *The Art of Memory* (Chicago: The University of Chicago Press, 1966), 75.

34. "The language of myth thus gives shape to spiritual consciousness and provides the armature and forms of imagination through which one may conceptualize 'the Whole' and bear it in mind at all times. Myth may therefore comprise and condition a mystical mentality- not by being transcended so much as by being fully subjectivized and lived." Michael Fishbane, *Biblical Myth and Rabbinic Mythmaking* (Oxford: Oxford University Press, 2003), 314.

35. The following explanation of kabbalistic imagery summarizes an argument published in an earlier article. Those interested in a fuller presentation of my argument, along with analysis of some of the Zohar's specific image strategies and a discussion of my perspective in relation to other scholars of kabbalistic symbol, are welcome to read the article: Ellen Haskell, "Metaphor, Transformation and Transcendence: Toward an Understanding of Kabbalistic Imagery in *Sefer hazohar.*" *Prooftexts: A Journal of Jewish Literary History* 28, no. 3 (2008): 335–62. As the reader will note, my views on this matter differ significantly from theories that understand kabbalistic images as interchangeable terms comprising codes for Biblical interpretation, as in the works of Arthur Green and Moshe Idel. Also in contrast with Idel, I emphasize contemplation as a

necessary corollary to theurgic action in theosophical Kabbalah (rather than emphasizing action over contemplation). Finally, my perspective on this matter diverges from Melila Hellner-Eshed in that I emphasize the symbol's ability to evoke mystical experience, rather than the symbol as a symptom of mystical experience. My thoughts on kabbalistic imagery are inspired by anthropological literature and critical theory (see notes 16, 31–32, 37–43, 46 above and below) as well as by the work of Elliot Wolfson and Michael Fishbane, both of whom acknowledge religious imagery's ability to inspire transformative experience; Arthur Green, "Shekhinah, the Virgin Mary, and the Song of Songs," 19, 43–44; Arthur Green, *Keter: The Crown of God in Early Jewish Mysticism* (Princeton, NJ: Princeton University Press, 1997), 151; Moshe Idel, *Absorbing Perfections: Kabbalah and Interpretation*, with a foreword by Harold Bloom (New Haven: Yale University Press, 2002), 50, 223, 272, 313; Moshe Idel, *Ascensions on High in Jewish Mysticism*, 18, 209, 214; Moshe Idel, *Kabbalah: New Perspectives* (New Haven: Yale University Press, 1988), 224; Hellner-Eshed, *A River Flows from Eden*, 341–51; Elliot Wolfson, *Language, Eros, Being*, 6–7, 27, 38–9; Michael Fishbane, *Biblical Myth and Rabbinic Mythmaking*, 314.

36. In her work on medieval Christian imagery, Mary Carruthers writes, "The image is used by its fashioner and, if it finds artistic form, by its audience as a cognitive tool. The first question one should ask of such an image is not "What does it mean?" but "What is it good for?" Carruthers, *The Craft of Thought*, 118.

37. Fernandez, *Persuasions and Performances*, 8; George Lakoff and Mark Johnson, *Metaphors We Live By*, (Chicago: The University of Chicago Press, 1981), 5.

38. This is similar to Roland Barthes' description of the power of myth, which transforms history because "driven to having either to unveil or to liquidate the concept, it [myth] will *naturalize* it." Roland Barthes, "Myth Today" in *Mythologies*, trans. Annette Lavers, 1st American edition (New York: Hill and Wang, 1972), 129. Sarah Kofman has similarly noted that metaphoric imagery can have a perceptible impact on the unconscious, particularly through its mythic associations. Sarah Kofman, *Camera Obscura of Ideology*, trans. Will Straw (np: Ithaca, NY: Cornell University Press, 1999), 53.

39. See Lakoff and Johnson, *Metaphors We Live By*, 49.

40. Jacques Lacan and Judith Butler have both observed that language affects self-perception because it actively constructs the ways in which we signify ourselves *to* ourselves, demonstrating a reciprocal interaction between the person and the language with which he engages. Jacques Lacan, "The Meaning of the Phallus," in *Feminine Sexuality*, trans. Jacqueline Rose and ed. Juliet Mitchell and Jacqueline Rose (New York: W. W. Norton and Pantheon Books, 1985), 78; Judith Butler, *Bodies That Matter: On the Discursive Limits of "Sex"* (New York: Routledge, 1993), 30. George Lakoff and Mark Johnson explain a similar effect, noting, "changes in our conceptual system do change what is real for us and affect how we perceive the world and act upon those perceptions." Lakoff and Johnson, *Metaphors We Live By*, 145–46. Also see David Stern, who notes that human images are some of the most complex ones that we can apply to divinity. David Stern, "*Imitatio Hominis*: Anthropomorphism and the Character(s) of God in Rabbinic Literature," *Prooftexts: A Journal of Jewish Literary History* 12 (1992): 157.

41. "The actors themselves become terms in their own logic of the concrete." Roy Rappaport, *Ecology, Meaning, and Religion* (Berkeley, CA: North Atlantic Books, 1979), 136. Rappaport is writing specifically of gendered metaphors, and notes that such metaphors can become socially problematic for just this reason.

42. All metaphoric use is culturally constrained, a fact noted by many scholars. See James Fernandez, "Introduction: Confluents of Inquiry," in *Beyond Metaphor: The Play of Tropes in Culture*, ed. James Fernandez, 1–13 (Stanford, CA: Stanford University Press, 1991), 9; Naomi Quinn, "The Cultural Basis of Metaphor," in *Beyond Metaphor: The Play of Tropes in Culture*, ed. James Fernandez, 56–93, 60; Terence Turner, ""We Are Parrots," "Twins Are Birds": Play of Tropes as Operational Structures," in *Beyond Metaphor: The Play of Tropes in Culture*, ed. James Fernandez, 121–58, 129; Elliot Wolfson, *Through a Speculum that Shines: Vision and Imagination in Medieval Jewish Mysticism* (Princeton, NJ: Princeton University Press, 1994), 66.

43. "These various images of the deity cannot be dismissed as 'just metaphors.' There is no idea that is not embodied in metaphors, and to be embodied in that way is to be caught up in a set of meanings and connotations that are woven into the very fabric of

an idea." Howard Eilberg-Schwartz, *God's Phallus and Other Problems for Men and Monotheism* (Boston: Beacon Press, 1994), 7. The claim that metaphor and imagery are central to human cognitive processes is widespread in scholarly literature. See especially Wolfson, *Through a Speculum that Shines*, 58; Lakoff and Johnson, *Metaphors We Live By*, xiii; Mary Douglas, *Natural Symbols: Explorations in Cosmology*, with a new introduction (np: London: Barrie & Rockliff, 1970; reprint, New York: Routledge, 1996), 38.

44. I am not claiming that this action is automatic. Obviously, an active reader who desires to let kabbalistic images inspire him to become a kabbalist himself will experience a far different result from reading this literature than a casual reader or curiosity seeker, both of whom may not be affected by these images at all.

45. I will return to this text and elaborate on it in Chapter 3. For an excellent perspective on how the Zohar's unusual imagery may be understood as symptomatic of its authors' mystical experiences, see Hellner-Eshed, *A River Flows from Eden*, 341–51. Hellner-Eshed also notes Zoharic symbol's power to inspire a journey of words, in which the text's reader participates. Ibid., 190–91. However, while Hellner-Eshed focuses on the Zohar as a record of its authors' mystical experiences and transformative states of consciousness, my work focuses on kabbalistic imagery's effects on its mindful readers. From this perspective, the Zohar's images are not only indicators of experience, but are also generators of experience.

46. Victor Turner, *The Forest of Symbols: Aspects of Ndembu Ritual* (Ithaca, NY: Cornell University Press, 1967), 103–106.

47. Gershom Scholem, *Major Trends in Jewish Mysticism*, with a foreword by Robert Alter (Jerusalem: Schocken Publishing House, Ltd., 1941; reprint, New York: Schocken Books Inc., 1995), 173.

48. Moshe Halbertal, *Concealment and Revelation: Esotericism in Jewish Thought and Its Philosophical Implications*, trans. Jackie Feldman (Princeton, NJ: Princeton University Press, 2007), 93–94; Boaz Huss, "*Sefer ha-Zohar* as Canonical, Sacred and Holy Text: Changing Perspectives of the Book of Splendor between the Thirteenth and the Eighteenth Centuries," *The Journal of Jewish Thought and Philosophy* 7 (1998): 272–73; Moshe Idel, "Naḥmanides: Kabbalah, Halakhah, and Spiritual Leadership," in *Jewish Mystical Leaders and Leadership in the Thirteenth Century*, ed. Moshe Idel

and Mortimer Ostow (Lanham, Maryland: Rowman & Littlefield Publishers, Inc., 2005), 15–96.

49. Huss, "*Sefer ha-Zohar* as Canonical, Sacred and Holy Text," 272–73.

50. Most contemporary scholars of Jewish mysticism accept that the Zohar is the product of group authorship, while some even suggest that it is the product of multiple groups. In either case, this collective quality makes the Zohar a truly unique lens through which to engage broad trends in classical Kabbalah. Yehuda Liebes, *Studies in the Zohar*, trans. Arnold Schwartz, Stephanie Nakache, and Penina Peli, (Albany, NY: SUNY Press, 1993), 85–113; Meroz, "Zoharic Narratives and Their Adaptations," 4–5, 15–22; Ronit Meroz, "The Path of Silence: An Unknown Story from a Zohar Manuscript," *European Journal of Jewish Studies* 1, no. 2 (2008): 320; Ronit Meroz, "And I Was Not There?: The Complaints of Rabbi Simeon bar Yohai According to an Unknown Zoharic Story," *Tarbitz* 71 (2002): 163–1993 [Hebrew]; Boaz Huss, *Like the Radiance of the Sky: Chapters in the Reception History of the Zohar and the Construction of Its Symbolic Value* (Jerusalem: Mosad Bialik, 2008), 43–44 [Hebrew]; Boaz Huss, "*Sefer ha-Zohar* as Canonical, Sacred and Holy Text," 268–271; Hellner-Eshed, *A River Flows from Eden*, 18–19; Elliot Wolfson, "The Anonymous Chapters of the Elderly Master of Secrets: New Evidence for the Early Activity of the Zoharic Circle," *Kabbalah: Journal for the Study of Jewish Mystical Texts* 19 (2009): 144–45, 173–75; Daniel Abrams, "The Invention of the *Zohar* as a Book: On the Assumptions and Expectations of the Kabbalists and Modern Scholars," *Kabbalah: Journal for the Study of Jewish Mystical Texts* 19 (2009): 89, 111–13, 139.

51. I am more interested in revealing divine nursing imagery's importance as an emerging religious theme and highlighting its relationship to its cultural context than I am in tracing all of the authors in whose works suckling imagery appears. In order to keep my focus on suckling's importance, rather than diverting myself into the complexities of Zoharic authorship, I have elected to use the Zohar to represent the collective thought of many authors at once. To put it differently, I am more interested in Mary Carruthers' question of what divine nursing imagery is "good for" (see note 36, above) than I am in which of the Zohar's many authors (whose individual

identities are the topic of much speculation) elected to use suckling imagery and which did not. Divine nursing imagery's prevalence in the Zohar is sufficient attestation of its importance, while the Zohar's link to the Gerona School's literature demonstrates its continuity with prior kabbalistic thought.

52. For a look at some interesting post-Zoharic texts that contain suckling imagery, including works by Moses Cordovero, Isaac Luria and the Maggid of Mezeritsch, see Daniel Abrams, *The Female Body of God in Kabbalah: Embodied Forms of Love and Sexuality in the Divine Feminine* (Jerusalem: The Hebrew University Magnes Press Ltd., 2004), 135–38. [Hebrew]

53. Readers interested in a more extensive application of metaphor theory to the Jewish nursing God image are welcome to consult a chapter I am contributing to a forthcoming group volume. There, I discuss a small selection of the materials addressed in chapters 2 and 3 of this book, demonstrating how metaphor and metonymy's complex interactions enable authors to craft compelling religious images. Ellen Haskell, "Bathed in Milk: Metaphors of Suckling and Spiritual Transmission in Thirteenth-Century Kabbalah," in *Figuring Religions: Comparing Ideas, Images, and Activities*, ed. Shubha Pathak (Albany, NY: SUNY Press, forthcoming).

Notes to Chapter 1

1. James Fernandez, *Persuasions and Performances: The Play of Tropes in Culture* (Bloomington, IN: Indiana University Press, 1986), 12, 25.

2. Paul Ricoeur asserts that "metaphoric utterances" communicate complex statements that bring broad reference fields (such as breastfeeding and spirituality) into creative conjunction. Paul Ricoeur, *The Rule of Metaphor: Multi-Disciplinary Studies of the Creation of Meaning in Language*, trans. Robert Czerny with Kathleen McLaughlin and John Costello (Toronto: University of Toronto Press, 1977), 299, 307.

3. Metonymy, the linguistic trope of contiguity, is in large part the force that makes these metaphoric connotations effective, providing the thick perceptual reality of metaphorical assertions. Metonymy's use of contiguity may be obvious, as in the classic

crown-for-king example, or it may be more obscure, like the relationship between funerals and the color black. (This colorful example is borrowed from Roman Jakobson's famous study.) See Roman Jakobson, "Two Aspects of Language and Two Types of Aphasic Disturbances," in *Fundamentals of Language*, ed. Roman Jakobson and Morris Halle, 2d rev. ed., 67–96 (The Hague, The Netherlands: Mouton, 1971), 83–4. As James Fernandez explains, "The complexity of expressive experience lies in the interplay of contiguity and similarity associations in the predications upon the pronouns participating in this experience." Fernandez, *Persuasions and Performances*, 43–44.

4. These works include the Babylonian Talmud, the texts included in the *Midrash Rabbah*, the *Midrash to the Psalms*, the *Pesiktot* and *Pirke de Rabbi Eliezer*. Gershom Scholem, *Major Trends in Jewish Mysticism*, with a foreword by Robert Alter (Jerusalem: Schocken Publishing House, Ltd., 1941; reprint, New York: Schocken Books Inc., 1995), 173–74.

5. My main source for dating rabbinic texts is H. L. Strack and Günter Stemberger, *Introduction to the Talmud and Midrash*, trans. and ed. Markus Bockmuehl np (Edinburgh, UK: T & T Clark Ltd., 1991; reprint, Minneapolis: Fortress Press, 1996, with emendations and updates).

6. The Babylonian Talmud will hereafter be abbreviated BT.

7. Brackets indicate implied words, unstated in the Hebrew text but necessary for a narrative's translation into English. They also indicate phrases that complete relevant Biblical references included only as partial citations. (The texts' traditional readers, who were well versed in Biblical narrative, would have supplied these completions automatically.) In addition, I have adopted a simplified form of punctuation within block quotations. Biblical quotes receive double quotation marks to highlight their importance, but speech is left without quotation marks. This system reflects the Hebrew and Aramaic source texts, which do not punctuate speech with quotation marks. Rarely, double quotation marks also surround a rabbinic text cited within a translated text or set off terms being specially presented.

8. It is interesting that Rabbi Levi, a third generation Palestinian Amora, appears in this text and in the Talmudic version of the story, as well as being cited by Rabbi Berekhya in the *Pesikta de Rav*

Kahana version. Although he voices different points of emphasis in the different texts, he does appear to be associated strongly with Sarah's miraculous suckling.

9. The expression *pathu* (they opened) is connected with rabbis giving teachings on scripture. I have left the term *open* intact to highlight the parallelism between Sarah's breasts' miraculous opening and the observers' awareness "opening."

10. The rabbis find every detail of Torah significant, so when they encounter unusual word choices in scripture, they creatively invest them with meaning. Dealing with textual inconsistencies and filling in the gaps left by sparse Biblical narratives are two important motivators for rabbinic interpretation.

11. I will have more to say about the identity of these God fearers below.

12. Of the remaining versions of this tale, *Pesikta de Rav Kahana* also contains the miraculous suckling theme, but the abundance of joy and nourishment derived from Sarah is used to signify God's future renewal of Jerusalem, rather than creating an origin myth for proselytes. *Pirke de Rabbi Eliezer*'s version does not address the origins of proselytes and instead employs vegetative imagery, comparing Sarah to a blossoming tree. This metaphor, derived from Ezekiel 17, is particularly interesting, because kabbalistic literature also blends human suckling imagery with vegetative imagery.

13. In Theodor and Albeck's critical edition, the text is found as *Genesis Rabbah* 53:7. Their version is almost exactly the same as the one translated above, with the addition of the sentence, "She suckles children, she suckles builders," rather than the explanation that the Torah verse does not read "child" in the singular. See J. Theodor, *Bereschit Rabbah: mit Kritischem Apparat und Kommentar*, 2nd printing with additional corrections by Ch. Albeck, vol. 1 (Jerusalem: Wahrmann Books, 1965), 564.

14. Babylonian Talmud *Berakhot* 64a reads, "Rabbi Eleazar said [that] Rabbi Ḥanina said: The students of the wise increase peace in the world. As it is said, 'And all of your children will be taught of the Lord, and great will be the peace of your children.' (Isaiah 54:13) Do not read, 'your children (*banayikh*),' but rather, 'your builders (*bonayikh*).'"

15. Michael Fishbane, "The Well of Living Water: A Biblical Motif and Its Ancient Transformations," in *"Sha'arei Talmon:" Studies in the*

Bible, Qumran, and the Ancient Near East Presented to Shemaryahu Talmon, ed. Michael Fishbane and Emanuel Tov with Weston W. Fields, 3–16 (Winona Lake, IN: Eisenbrauns, 1992), 4–6. Fishbane includes many other relevant examples of this Biblical motif in his essay.

16. Terence Turner. ""We Are Parrots," "Twins are Birds": Play of Tropes as Operational Structure" in *Beyond Metaphor: The Theory of Tropes in Anthropology*, ed. James Fernandez, 153 (Stanford, CA: Stanford University Press, 1991).

17. As Roland Barthes notes, socially relevant myths can transform history because "driven to having either to unveil or to liquidate the concept, it [myth] will *naturalize* it." Roland Barthes, *Mythologies*, trans. Annette Lavers, 1st American edition (New York: Hill and Wang, 1972), 129. These are Barthes' italics.

18. Shaye J. D. Cohen. *The Beginnings of Jewishness: Boundaries, Varieties, Uncertainties*, Hellenistic Culture and Society, ed. Anthony W. Bulloch, Erich S. Gruen, A. A. Long, and Andrew F. Stewart (Berkeley, CA: University of California Press, 1999), 341; Martin Goodman, *Mission and Conversion: Proselytizing in the Religious History of the Roman Empire* (Oxford: Clarendon Press, 1994), 45–46; Louis Feldman, *Jew and Gentile in the Ancient World: Attitudes and Interactions from Alexander to Justinian* (Princeton, NJ: Princeton University Press, 1993), 334–35; Seth Schwartz, "Language, Power and Identity in Ancient Palestine," *Past and Present* 148 (1995): 34.

19. Shaye Cohen suggests that the idea of conversion to Judaism emerged as a cultural analogue to the process of "converting" to Hellenism. Louis Feldman similarly makes the point that as the Jewish diaspora spread, it may have become increasingly important for Jews to define and explain themselves as a defense against assimilation into more numerous cultural groups. Joseph Rosenbloom makes similar suggestions. Cohen, *The Beginnings of Jewishness*, 134–35; Feldman, *Jew and Gentile in the Ancient World*, 334–35; Joseph R. Rosenbloom, *Conversion to Judaism: From the Biblical Period to the Present* (Cincinnati, OH: Hebrew Union College Press, 1978), 39.

20. Goodman, *Mission and Conversion*, 46, 121–25.

21. Cohen, *The Beginnings of Jewishness*, 156, 263. This lengthy Mishnaic passage requires a great deal of legal explication that is

not appropriate in the context of this book. I recommend seeing Cohen's excellent discussion for further information. Ibid.,
273–76.

22. Ibid., 156, 272. Martin Goodman also dates the earliest evidence
of the matrilineal principle to the *Mishna's* appearance in the early
third century, providing a similar time frame for the principle's
development. Goodman, *Mission and Conversion*, 120–21.

23. Not everyone agrees with this time frame for the matrilineal prin-
ciple. Mayer Gruber claims that the principle originated in the late
Bronze Age, rather than the Hellenistic period. See Mayer I. Gru-
ber, "Matrilineal Determination of Jewishness: Biblical and Near
Eastern Roots," in *Pomegranates and Golden Bells: Studies in Bibli-
cal, Jewish, and Near Eastern Ritual, Law, and Literature in Honor of
Jacob Milgrom*, ed. David Noel Freedman, Avi Hurvitz and David
P. Wright, 437–43 (Winona Lake, IN: Eisenbrauns, 1995).

24. Goodman, *Mission and Conversion*, 121; Cohen, *The Beginnings of
Jewishness*, 298–99, 306–307.

25. Cohen locates the texts that become the bases for this principle in
M. *Qiddushin* 3:13, M. *Yevamot* 12:5, M. *Yevamot* 7:5 and T. *Qiddushin* 4:16. For a discussion of these sources, see Ibid., 273–78.

26. Feldman, *Jew and Gentile in the Ancient World*, 338–39. See Feldman's text for extensive examples of rabbinic writings on proselytes
and their status within the Jewish community.

27. Ibid., 339–40.

28. Cohen, *The Beginnings of Jewishness*, 161. See Cohen for documentation of various inscription sources.

29. Ibid., 333. Joseph Rosenbloom also notes the ambiguous rabbinic
attitude toward proselytes. Rosenbloom, *Conversion to Judaism*,
40–42. At least one scholar has argued that the rabbis do not make
any truly hostile comments about proselytes, claiming that even
the BT *Qiddushin* text comparing proselytes to scabs is intended to
indicate a political difficulty, rather than a religious one. See William Braude, *Jewish Proselytizing: In the First Five Centuries of the
Common Era the Ages of the Tannaim and Amoraim*, (Providence,
RI: Brown University, 1940), 47–48.

30. The first opinion is found in Feldman's work, with Rosenbloom
supporting the idea of an early Jewish proselytizing campaign. The
second view is Goodman's, and arises from his observation that
conversion was a complex and conflicted topic within rabbinic

circles. Cohen takes a similar stance to Goodman's in his book *The Beginnings of Jewishness,* the main topic of which is Jewish self-definition. See Feldman, *Jew and Gentile in the Ancient World,* 338–39, 341; Rosenbloom, *Conversion to Judaism,* 39; Goodman, *Mission and Conversion,* 129–53; Cohen, *The Beginnings of Jewishness,* 140–238.

31. For an extensive discussion of these texts, see Cohen, *The Beginnings of Jewishness,* 198–238.

32. Ibid., 210–11, 223, 236. Cohen's reasons for this dating involve both textual and social concerns.

33. See Rosenbloom, *Conversion to Judaism,* 60.

34. See Feldman, *Jew and Gentile in the Ancient World,* 344–45. I prefer the more literal translation "fearers of heaven." For Feldman's theory, see Louis Feldman, "Jewish "Sympathizers" in Classical Literature and Inscriptions," *Transactions and Proceedings of the American Philological Association* 81 (1950): 207.

35. Feldman, *Jew and Gentile in the Ancient World,* 344. The respectful use of "G-d" appears in Feldman's book, and I have retained it in this quotation.

36. Ibid., 358–61. Goodman cites similar dates, noting that there is not much evidence the Jewish community formally recognized God fearers before the second century. Goodman, *Mission and Conversion,* 47.

37. The distinction between Jews, proselytes, and God fearers was clarified by the discovery of inscriptions at Aphrodisias that list the three categories separately. Goodman, *Mission and Conversion,* 118; Cohen, *The Beginnings of Jewishness,* 171; Feldman, *Jew and Gentile in the Ancient World,* 367–69.

38. The Sarah stories show that metaphors are not simply literary devices, but can also be sources of social transformation. As James Fernandez explains, a metaphor is a "strategic predication upon an inchoate pronoun . . . which makes a movement and leads to performance." Fernandez, *Persuasions and Performances,* 8. Strong images change the ways that people think, and these changes are reflected in their behavior. Metaphors representing conceptual changes alter people's perceptions of what is happening around them and ultimately influence how an audience interprets a situation's reality. These altered perceptions then allow groups to translate their new interpretations into actions. George Lakoff and

Mark Johnson, *Metaphors We Live By* (Chicago: The University of Chicago Press, 1981), 145–46; David Edge, "Technological Metaphor and Social Control," *New Literary History* 6, no. 1 (1974): 136.

39. While it is difficult to know the precise identity of the rabbis' audience for this message, the Sarah texts were at least intended to persuade an internal rabbinic audience.

40. Feldman, *Jew and Gentile in the Ancient World*, 103.

41. For further examples, see Cohen, *The Beginnings of Jewishness*, 328–39; Goodman, *Mission and Conversion*, 145; Rosenbloom, *Conversion to Judaism*, 35.

42. Feldman notes that conversion may have been especially popular among women either because they didn't have to undergo the process of circumcision or because they were "attracted by the relatively more elevated position in Judaism." Feldman, *Jew and Gentile in the Ancient World*, 438. Also see Goodman, *Mission and Conversion*, 328, 330, 405, 407.

43. This teaching is found in BT *Avodah Zarah* 26a. The word I translate as "gentile" in the *Exodus Rabbah* 1:25 passage is actually *kutit* (a Cuthean woman). BT *Avodah Zarah* 26a uses the term *ovedet kokhavim* (star-worshipper), making it clearer that the teaching's central issue is idolatry (or at least gentile identity), rather than nationality. It is possible that *ovedet kokhavim* is a later term included by Jewish editors as an act of self-censorship, in which case the text more likely refers to gentiles in general, rather than to those who specifically incorporate statues in religious practice. Resolving this issue is beyond the scope of the project.

44. In this context, *Shekhinah* refers to the divine presence, rather than to the feminine *sefirah*.

45. The significant excerpt of BT *Sotah* 12b reads, "'And his sister said to Pharaoh's daughter, Shall I go and call for you a wet-nurse woman of the Hebrews, [and she will suckle the child for you?'] (Exodus 2:7). And what is the difference of a woman of the Hebrews? It teaches that she took Moses around to all the Egyptian women, but he did not suckle. He said: A mouth that in the future shall speak with the *Shekhinah*, shall it suckle an unclean (*tame'*) thing? This is as it is written: 'To whom shall he teach knowledge [and who shall he make understand tradition? Those who are weaned from milk, removed from the breasts'] (Isaiah 28:9). To

whom shall he teach knowledge and who shall he make understand tradition? To those who are weaned from milk and to those removed from the breasts." While this version is more concise, the key scriptural verses framing the narrative (Exodus 2:7 and Isaiah 28:9) are the same. The Talmudic version does not provide terminology for Moses' rejection of the Egyptians. The speaker's identity is also ambiguous. Is Moses explaining his own future, or is it God who does not want the infant's prophetic mouth defiled? Despite these differences, the parallel is clear and striking.

46. Strack and Stemberger, *Introduction to the Talmud and Midrash*, 309.

47. Rabbi Yudan is a fourth generation Amora, Rabbi Berekhya a fifth generation Amora, and Rabbi Abbahu a third generation Amora (c 300 CE). Marc Bregman has done extensive work on this passage and its treatment of masculine breastfeeding in rabbinic literature. Marc Bregman, "Mordekhai the Milkman" (lecture, The University of North Carolina at Greensboro, Greensboro, NC, Fall, 2008).

48. Bregman notes that this clean male milk is included in a rabbinic list of things that are not normally consumed, complicating Rabbi Abbahu's explanation. See Mishna *Makhshirim* 6:4. Bregman, "Mordekhai the Milkman."

49. Bregman notes that this text's variation seems to be a later addition to the Mordekhai breastfeeding motif, since no other rabbinic text mentions a wife for the Jewish hero. Bregman, "Mordekhai the Milkman."

50. Another rabbinic text that deals with the theme of a male suckling a child is BT *Shabbat* 53b, which contains a story of a man whose wife dies, leaving behind a child. The man is too poor to hire a wet nurse, so a miracle is done for him. "His breasts were opened like the two breasts of a woman, and he suckled his son." The rabbis thereafter disagree about whether he is a great man, to have such a miracle performed for him, or whether he is a lowly man, because the order of creation was changed for him. Marc Bregman has documented modern cases that prove fatherly suckling is a biological possibility. Bregman, "Mordekhai the Milkman."

51. Presumably, Abraham uniting the world's peoples relates to his teaching them Judaism.

52. Technically, the Biblical Abraham is not a Jew, since he behaves in pre-halakhic ways during the Genesis narrative and exists prior

to receiving the law at Sinai. He functions instead as a religious founding father. The rabbis, however, chose to ascribe Jewish identity to him, reading him through the lens of their own religious experience.

53. See Lakoff and Johnson, *Metaphors We Live By*, 46–47.

54. The Zoharic authorship also employs similar themes and expressions in the late thirteenth century. Zohar 2:80b interprets Song 8:8's "little sister" both as the divine Assembly of Israel (another name for *Shekhinah*), who is the Holy One's sister *and* as the human assembly of Israel that approaches Mount Sinai to receive the Torah. This passage states: "Rabbi Abba opened: 'We have a little sister and she has no breasts. What will we do for our sister on the day that she is spoken for?' (Song 8:8). 'We have a little sister': this is the Assembly of Israel, who is called the sister of the Holy One, blessed be He. 'And she has no breasts': this teaches us that at the time that Israel approached Mount Sinai, there were no merits or good deeds in them to protect them." In this kabbalistic passage, lack of breasts (rather than the lack of proper breastfeeding) is explicated as a lack of good deeds. Suckling, a term the Zoharic authorship prefers for the passage of blessings and divine influence, is not present. Thematically, suckling good deeds from a mother is transferred to the mystical act of suckling blessings from God.

55. *Numbers Rabbah* was redacted in Provence, very close to the time when the earliest kabbalistic texts appeared. Ḥananel Mack has identified *Numbers Rabbah* as a foundational text for early Kabbalah. See Ḥananel Mack, "Midrash Bamidbar Rabbah and the Beginning of Kabbalah in Provence." In *Myth in Judaism*, ed. Haviva Pedaya, 80, 94, vol. 4 of *Eshel Beer-Sheva: Occasional Publications in Jewish Studies*. Jerusalem: Mosad Bialik for Ben-Gurion University of the Negev Press, 1996.

56. The Hebrew term suckling (*yeniqah*) has meanings beyond breastfeeding, such as absorbing and drawing sustenance or sap. It is possible that these vegetative connotations inspired the text's suckling interpretation. For example, BT *Bava Batra* 71b discusses the status of trees that suckle from a sanctified field. It seems that the field's sanctity is transmitted to the trees that draw from it, providing an interesting parallel to the metaphor of religious transmission via suckling from a human mother. This vegetable-suckling motif is also found in the Zohar, a topic addressed in chapter 3. However,

suckling's human associations are clearly present in *Pesikta Rabbati* 7:9 where the tribal ancestors suckle Jacob's blessing, a religious quality received from a parental figure.

57. Mack notes that some of the earliest sources to cite *Numbers Rabbah* are the kabbalists Ezra and Azriel of Gerona. The work is also closely associated with the twelfth century kabbalistic text *Sefer ha-Bahir*. Mack, "Midrash Bamidbar Rabbah and the Beginning of Kabbalah in Provence," 88–90.

58. Ivan Marcus's book, *Rituals of Childhood*, provides detailed analysis of a medieval ritual marking such a transition. Ivan Marcus, *Rituals of Childhood: Jewish Acculturation in Medieval Europe* (New Haven, CT: Yale University Press, 1996).

59. Admiel Kosman has shown that rabbinic literature uses suckling as a metaphor for the transmission of Oral Law, noting the close relationship between Torah and mother's milk. He suggests that this metaphor highlights the sensitive and receptive qualities of the scholar engaged in Torah learning. Admiel Kosman, "The Female Breast and the Male Mouth: A Talmudic Vignette (BT *Bava Batra* 9a-b)," *Jewish Studies Quarterly* 11, no. 4 (2004): 305–307.

60. Another example of the suckling as Torah transmission theme is found in *Numbers Rabbah* 4:2, which reads, "You do not have a man in Israel who humbled himself for the commandments more than David. Thus it was that he said before God: 'God, my heart was not haughty' (Psalms 131:1), at the time that Samuel anointed me as king. 'And my eyes were not lofty' (Psalms 131:1), at the time that I killed Goliath. 'And I did not proceed in great matters' (Psalms 131:1), at the time that I was restored to my kingdom. 'Or in wonders beyond me' (Psalms 131:1), at the time that I brought up the Ark. 'Have I not smoothed myself and quieted my soul like a weaned child with its mother?' (Psalms 131:2). As this child is not ashamed to be uncovered before his mother, thus have I smoothed my soul before you so that I was not ashamed to humble myself before you to honor you. 'Like a weaned child is my soul upon me' (Psalms 131:2). For as the child comes forth from the belly of his mother and does not have within him a spirit too proud to suckle from the breasts of his mother, so is my soul upon me, that I am not ashamed to study Torah, even from the least of Israel." This passage is paralleled by *Midrash on Psalms* 131:2, another late text that dates to the thirteenth century. The

two passages are almost exact parallels, except for a few linking words. In *Numbers Rabbah's* version, the context is a discussion of 2 Samuel 6:20, in which David's dancing angers his wife Mikhal and he responds by defending his humility. Here, suckling is not an explicit metaphor for Torah learning, since David is showing humility by declaring that he is not ashamed to learn Torah from "the least of Israel." Still, it is interesting that the interpreter, as in the earlier Talmudic text, chooses this particular analogy and aligns suckling with Torah learning. For *Numbers Rabbah's* connection to the early kabbalists, see Mack, "Midrash Bamidbar Rabbah and the Beginning of Kabbalah in Provence," 80, 94.

61. "Those who serve the stars" refers to pagans.

62. *Genesis Rabbah* 1:1 also links Proverbs 8:30 and Numbers 11:12 in a discourse on *amon/omen*, but there the terms seem to imply the definitions *tutor, workman,* or *tool*.

63. These Jewish thinkers need not have been consciously aware of using one set of religious images to inspire another. Rather, the process reflects Jewish literature's strong intertextual character, which allows ideas and images to be expanded over time and developed according to changing cultural and historical circumstances.

64. A variant of the Sarah story is also found in Zohar 1:10b, but in that context it is a cautionary tale about hospitality to the poor. In the Zohar, spiritual transmission is removed from the human context of an earthly woman suckling her child and refocused on God's dynamic inner life.

Notes to Chapter 2

1. The edition of Ezra's text used for my translation is: Charles Chavel, ed., "*Perush le-Shir ha-Shirim,*" in *Kitve Rabenu Moshe ben Naḥman*, vol. 2 (Jerusalem: Mosad ha-Rav Kook, 2002), 473–518. Seth Brody provides a helpful English translation of a manuscript version of Ezra's commentary (the Jewish Theological Seminary's Lutzki 1059), to which I refer below. Seth Brody, ed. and trans., *Rabbi Ezra ben Solomon of Gerona: "Commentary on the Song of Songs" and Other Kabbalistic Commentaries*, with an introduction by Arthur Green, Commentary Series, ed. E. Ann Matter

(Kalamazoo, MI: Medieval Institute Publications for The Consortium for the Teaching of the Middle Ages, 1999).

2. The following documents provide source texts for my translations. Gershom Scholem, ed., *"Perush Sefer Yetzirah,"* in *Ha-Kabbalah bi-Provans: Ḥug ha-Rabad u-Veno R. Yitzḥak Sagi Nahor*, appendix 1: 1–18 (Jerusalem: Akademon, 1969); Mark Sendor, "The Emergence of Provençal Kabbalah: Rabbi Isaac the Blind's "Commentary on *Sefer Yetzirah*," 2 vols. (PhD. diss., Harvard University, 1994); Reuven Moshe Margaliot, ed. *Sefer ha-Bahir* (Jerusalem: Mosad he-Rav Kook, 1994); Charles Chavel, *"Perush le-Shir ha-Shirim."*

3. Both Rabbi Isaac the Blind and his father, Rabbi Abraham ben David of Posquières (d. 1198), were said to have received revelations from the prophet Elijah. Their disciples were largely responsible for transporting Kabbalah from southern France to northern Spain, where it entered its next developmental phase. Gershom Scholem, *Origins of the Kabbalah*, ed. R. J. Zwi Werblowsky, trans. Allan Arkush, 1st English translation (np Philadelphia, PA: The Jewish Publication Society, 1987; reprint, Princeton, NJ: Princeton University Press, 1990), 37, 253.

4. See Sendor, "The Emergence of Provençal Kabbalah," vol. 1, 14–15. For an example of Jewish literary production in eleventh- and twelfth-century France, see Ḥananel Mack, who has demonstrated that there are close ties between *Numbers Rabbah* (which was redacted in twelfth century France) and early kabbalistic literature, with some of the earliest citations of this *midrash* found in the works of Ezra of Gerona, Isaac's student. Mack also demonstrates a close connection between *Numbers Rabbah* and *Sefer ha-Bahir*. Ḥananel Mack, "Midrash Bamidbar Rabbah and the Beginning of Kabbalah in Provence," in *Myth in Judaism*, ed. Haviva Pedaya, 78, 94, vol. 4 of *Eshel Beer-Sheva: Occasional Publications in Jewish Studies* (Jerusalem: Mosad Bialik for Ben-Gurion University of the Negev Press, 1996). Also, see Scholem, *Origins of the Kabbalah*, 17.

5. Isaac's influential teachings spread via his disciples. Many of the next generation's premier kabbalists received teachings from him. He was also the first kabbalist to apply the terminology of 1 Chronicles 29:11 to the *sefirot*, establishing normative terms for the divine gradations. See Scholem, *Origins of the Kabbalah*,

254, 263; Sendor, "The Emergence of Provençal Kabbalah," vol. 1, 1–43; Yechiel Goldberg, "Spiritual Leadership and the Popularization of Kabbalah in Medieval Spain," *The Journal for the Study of Sephardic and Mizrahi Jewry* 2, no. 2 (2009): 3–5; Moshe Idel, "Naḥmanides: Kabbalah, Halakhah, and Spiritual Leadership," in *Jewish Mystical Leaders and Leadership in the Thirteenth Century*, ed. Moshe Idel and Mortimer Ostow, 15–96 (Lanham, MD: Rowman & Littlefield Publishers, Inc., 2005), 16–59, 84; Moshe Halbertal, *Concealment and Revelation: Esotericism in Jewish Thought and Its Philosophical Implications*, translated by Jackie Feldman (Princeton, NJ: Princeton University Press, 2007), 71–73.

6. Scholem, *Origins of the Kabbalah*, 253–54.

7. Scholem suggests a period between the second and the sixth centuries for this text's composition. Scholem, *Origins of the Kabbalah*, 25. Yehuda Liebes locates *Sefer Yetzirah*'s composition in the first century of the Common Era. Yehuda Liebes, *Torat ha-Yetzirah shel Sefer Yetzirah* (Tel Aviv: Schocken Publishing House Ltd., 2000), 229–37 [Hebrew]. However, A. Peter Hayman and Steven Wasserstrom date the text later, in the ninth century. A. Peter Hayman, *Sefer Yeṣira: Edition, Translation and Text-Critical Commentary*, (Tübingen, Germany: Mohr Siebeck, 2004), 7; Steven Wasserstrom, "Further Thoughts on the Origins of Sefer Yesirah," *Aleph: Historical Studies in Science and Judaism* 2 (2002): 201–21.

8. For *Sefer Yetzirah*'s focus on numerical and alphabetic creativity, see Moshe Idel, *Absorbing Perfections: Kabbalah and Interpretation*, with a foreword by Harold Bloom (New Haven, CT: Yale University Press, 2002), 36–37. For *Sefer Yetzirah* as the source of kabbalistic terminology, see Scholem, *Origins of the Kabbalah*, 25–27. Elliot Wolfson has convincingly demonstrated that the tenth-century Italian writer Shabbetai Donnolo interpreted *Sefer Yetzirah*'s *sefirot* as divine aspects or entities, rather than as numbers, in his commentary *Sefer Ḥakhmoni* (written in 946 or 982 CE). While this commentary is not kabbalistic, it represents an important theosophic usage of the term "*sefirot*" that predates Kabbalah's earliest texts. Elliot Wolfson, "The Theosophy of Shabbetai Donnolo, with Special Emphasis on the Doctrine of *Sefirot* in His *Sefer Hakhmoni*," *Jewish History* 6:1–2, The Frank Talmage Memorial Volume (1992): 286–301.

9. Scholem, *Origins of the Kabbalah*, 282–83; Sendor, "The Emergence of Provençal Kabbalah," vol. 1, 126–29.

10. Scholem, *Origins of the Kabbalah*, 299. For a detailed overview of Isaac's life and theology, see Ibid., 248–309. For a thorough discussion of R. Isaac's theology in *Commentary on Sefer Yetzirah*, see Sendor, "The Emergence of Provençal Kabbalah," vol. 1, 109–374.

11. Sendor, "The Emergence of Provençal Kabbalah," vol. 1, 120–29.

12. *Em ha-derekh* is probably a reference to Ezekiel 21:26, where a crossroads is referred to as a "mother of the way (*em ha-derekh*)." "There" seems to refer to *Ḥokhmah*, the source or root of the paths and their complex images.

13. This passage comments on *Sefer Yetzirah* 1:1. Gershom Scholem, ed., "*Perush Sefer Yetzirah*," 1.

14. This topic is characteristic of Isaac's work, which tends to emphasize the dynamics of the three highest *sefirot*: *Keter* (Crown), *Ḥokhmah* (Wisdom) and *Binah* (Understanding). See *Sefer Yetzirah*, chapter 1, for the thirty-two paths of Wisdom.

15. The letter *alef* is the first letter of the element air *(avvir)*, while *mem* is the first letter of the element water *(mayim)*, and *shin* corresponds to the last letter of the element fire *(esh)*, whose first letter, *alef*, has already been used to represent air. For a more detailed overview of the three alphabetic mothers, including a brief description of their importance in medieval Jewish interpretation, see Liebes, *Torat ha-Yetzirah shel Sefer Yetzirah*, 17–19.

16. *Sefer Yetzirah* 1:1 also contains the divine name *El Shaddai*, whose association with divine suckling and satiation stems from the punning relationship between the name *El Shaddai* and the words "enough" *(day)* and "breasts" *(shadayim)*. This pun may also have helped to suggest the suckling metaphor to Isaac. The same pun is used in the Zohar and in the work of the thirteenth-century kabbalist Joseph ben Abraham Gikatilla to help explain the relationship between God and humanity, as will be discussed in chapter 3.

17. And in fact, many kabbalistic texts that use the suckling metaphor move freely between the term's anthropomorphic and vegetative usages.

18. When approaching Isaac the Blind's complex literary imagery, it is interesting to note Moshe Idel's statement that this mystic's work consists mainly of "dry, monosemic, theosophical symbols," which

Idel claims as a result of Isaac's avoiding a midrashic approach to interpretation. While the interpretive strategies Isaac brings to bear upon *Sefer Yetzirah* are certainly different from the interpretive strategies of *midrash*, I believe that the play of interwoven images and connotations in this passage effectively demonstrates that Isaac's work is anything but dry and monosemic. See Idel, *Absorbing Perfections*, 232.

19. Sendor, "The Emergence of Provençal Kabbalah," vol. 2, 13–14, n31; Y. Goldberg, "Spiritual Leadership and the Popularization of Kabbalah in Medieval Spain."47; Daniel Abrams, *The Female Body of God in Kabbalah: Embodied Forms of Love and Sexuality in the Divine Feminine* (Jerusalem: The Hebrew University Magnes Press Ltd., 2004), 125. [Hebrew]

20. Ivan Marcus, *Rituals of Childhood: Jewish Acculturation in Medieval Europe* (New Haven, CT: Yale University Press, 1996), 43, 75–76.

21. Hellner-Eshed notes that thirteenth-century Kabbalah continues to locate the essence of mystical life in the emotional sphere of the heart, rather than in the intellectual realm of knowledge. Furthermore, given that Haviva Pedaya has demonstrated a connection between mystical experience, automatic speech, and Isaac the Blind's teachings, it is intriguing to speculate whether there may be a connection between Isaac's suckling and mystical experience. Melila Hellner-Eshed, *A River Flows from Eden: The Language of Mystical Experience in the Zohar* (Stanford, CA: Stanford University Press, 2005), 68–9; Haviva Pedaya, "Aḥuzim ba-Dibbur: Li-Vruro shel ha-Defus ha-Mitpa'el etzel Rishonei ha-Mekubbalim," *Tarbitz* 65 (1996): 567, 580–81, 588.

22. For an explanation of this process in relation to myth, see Roland Barthes, *Mythologies*, trans. Annette Lavers, 1st American edition (New York: Hill and Wang, 1972), 129.

23. Sendor, "The Emergence of Provençal Kabbalah," vol. 1, 208–209.

24. Ibid., vol. 1, 224.

25. The nature of this "it" is uncertain. However, "it" most likely refers to being itself. See Sendor, "The Emergence of Provençal Kabbalah," vol. 2, 129–30.

26. My translation follows Sendor, "The Emergence of Provençal Kabbalah," vol. 2, 130–31. This phrase is difficult to translate, because it is unclear whether the abbreviation *am'* in this sentence is intended to mean "mothers" (*imot*) or "it [the text] says" (*amar*).

(All these terms begin with *alef.*) As Sendor notes, the "mothers" reading recapitulates the message of the sentence directly prior to this one and fits nicely into the fabric of the passage as a whole.

27. In this case, "it" probably means *Sefer Yetzirah* itself, which describes how the Mothers relate to world, year and soul in chapter 2:2–5. This passage comments on *Sefer Yetzirah* 3:2 and is located in Scholem, ed., "*Perush Sefer Yetzirah,*" 13.

28. For another discussion of how Mothers, Fathers, and separate entities are joined together in the divine flow, see Sendor, "The Emergence of Provençal Kabbalah," vol. 1, 126. Sendor explains that the Mothers and Fathers enjoy continuous overflow, while the separated beings receive divine substance discontinuously.

29. There are also passages in the Commentary where suckling is not associated with anthropomorphic imagery at all. The most notable occur in chapter 1, where suckling is associated with the image of *Ḥokhmah* as a brain (and possibly with phallic imagery) and in chapter 2, where it is associated with vegetable imagery. See Scholem, ed., "*Perush Sefer Yetzirah,*" 2, 9.

30. This move is characteristic of kabbalistic theology, which often takes prior rabbinic images and reapplies them to God's sefirotic interior life.

31. James Fernandez, *Persuasions and Performances: The Play of Tropes in Culture* (Bloomington, IN: Indiana University Press, 1986), 191–208.

32. Elliot Wolfson, "By Way of Truth: Aspects of Nahmanides' Kabbalistic Hermeneutic," *AJS Review* 14, no. 2 (1989): 178; Daniel Abrams, "The Condensation of the Symbol 'Shekhinah' in the Manuscripts of the *Book Bahir,*" *Kabbalah: Journal for the Study of Jewish Mystical Texts* 16 (2007): 23.

33. Scholem, *Origins of the Kabbalah*, 56, 123; Gershom Scholem, *On the Kabbalah and Its Symbolism*, with a foreword by Bernard McGinn, trans. Ralph Manheim (New York: Schocken Books Inc., 1965; reprint, New York: Schocken Books, 1996), 90; Peter Schäfer, *Mirror of His Beauty: Feminine Images of God from the Bible to the Early Kabbalah,* (Princeton, NJ: Princeton University Press, 2002), 119, 235–37; Sendor, "The Emergence of Provençal Kabbalah," vol. 1, 288–89; Moshe Idel, *Kabbalah and Eros* (New Haven, CT: Yale University Press, 2005), 52; Elliot Wolfson, *Language, Eros, Being: Kabbalistic Hermeneutics and Poetic Imagination*

(New York: Fordham University Press, 2005), 146–47; Ronit Meroz, "On the Time and Place of Some Passages in *Sefer ha-Bahir*," *Da'at* 49 (2002), 150–65, 175; Halbertal, *Concealment and Revelation*, 69; Abrams, "The Condensation of the Symbol 'Shekhinah' in the Manuscripts of the *Book Bahir*," 8–12, 23–25; Daniel Abrams, "The Virgin Mary as the Moon That Lacks the Sun: A Zoharic Polemic Against the Veneration of Mary," *Kabbalah: Journal for the Study of Jewish Mystical Texts* 21 (2010): 11–12. The earliest known manuscript of the Bahir is Munich 209, which was copied in 1298 in a Spanish script. Daniel Abrams, *The Book Bahir: An Edition Based on the Earliest Manuscripts*, with an introduction by Moshe Idel (Los Angeles, CA: Cherub Press, 1994), 11.

34. *Sefer ha-Bahir* was known to some medievals as the *Midrash of Rabbi Nehunya ben Haqanah* and erroneously attributed to this second century sage. Scholem, *Origins of the Kabbalah*, 39; Schäfer, *Mirror of His Beauty*, 123.

35. Examples of these standard sefirotic terms include the names *Hokhmah* and *Binah*. Scholem, *Origins of the Kabbalah*, 124, 131. Daniel Abrams believes that rather than representing kabbalistic theology's first coherent presentation, the form of the Bahir known to scholars represents a thirteenth-century reworking of kabbalistic principles into the Bahir, which was originally a far more fluid document. Abrams, "The Virgin Mary as the Moon That Lacks the Sun," 11–12; Abrams, "The Condensation of the Symbol 'Shekhinah' in the Manuscripts of the *Book Bahir*," 8–10, 11–12.

36. Gershom Scholem, *On the Mystical Shape of the Godhead: Basic Concepts in the Kabbalah*, trans. Joachim Neugroschel (New York: Schocken Books, 1991), 162; Scholem, *On the Kabbalah and Its Symbolism*, 105–6; Scholem, *Origins of the Kabbalah*, 162–63; Schäfer, *Mirror of His Beauty*. (Schäfer's book discusses the feminine divine's development in its historical contexts.) Also see Arthur Green, "Shekhinah, the Virgin Mary, and the Song of Songs: Reflections on a Kabbalistic Symbol in Its Historical Context," *AJS Review* 26, no. 1 (2002): 21. Moshe Idel and Daniel Abrams challenge this view of the Bahir's gender innovation regarding *Shekhinah*, particularly in relation to Schäfer and Green's ideas about Marian influence on the feminine divine. See Idel, *Kabbalah and Eros*, 46; Abrams, "The Virgin Mary as the Moon That Lacks the Sun," 11–12, 15–16, 21–24; Abrams, "The Condensation of the Symbol 'Shekhinah' in the Manuscripts of the *Book Bahir*," 7–10, 42.

37. Daniel Abrams suggests that the *Shekhinah*'s important role in the Bahir is largely the product of later kabbalists with a better-developed concept of *Shekhinah* projecting their ideas into the text. Daniel Abrams, "The Condensation of the Symbol 'Shekhinah' in the Manuscripts of the *Book Bahir*," 8–15.

38. This concept is based on a reading of Proverbs 2:3, "You shall call Understanding (*Binah*) Mother." Detailed studies of feminine images in the Bahir have been undertaken by Gershom Scholem and Peter Schäfer. Scholem, *On the Mystical Shape of the Godhead*, 140–96; Schäfer, *Mirror of His Beauty*.

39. Scholem, *Origins of the Kabbalah*, 80; Schäfer, *Mirror of His Beauty*, 120.

40. Scholem, *Origins of the Kabbalah*, 261.

41. Abrams, "The Condensation of the Symbol 'Shekhinah' in the Manuscripts of the *Book Bahir*," 23; Daniel Abrams, "The Invention of the *Zohar* as a Book: On the Assumptions and Expectations of the Kabbalists and Modern Scholars," *Kabbalah: Journal for the Study of Jewish Mystical Texts* 19 (2009): 111.

42. In Exodus 17, the people of Israel prevail during the battle with Amalek while Moses holds up his hand. Zohar 2:65b–66a uses the battle with Amalek to provide context for the image of a nursing, feminine divine. I will discuss this text in chapter 3.

43. In Daniel Abrams' critical edition of the Bahir, which is based on the earliest available manuscripts, these passages are found between Bahir 93 and Bahir 94. While Abrams' critical edition is an important scholarly resource, I have chosen to use the Margaliot edition as the source for my translation because of its greater availability to those who may wish to refer to these text passages in Hebrew. Other than their placement in the work as a whole, there are no significant differences between the two editions' versions of these passages. See Abrams, *The Book Bahir*.

44. The idea of *zekhut avot* (merit of the patriarchs) is found in rabbinic literature. For a few classical rabbinic examples, see Babylonian Talmud *Berakhot* 27b, *Genesis Rabbah* 60:2, 70:8, and 74:12, and *Leviticus Rabbah* 29:7. For medieval examples, see *Exodus Rabbah* 40:4 and *Numbers Rabbah* 11:2.

45. These sefirotic associations (including that of Isaac with Fear and Jacob with Peace and Truth) are common in kabbalistic literature and have roots in Biblical and rabbinic writings. For a few rabbinic examples, see *Genesis Rabbah* 39:6, 73:2, and 79:1–3, *Leviticus*

Rabbah 1:4, and *Pesikta de-Rav Kahana* 19:3. Also see Genesis 31:42 and Micah 7:20 for source texts.

46. Hellner-Eshed notes that in the Zohar, "The white light is the most profound expression of divine *ḥesed.*" She associates this light with an undifferentiated experience of divinity beyond language. Hellner-Eshed, *A River Flows from Eden*, 273. For a longer discussion of kabbalistic color symbolism, see chapter 3, below.

47. The sixth *sefirah* is more commonly referred to as *Tif'eret* or *Raḥamim* in later literature.

48. Mark Verman, *The Books of Contemplation: Medieval Jewish Mystical Sources* (Albany, NY: SUNY Press, 1992), 24.

49. This community of kabbalists, whose other leading figure was Rabbi Azriel of Gerona, flourished in the first half of the thirteenth century. For an interesting look at Gerona's differing kabbalistic schools, one of which centered around Ezra and Azriel, and the other of which was led by Naḥmanides, see Idel, "Naḥmanides: Kabbalah, Halakhah, and Spiritual Leadership," 15–96. Also see Boaz Huss, "*Sefer ha-Zohar* as Canonical, Sacred and Holy Text: Changing Perspectives of the Book of Splendor between the Thirteenth and the Eighteenth Centuries," *The Journal of Jewish Thought and Philosophy* 7 (1998): 272–73. For more extensive analyses of how Ezra and Azriel's ideas about transmitting Kabbalah to a broad audience differed from Naḥmanides' opinions on kabbalistic secrecy, see Halbertal, *Concealment and Revelation*, 69–92; Wolfson, "By Way of Truth," 104–110, 154.

50. Yechiel Goldberg has convincingly demonstrated that Ezra understood actively disseminating his kabbalistic teachings to be a religious duty. His goal was to renew Jewish scholarship and hope, which he believed would lead ultimately toward redemption. Goldberg, "Spiritual Leadership and the Popularization of Kabbalah in Medieval Spain, " 3–5, 52–55. Moshe Halbertal credits Ezra and Azriel with changing the nature of kabbalistic transmission and making the teachings of Kabbalah much more open and available. Halbertal, *Concealment and Revelation*, 77.

51. Ezra's *Commentary on the Song of Songs* has a history of authorial controversy. It was erroneously attributed to the more famous kabbalist Naḥmanides as early as 1387, and was often printed under his name. The work was also attributed to Azriel of Gerona. It is, in fact, the work of R. Ezra. However, in the source for my

translation the Commentary is again collected among the works of Naḥmanides. Charles Chavel, "*Perush le-Shir ha-Shirim*," 473–518. For a history of this confusion, see Scholem, *Origins of the Kabbalah*, 371. Georges Vajda also attributes the work to Rabbi Ezra. Georges Vajda, *L'amour de Dieu dans la Théologie Juive du Moyen Age*, Études de Philosophie Médiévale, ed. Étienne Gilson, no. 46 (Paris: Librairie Philosophique J. Vrin, 1957), 195. As a result of these efforts, the work is now consistently attributed to its proper author. See Brody, *Rabbi Ezra ben Solomon of Gerona: "Commentary on the Song of Songs" and Other Kabbalistic Commentaries*, 9–10.

52. Scholem, *Origins of the Kabbalah*, 374.

53. Scholem, *Origins of the Kabbalah*, 394; Goldberg, "Spiritual Leadership and the Popularization of Kabbalah in Medieval Spain, " 3–5; Idel, "Naḥmanides: Kabbalah, Halakhah, and Spiritual Leadership," 32–34; Halbertal, *Concealment and Revelation*, 71. This controversy between Ezra and his prestigious teacher illustrates Kabbalah's growing appeal and its spread beyond the elite esoteric community. A broader audience for Kabbalah is associated with the mid-thirteenth century Geronese kabbalists. The fact that a Geronese author could stir such an impassioned response in the Provençal community also illustrates the close ties between the Jews of southern France and northern Spain during this period. Both regions were held by the Crown of Aragon until 1258. See Scholem, *Origins of the Kabbalah*, 365–66, 393–94. For an extensive analysis of the controversy regarding kabbalistic leaders revealing or concealing kabbalistic secrets in the thirteenth century and of Ezra's role in this controversy (as well as a close look at Isaac's letter), see Goldberg, "Spiritual Leadership and the Popularization of Kabbalah in Medieval Spain, " 1–59.

54. Ezra's use of the Bahir relates to a growing trend among Geronese kabbalists to rely on a growing literary corpus for kabbalistic knowledge, rather than focusing primarily on oral tradition, as did the school surrounding Nahmanides. Halbertal, *Concealment and Revelation* 93–94; Idel, "Naḥmanides: Kabbalah, Halakhah, and Spiritual Leadership," 22–25, 85–87.

55. This statement is located in Ezra's digression on Psalm 104:1, which is embedded within his Song Commentary. See Chavel, "*Perush le-Shir ha-Shirim*," 505. "Causes" (*ilot*) is a philosophical term that

here refers to the *sefirot*. Using the Jewish Theological Seminary's manuscript Lutzki 1059, rather than the Chavel version to which I have access, Seth Brody offers an alternative version of this phrase, which reads, "each Cause and attribute nurses like an infant." It is intriguing to speculate on Ezra's use of overt child imagery for the *sefirot* as they suckle from *Ḥokhmah*. If the Lutzki manuscript contains the word *infant* (as opposed to a clarification by Brody, for which I can see no reason) Ezra is using anthropomorphic suckling imagery in a particularly clear and daring manner. Brody, *Rabbi Ezra ben Solomon of Gerona: "Commentary on the Song of Songs" and Other Kabbalistic Commentaries*, 110.

56. This statement is found in the Commentary on Song 6:3. Chavel, "*Perush le-Shir ha-Shirim*," 504.

57. I am using both "divine overflow" and "divine energy" to represent the kabbalistic term *shefaʿ*, which refers to a divine outpouring of an ineffable nature.

58. Ibid., 504. The passage containing these quotations (found in the Commentary on Song 6:2) reads: "'And to gather lilies' (Song 6:2). This refers to [the gradation of] Thought, the light of *Ḥokhmah* to [the] six extremities. And all of this [occurs] in the days of the exile, when there is no sacrifice or thanksgiving or meal offering. And [as a consequence] the spiritual things ascend and are drawn up to the place of their suckling (*yeniqtam*). And thus it says, 'For because of evil the righteous one is taken away (*neʿesaf*)' (Isaiah 57:1). And for this reason it is necessary to strive and cause to emanate and to draw the blessing to the Fathers, so that there be a drawing for the children. And here [in this verse] the emanation and the drawing are called gathering." Ezra uses Isaiah 57:1 to explain that sin inspires the *sefirot* to flee from the human world. The term used for "taken away" (*neʿesaf*) can also mean "gathered up," indicating sefirotic upward movement.

59. Nursing imagery appears in connection with Ezra's interpretations of Song 1:3, 1:4, 2:2, 3:8, 6:2, three times during his digression on Psalm 104, and in connection with Song 7:9, 8:1, and 8:8.

60. Chavel, "*Perush le-Shir ha-Shirim*," 513.

61. Ibid.

62. The phrase "the spirit of the living God" may also serve as an epithet for *Ḥokhmah* in this passage. In my opinion, the phrase

signifies both the place of suckling (*Ḥokhmah*) and the substance being suckled (divine overflow).

63. Ibid., 514.

64. The Oral Torah and the tenth *sefirah* are frequently associated with each other in kabbalistic literature. This is because the tenth *sefirah* acts as a gateway between the human and divine realms, just as the Oral Torah serves as a gateway to God for the Jewish people.

65. This description of the Written and Oral Torahs as the tenth *sefirah*'s two breasts is unusual. In Kabbalah, the Oral Torah is generally associated with the feminine Assembly of Israel, while the Written Torah is associated with the masculine sixth *sefirah*, *Tif'eret*. This formulation is found in texts as early as *Sefer ha-Bahir* and the writings of Isaac the Blind. However, Ezra's attribution of both Written and Oral Torah to the final *sefirah* works well with the Song's imagery and the physical duality of female breasts. See Scholem, *On the Kabbalah and Its Symbolism*, 47–49; Isaiah Tishby and Fischel Lachower, eds., *The Wisdom of the Zohar: An Anthology of Texts*, trans. David Goldstein, vol. 3 (Washington D.C.: The Littman Library of Jewish Civilization, 1989), 1085–86. For an interesting reading of the *Shekhinah*'s two breasts in relation to the ninth *sefirah Yesod*'s more phallic symbolism and as channels for transmitting divine Mercy and Judgment, see Abrams, *The Female Body of God in Kabbalah*, 127–28.

66. This is a prime example of image-based intertextuality in Jewish thought. Ezra presents a complex theological image drawn from multiple sources in Jewish literature's extensive repertoire.

67. In its Biblical context this is a statement of hope. Here, Ezra reads the phrase in a curiously inverted manner to represent the people of Israel going forth into exile from the land of Israel and the place of Torah.

68. Chavel, "*Perush le-Shir ha-Shirim*," 514. For another analysis of this passage that focuses on Ezra's views regarding knowledge among thirteenth-century Jews, see Goldberg, "Spiritual Leadership and the Popularization of Kabbalah in Medieval Spain," 45–47.

69. See *Genesis Rabbah* 39:3 and *Song of Songs Rabbah* on Song 8:8, in chapter 1, above.

70. Ezra's concern with providing hope to the Jewish community also inspired his decision to make kabbalistic teachings more broadly

available. Goldberg, "Spiritual Leadership and the Popularization of Kabbalah in Medieval Spain." 21–22.

71. Arthur Green notes, "As the earliest Kabbalistic commentary to the Song of Songs, R. Ezra's work may be seen as one that had a truly pivotal influence on the future development of Jewish mysticism. . . . The Zohar, composed in Castile some forty to fifty years after this work, is replete on nearly every page with allusions to the Canticle. . . . This transition from the very earthly setting of the Canticle itself to the realm of sublime symbolism was brought about largely through the influence of R. Ezra's work." Arthur Green, "Editor's Note" in Seth Brody, trans., *Rabbi Ezra ben Solomon of Gerona: "Commentary on the Song of Songs" and Other Kabbalistic Commentaries*, with an introduction by Arthur Green (Kalamazoo, MI: Medieval Institute Publications for The Consortium for the Teaching of the Middle Ages, 1999), 7–8. Isaiah Tishby and Fischel Lachower also acknowledge that Ezra's Commentary is an important source text for the Zoharic authorship. Tishby and Lachower, *The Wisdom of the Zohar*, 80.

72. This reference is not actually present in *Exodus Rabbah*, and appears to be an incorrect citation (at least according to the *Exodus Rabbah* version available today). A similar passage, however, can be found in *Leviticus Rabbah* 20:10.

73. Chavel, "*Perush le-Shir ha-Shirim*," 486.

74. The concept of deriving spiritual nourishment from *Shekhinah* is also found in early rabbinic writings such as BT *Berakhot* 17a and in the literature of *Merkavah* mysticism. See Ira Chernus, *Mysticism in Rabbinic Judaism: Studies in the History of Midrash*, Studia Judaica, ed. E. L. Ehrlich, no. 11 (New York: Walter de Gruyter, 1982), 75–6.

75. *Zan* is also used to describe spiritual nourishment derived from suckling in the Zohar, as shall be seen in chapter 3.

76. Proverbs 16:15 contrasts a king's favor with a king's wrath. It is unclear whether the verse necessarily implies the divine King, since it may also be understood as referencing a human king. Light imagery is also common in kabbalistic descriptions of the divine overflow. For Zoharic examples, see Hellner-Eshed, *A River Flows from Eden*, 233, 237, 256, 269–71.

77. As noted above, the reference is actually not from *Exodus Rabbah*, but a similar passage can be found in *Leviticus Rabbah* 20:10.

78. For one example of this usage, see the Commentary on Song 6:2, in which Ezra takes care to remind his readers that "to graze" means for *Tif'eret* "to satiate itself (*lehistapeq le-'atzmo*) and to draw the splendor to the gardens, with the *Shekhinah*." See Chavel, "*Perush le-Shir ha-Shirim*," 504.

79. For a discussion of *oneg*, a term related to Ezra's *ta'anug*, and its role in Jewish mysticism, see Hellner-Eshed, *A River Flows from Eden*, 280–82.

80. As shall be seen in chapter 3, the Zohar explicitly links suckling and satiation, drawing its own conclusions from Ezra's writings.

81. Ezra's suckling theology mirrors Isaac's schema of divine overflow, in which the *sefirot* are continuously immersed in the divine substance and lower beings receive divine overflow discontinuously. Sendor, "The Emergence of Provençal Kabbalah," vol. 1, 127–29.

82. As Joel Hecker notes, there is an increased understanding of mystical concepts when their description draws not only on a common text, but on the experience of our own bodies as well. Joel Hecker, "Eating Gestures and the Ritualized Body in Medieval Jewish Mysticism," *History of Religions* 40, no. 2 (2002): 128. Rachel Fulton argues that medieval Christian commentary "demanded of its authors a comprehensive engagement with the Word of God not only as language . . . but also as experience . . . it was only through such experience (both solitary and communal) that the Word of God could be truly understood." Rachel Fulton, *From Judgment to Passion: Devotion to Christ and the Virgin Mary, 800–1200* (New York: Columbia University Press, 2002), 294. Similarly, Lakoff and Johnson write, "symbolic metonymies that are grounded in our physical experience provide an essential means of comprehending religious and cultural concepts." George Lakoff and Mark Johnson, *Metaphors We Live By*, (Chicago: The University of Chicago Press, 1981), 40. Victor Turner points out that because the human body is a complex structure, it easily lends itself to symbolizing other complex structures. He also notes that these sorts of anthropomorphic metaphors can be deeply emotional. Victor Turner, *The Forest of Symbols: Aspects of Ndembu Rituals* (Ithaca, NY: Cornell University Press, 1967), 142, 150. Finally, see David Stern, "*Imitatio Hominis*: Anthropomorphism and the Character(s) of God in Rabbinic Literature," *Prooftexts: A Journal of Jewish Literary History* 12 (1992): 157.

83. Michael Jackson, "Thinking through the Body: An Essay on Understanding Metaphor," *Social Analysis* 14 (1983): 132.

Notes to Chapter 3

1. The edition of *Sefer ha-Zohar* used in this study is Reuven Moshe Margaliot, ed., *Sefer ha-Zohar al Ḥamishah Ḥumshei Torah*, 3 vols. (Jerusalem: Mosad ha-Rav Kook, 1999). All translations are my own, unless otherwise stated.
2. While Gershom Scholem considered the Zohar's distinctive Aramaic a linguistic choice intended to reinforce the work's purportedly ancient character, several modern scholars have shown it to be part of a larger corpus of esoteric literature composed in Aramaic, and thus not necessarily directed at convincing readers of a supposedly ancient provenance. Most of the Zohar seems to have been composed between 1280 and 1286, although some sections may have been written earlier. The Zoharic authors continued writing and revising various textual sections throughout the early 1290s. Dating the Zohar's different parts with precision is a topic of scholarly debate. See Gershom Scholem, *Major Trends in Jewish Mysticism*, with a foreword by Robert Alter (Jerusalem: Schocken Publishing House, Ltd., 1941; reprint, New York: Schocken Books Inc., 1995), 163–8, 188. Also see Isaiah Tishby and Fischel Lachower, ed., *The Wisdom of the Zohar: An Anthology of Texts*, trans. David Goldstein, vol. 1 (Washington DC: The Littman Library of Jewish Civilization, 1989), 91–96; Yehuda Liebes, *Studies in the Zohar*, trans. Arnold Schwartz, Stephanie Nakache, and Penina Peli, (Albany, NY: SUNY Press, 1993), 11–12, 85–86; Yehudah Liebes, "Hebrew and Aramaic as Languages of the Zohar," translated by Daphne Freedman and Ada Rapoport-Albert, *Aramaic Studies* 4, no. 1 (2006): 35–52; Charles Mopsik, "Late Judeo-Aramaic: The Language of Theosophic Kabbalah," translated by Ariel Klein, *Aramaic Studies* 4:1 (2006): 21–33; Ada Rapoport-Albert and Theodore Kwasman, "Late Aramaic: The Literary and Linguistic Context of the Zohar," *Aramaic Studies* 4, no. 1 (2006): 5–19.
3. This form of mysticism is also known as *ma'aseh merkavah*, the work of the divine Chariot.
4. Zohar 1:247b.

5. Scholem, *Major Trends in Jewish Mysticism*, 156.

6. For a description of the Zohar's "canonization" as the central text of Jewish mysticism, see Tishby and Lachower, *The Wisdom of the Zohar*, vol. 1, 25–30.

7. Rapoport-Albert and Kwasman, "Late Aramaic," 7. The two printed editions also exhibit differences, such as sections containing similar content but printed in Hebrew in one edition and Aramaic in the other edition. Yehudah Liebes sees this as further evidence for the diversity of Zoharic authorship. Liebes, "Hebrew and Aramaic as Languages of the Zohar," 42. Also see Elliot Wolfson, "The Anonymous Chapters of the Elderly Master of Secrets: New Evidence for the Early Activity of the Zoharic Circle," *Kabbalah: Journal for the Study of Jewish Mystical Texts* 19 (2009): 173–74; Daniel Abrams, "The Invention of the *Zohar* as a Book: On the Assumptions and Expectations of the Kabbalists and Modern Scholars," *Kabbalah: Journal for the Study of Jewish Mystical Texts* 19 (2009): 8–15, 27–32, 89–90, 105–13; Boaz Huss, "*Sefer ha-Zohar* as Canonical, Sacred and Holy Text: Changing Perspectives of the Book of Splendor between the Thirteenth and the Eighteenth Centuries," *The Journal of Jewish Thought and Philosophy* 7 (1998): 282–83.

8. Scholem, *Major Trends in Jewish Mysticism*, 156–204.

9. For a detailed and compelling presentation of this theory, see Liebes, *Studies in the Zohar*, 85–138. Also see Ronit Meroz, "Zoharic Narratives and Their Adaptations," *Hispania Judaica* 3 (2000): 4; Ronit Meroz, "The Path of Silence: An Unknown Story from a Zohar Manuscript," *European Journal of Jewish Studies* 1, no. 2 (2008): 320; Ronit Meroz, "And I Was Not There?: The Complaints of Rabbi Simeon bar Yohai According to an Unknown Zoharic Story," *Tarbitz* 71 (2002): 163–93 [Hebrew]; Boaz Huss, *Like the Radiance of the Sky: Chapters in the Reception History of the Zohar and the Construction of Its Symbolic Value* (Jerusalem: Mosad Bialik, 2008), 43–44 [Hebrew]. Melila Hellner-Eshed accepts a modified version of Liebes' theory, approving of the possibility of group authorship, while reluctant to deny the possibility of a single author's charismatic and directorial force. She suggests that a single author may be responsible for the Zohar's narrative layers. Melila Hellner-Eshed, *A River Flows from Eden: The Language of Mystical Experience in the Zohar* (Stanford CA: Stanford University Press, 2005), 18–19.

10. See Wolfson, "The Anonymous Chapters of the Elderly Master of Secrets," 144–45, 173–75; Abrams, "The Invention of the *Zohar* as a Book," 89, 111–13, 139; Huss, "*Sefer ha-Zohar* as Canonical, Sacred and Holy Text," 268–71; Huss, *Like the Radiance of the Sky*, 43–44; Meroz, "Zoharic Narratives and Their Adaptations," 4–5, 15–22; Meroz, "The Path of Silence," 320. Daniel Abrams has even suggested that the Zohar, "is best appreciated as a literary and religious process instead of an act of single or multiple authorship in Castile." Abrams, "The Invention of the *Zohar* as a Book," 139.

11. While I have chosen to focus in this chapter specifically on suckling imagery in relation to the *sefirot*, the theme of Torah as a nursing mother also has its place in the Zohar. For a good example, see Zohar 3:166b, in which Rabbi Shimon bar Yoḥai speaks of the Torah as a lover (citing Proverbs 5:19) and as the source of suckling. Eitan Fishbane analyzes this text, using it to illustrate the important role emotion plays in the disclosure of Zoharic secrets. Eitan Fishbane, "Tears of Disclosure: The Role of Weeping in Zoharic Narrative," *The Journal of Jewish Thought and Philosophy* 11, no. 1 (2002): 42–47.

12. "Another place" refers to the *sefirot Netzaḥ* and *Hod*, which are often (though not always) considered the sources of prophecy in Kabbalah.

13. In its Biblical context, Isaiah 22:1 begins a prophetic pronouncement against the people of Jerusalem in which the "Valley of Vision" refers to a location that is also mentioned in Isaiah 22:5 as a battle site.

14. The root *sh.r.y.* is used in both situations.

15. Joel Hecker writes, "Nourishment imagery is used throughout the kabbalah as a metaphor signifying the flow of divine blessings from the upper worlds to the lower." Hecker notes the relationship between nourishment and suckling, but focuses on divine nourishment's sexual connotations rather than its parent-child implications. Joel Hecker, *Mystical Bodies, Mystical Meals: Eating and Embodiment in Medieval Kabbalah*, ed. Dan Ben-Amos (Detroit, MI: Wayne State University Press, 2005), 3–4.

16. Divine overflow's transmission and reception are often associated with light imagery in kabbalistic literature. In this context, the suckling metaphor is enriched with additional light imagery

to express the idealized relationship between humanity and divinity during Temple times. Hellner-Eshed notes that Zoharic divine descriptions, "regularly interchange with images of light and those of water." Hellner-Eshed, *A River Flows from Eden*, 274.

17. See chapter 2 for a discussion of this term in Ezra's Commentary on Song 1:7.

18. "And the Lord spoke to Moses face to face, as a man speaks to his friend. And he returned to the camp. And his servant, Joshua son of Nun, a youth, did not depart from within the Tent." (Exodus 33:11)

19. Moses is understood as married to *Shekhinah*, while Joshua is instead united with the level *youth*, a term with which the Zohar refers to the angel Metatron, who is also considered *Shekhinah's* son. Thus, Joshua is likened to Her son. The "tent that will not wander" from Isaiah 33:20 is interpreted to mean *Shekhinah*. In the Biblical verse, the phrase is used to speak of earthly Jerusalem. The *Shekhinah*, however, is associated with the heavenly Jerusalem, dwelling place of the people Israel.

20. This is the angel Metatron, whom the Zohar often calls a "youth." See below for further discussion of this interesting figure.

21. This passage has been abbreviated for the sake of focus on the suckling mother image, rather than on the context of the passage as a whole.

22. For an informative essay on the Zohar's concept of evil, see Tishby and Lachower, *The Wisdom of the Zohar*, vol. 2, 447–74.

23. For discussions of Metatron's role in early Jewish mysticism, see Scholem, *Major Trends in Jewish Mysticism*, 67–70; Andrei Orlov, "Titles of Enoch-Metatron in *2 Enoch*," *Journal for the Study of the Pseudepigrapha* 18 (1998): 71–86; Andrei Orlov, *The Enoch-Metatron Tradition*, Texts and Studies in Ancient Judaism, ed. Martin Hengel and Peter Schäfer (Tübingen, Germany: Mohr Siebeck, 2005).

24. Moshe Idel, *Absorbing Perfections: Kabbalah and Interpretation*, with a foreword by Harold Bloom (New Haven, CT: Yale University Press, 2002), 141–42; Arthur Green, *Keter: The Crown of God in Early Jewish Mysticism* (Princeton, NJ, Princeton University Press, 1997), 37–38, 91–92. For more extensive writings on Metatron's role in various bodies of Jewish mystical literature, see Daniel Abrams, "The Boundaries of Divine Ontology: The Inclusion

and Exclusion of Metatron in the Godhead," *Harvard Theological Review* 87, no. 3 (1994): 291–321; Moshe Idel, "Enoch is Metatron," *Immanuel* 24/5 (1990): 220–40; Elliot Wolfson, "Metatron and Shi'ur Qomah in the Writings of Haside Ashkenaz," in *Mysticism, Magic, and Kabbalah in Ashkenazic Judaism: International Symposium Held in Frankfurt a.M. 1991*, ed. Karl Erich Grözinger and Joseph Dan, 60–92 (New York: Walter de Gruyter, 1995).

25. In some kabbalistic traditions, Metatron is conflated with the *Shekhinah* and represents the lowest *sefirah*. The Zohar, a text that rarely fails to offer multiple theological perspectives, presents him both as part of the tenth *sefirah* and as a fully separate leader of the angelic host. Abrams, "The Boundaries of Divine Ontology," 307–15.

26. "Youth" is one of Metatron's most important titles in *hekhalot* literature. It is derived from Proverbs 22:6 "*ḥanokh le-na'ar* (train a youth)", read as "Enoch [was made] into the Youth." Orlov, "Titles of Enoch-Metatron in *2 Enoch*," 80. For an extensive discussion of Metatron's role in the Zohar, including the doctrine of his periodic rejuvenation within *Binah* (the idea that Metatron ages and is rejuvenated provides another reason for his title "youth") and speculation on his status as a holy being emanated from *Shekhinah*'s light, see Tishby and Lachower, *The Wisdom of the Zohar*, vol. 2, 626–31. Andrei Orlov also notes the tradition of Metatron's periodic rejuvenation. Orlov, "Titles of Enoch-Metatron in *2 Enoch*," 80.

27. For a close look at another text that deals with *Shekhinah* as the Tent of Meeting (which only Moses enters while the rest of the prophets stand outside) see Daniel Abrams' analysis of Joseph ben Abraham Gikatilla's *Sha'arey Tzedeq* 4b-5a. This text also contains suckling imagery, to which I will return later in this chapter. Daniel Abrams, *The Female Body of God in Kabbalah: Embodied Forms of Love and Sexuality in the Divine Feminine* (Jerusalem: The Hebrew University Magnes Press Ltd., 2004), 132–35.

28. As a human being, Joshua might be thought to suckle discontinuously, as do the lower beings in the teachings of Isaac the Blind and Ezra of Gerona. Instead, Joshua's continuous suckling emphasizes his special spiritual status.

29. *Binah*, the feminine third *sefirah*, is not often associated with Judgment since she is one of the three uppermost *sefirot* that exist closest to the mystery of unknowable God (*Ein Sof*).

30. For a textual example of *Shekhinah* channeling different properties that also employs the suckling metaphor among the *sefirot*, see Zohar 3:184a.

31. In the Zohar, kabbalistic "marriage" to *Shekhinah* can also describe a desirable state accessible to less prestigious figures than Moses. For an example of such a liaison, see Zohar 1:49b-50a, in which a man's ideal state involves his positioning between a human female below and a divine female above. In this particular case, the kabbalist's human wife enables his connection with his divine spouse.

32. "It" refers to the ninth *sefirah*, which is called *Tzaddiq* (Righteous One) in this passage, but is often named *Yesod* (Foundation).

33. A related formulation of this text's theological imagery is found in Ezra of Gerona's *Commentary on the Song of Songs* 1:3, in which Israel is said to suckle from the trunk of the tree that is the *sefirah Tif'eret*, comprised of the *sefirot Yesod* and *Malkhut*. The Zoharic version, however, is far more extensive and contains more interesting imagery.

34. This passage references Genesis 2:10, "A river goes forth from Eden to give drink to the garden," which Melila Hellner-Eshed has identified as an extremely important passage for the Zohar. She connects this passage with the movements of divine reality and divine consciousness, the creation and sustaining of other realities, processes of human consciousness, and sexual symbolism. Hellner-Eshed, *A River Flows from Eden*, 235–37.

35. "Inherit" (*yartin*) also bears connotations of conquering and taking possession. Like inheriting, however, these are cultural actions performed in an anthropomorphic context.

36. This passage also recalls Biblical texts cited in chapter 1 (such as Jeremiah 17:13) that describe God as a fount of living water. The motif of the well or spring as a source of divine wisdom, sustenance, and salvation is ancient. For an analysis of this motif from Biblical literature through early medieval midrash, see Michael Fishbane, "The Well of Living Water: A Biblical Motif and Its Ancient Transformations," in *"Sha'arei Talmon:" Studies in the Bible, Qumran, and the Ancient Near East Presented to Shemaryahu Talmon*, ed. Michael Fishbane and Emanuel Tov with Weston W. Fields, 3–16 (Winona Lake, IN: Eisenbrauns, 1992).

37. These names are citations of Exodus 3:14, "I will be what I will be." (*Ehyeh Asher Ehyeh*.) The Zohar understands each unit as a

divine name representing a stage in concealed divinity's revelation through the *sefirot*. Here, *Ehyeh* seems to refer to *Keter*, the first, highest and most concealed of the *sefirot*.

38. At this point, the explanation of divine names and their relationships with the *sefirot* continues at length.

39. The Nothing (*Ayin*) being hinted at is an allusion to *Ein Sof* (Without End), a kabbalistic way of referring to divinity as infinite, indescribable, and unknowable.

40. *Yotze'* (goes forth) is in the present tense, while *yatza'* (went forth) is in the past tense. The Zohar reads this Biblical phrase and its use of the present tense to imply continuous action. Melila Hellner-Eshed notes that Genesis 2:10 is extremely important in the Zohar, where it is cited numerous times. She considers it a special code phrase that signifies both a change in the Zohar's "hermeneutical registers" and a reminder to the reader of the Zohar's ultimate motivation to seek the divine flow that underlies reality. She understands the verse's use of the present tense as the source of its ongoing fascination for the Zoharic authorship. Hellner-Eshed, *A River Flows from Eden*, 229–31. For a lengthy discussion of this verse's symbolism within the Zohar and its relationship to mystical consciousness, see Ibid., 229–51.

41. *Ra'yati* can also be translated as "my desired one."

42. These "three" are the Tetragrammaton's three other letters. In this passage, the sefirotic structure's unfolding represents the revelation of the four-letter divine name.

43. This discussion's prelude is located in Zohar 3:65a.

44. A parallel teaching found in the kabbalistic text *Sha'arey Orah* (*Gates of Light*) by Joseph ben Abraham Gikatilla helps to clarify the letter *Yud's* ambiguous role in this passage. In his chapter on the sixth *sefirah*, Gikatilla explains that *Yud* alludes to the second *sefirah*, *Hokhmah*, but only the *Yud's* crown (its upstroke) alludes to the first *sefirah*, *Keter*, and beyond to *Ein Sof*. As in Zohar 3:65a-b, the letter *He'* represents *Binah*, the source of divine overflow to the lower *sefirot*. Gikatilla's text, however, lacks the feminine imagery found in the Zoharic text. See Joseph ben Abraham Gikatilla, *Sha'arey Orah*, vol. 1 (Jerusalem: Mosad Bialik, 1980), 188. Gikatilla was a late thirteenth-century kabbalist who may have been part of the group that composed the Zohar. He was almost certainly a member of the group surrounding Moses de León. For

discussions of Gikatilla's relationship to Moses de León, see Liebes, *Studies in the Zohar*, 99–103; Scholem, *Major Trends in Jewish Mysticism*, 194–96.

45. Hellner-Eshed notes that positive emotions play an important role in Zoharic spirituality. These emotions are often connected to contact with the divine river. Hellner-Eshed, *A River Flows from Eden*, 276, 279.

46. *Hokhmah*, the second *sefirah*, is gendered masculine in Kabbalah, despite the word's feminine form and Wisdom's feminine associations in rabbinic and Biblical literature.

47. "Might" (*Gevurah*) corresponds to the fifth *sefirah*, which is also called Judgment (*Din*). In Kabbalah, the color red is often associated with divine Judgment, while white is associated with Mercy.

48. Suckling imagery's presence in a discussion of the divine countenance is interesting, because it implies that the suckling-as-spiritual-transmission metaphor is connected to kabbalistic ideas about divine revelation (a connection also developed in Zohar 1:203a, where the prophets suckle from *Shekhinah*). Milk's peculiar juxtaposition with God's countenance is achieved by interpreting Song 5:13's poetic statement, "his eyes are like doves by streams of water, bathed in milk," which itself combines eye imagery with milk imagery. The Zohar changes the relationships between the two, reading the eyes as either sefirotic or angelic powers. Jewish exegetes generally understand this Biblical verse's male as a divine representation, making the Song text a fitting source for describing the divine countenance. The Song verse also provides a means with which to apply milk imagery to *Binah*.

49. Why does this passage contain explicit milk imagery, while other Zoharic passages and earlier kabbalistic writings seem to avoid it? Aside from the convenient color symbolism that makes milk's inclusion directly relevant to the passage's imagery and recalls *Sefer ha-Bahir*'s association of milk with Mercy, perhaps the uppermost *sefirot* are far enough removed from associations with physical women that such expressions are deemed safe for religious use. The radical anthropomorphic quality of a God who breastfeeds milk throughout the sefirotic system is tempered by the sublimely remote quality of the highest *sefirot*. The Zohar's attitude toward human women is complex; the image of God as a breastfeeding mother is not a glorification of femininity in general. This remote

region of divinity may be safe ground for feminine anthropomorphism precisely because of it supernal distance.

50. For examples of kabbalistic color symbolism, see Zohar 3:248a-b, which describes the redness of *Din*/Judgment (the fifth *sefirah*, also called Might) and the whiteness of *Hesed*/Mercy (the fourth *sefirah*). There, *Shekhinah* takes on both colors under various circumstances. The beautiful passage citing Song 2:2 at the Zohar's beginning (Zohar 1:1a) also uses white and red symbolism in association with *Shekhinah*. For additional examples, see Zohar 1:9a and Zohar 1:221a. Hellner-Eshed has noted that the Zohar's portrayal of the divine countenance is characterized by a continuous transposition between *Hesed*/whiteness and *Din*/redness. Hellner-Eshed, *A River Flows from Eden*, 272. In addition, these color associations were sometimes used in contemplative visualization of the *sefirot*. Moshe Idel, *Kabbalah: New Perspectives* (New Haven, CT: Yale University Press, 1988), 106.

51. The term *sumqa'*, used in this passage to describe the heavenly eyes' color under Judgment's influence, implies an eye-inflammation cured by the divine milk's flow. This representation of breast milk's effectiveness in curing redness is especially interesting because of human milk's proven antibiotic properties. Milk was used in the ancient world as a treatment for illnesses, including eye infections. Drinking human milk for therapeutic purposes was also recommended by Galen, whose medical theories would have been known to the medievals. Julie Laskaris, "Nursing Mothers in Greek and Roman Medicine," *American Journal of Archaeology* 112 (2008): 460, 462.

52. Hellner-Eshed, *A River Flows from Eden*, 271–73. Also, see Hellner-Eshed's analysis of Zohar 3:136b from the *Idra' Rabba'*. This text bears many similarities to Zohar 2:122b, which Hellner-Eshed also briefly discusses. Ibid., 273.

53. Ibid., 350.

54. Ibid., 271–72.

55. Ibid., 271.

56. My perspective on this type of Zoharic imagery differs significantly from Hellner-Eshed's. She understands these mixed images as non-narrative (or even antinarrative) mythic elements that are cast at the reader in the hopes that one or another will resonate, suggesting that the Zohar's mystical author is attempting to convey an

experience beyond language. I would suggest instead that these strange mixtures of images represent a deliberate authorial strategy designed to inspire the reader's own contemplative experience, which may or may not be linguistically based. (Which is not to say that these images cannot have been inspired originally by an authorial mystical experience.) See Ibid., 350.

57. Sarah Kofman has observed that applying multiple metaphors often helps to express concepts whose complexity extends beyond a single metaphoric field of connotations. Victor Turner asserts that dissimilar images, when juxtaposed, provoke contemplation and consideration of the combined elements, highlighting the familiar by linking it with the strange. Sarah Kofman, *Camera Obscura of Ideology*, trans. Will Straw (np: reprint, Ithaca: Cornell University Press, 1999), 29; Victor Turner, *The Forest of Symbols: Aspects of Ndembu Ritual* (Ithaca, NY: Cornell University Press, 1967), 106.

58. The Book of Rav Hamnuna Sava, from which this teaching claims to derive, appears to be a fictional source cited by the Zoharic authorship. No such text is known to modern scholarship. According to the Talmud, Hamnuna Sava was a Babylonian *amora*. In the Zohar, he is a mysterious personality, appearing to the mystical companions at odd times as an old man who gives profound teachings. The Zohar's Rabbi Shimon bar Yoḥai cites authoritative interpretations from his (fictitious) work. Tishby and Lachower, *The Wisdom of the Zohar*, vol. 1, 60, 81; Scholem, *Major Trends in Jewish Mysticism*, 174. The term *be-re'uta'* has connotations of feeding, pasturing, and grazing, as well as taking pleasure. Here, it is probably inspired by the text's exegesis of Song 1:7 "Where do you pasture (*tir'eh*)?"

59. The text expresses discomfort with its suggestion that God could exist in an imperfect state by using the term *kivyakhol* (it is as though). In rabbinic literature, this term is often attached to theological teachings that the rabbis perceive as daring. *Kivyakhol* thus serves as a way for exegetes to tentatively express ideas that may seem potentially blasphemous. For a fuller explanation of *kivyakhol*, see Michael Fishbane, *Biblical Myth and Rabbinic Mythmaking* (Oxford: Oxford University Press, 2003), 325–401.

60. See chapter 2's discussion of Ezra's Commentary on Song 1:7.

61. For further description of positive emotions stressed by the Zohar, see Hellner-Eshed, *A River Flows from Eden*, 279–85.

62. The citation Jeremiah 25:30 is used to make a similar exegetical point in Zohar 3:74b. There, Israel's human sin causes disunity within divinity, interrupting the flow of blessings from *Binah*. In this passage, as in Zohar 3:17a, God's "dwelling" is understood as the tenth *sefirah*. This interpretive shift, which transforms Jeremiah 25:30 from divine anger to divine anguish, is a prevalent theme in aggadic literature as well. For a full discussion of this motif in Jewish literature, see Michael Fishbane, *The Exegetical Imagination: On Jewish Thought and Theology* (Cambridge, MA: Harvard University Press, 1998), 26–29, 35–39. For additional illumination on divine emotion and characterization in rabbinic literature, see David Stern, "*Imitatio Hominis*: Anthropomorphism and the Character(s) of God in Rabbinic Literature," *Prooftexts: A Journal of Jewish Literary History* 12 (1992): 151–74.

63. Both of these texts are presented in chapter 1. The BT text is located in the footnotes.

64. Caroline Walker Bynum, *Fragmentation and Redemption: Essays on Gender and the Human Body in Medieval Religion* (New York: Zone Books, 1992), 108–9, 116–17, 218.

65. *Ahavah* (Love) is taken as a divine name in this text, signifying the *sefirah* Ḥesed. This naming is clear to the reader because the printed text marks divine names in a distinctive way.

66. Margaliot provides this textual alternative in parentheses. I have retained it in my translation because it helps to clarify the rest of the passage.

67. In this passage, the term *palace* represents a *sefirah*.

68. Abraham is linked to divine Mercy and compassion in both rabbinic and kabbalistic literature. For an example, consider *Pesikta de Rav Kahana* 19:3, in which Abraham is described as the most compassionate patriarch and his argument with God regarding mercy for Sodom is discussed. Also recall Bahir 136–37, which connects Abraham with the fourth *sefirah*.

69. This passage describes divine suckling's nourishment and satiation in terms already encountered in this study. Zohar 1:203a uses the root *z.v.n.* to describe nourishment received via suckling (see above), as does Ezra of Gerona in his *Commentary on the Song of Songs* 1:7 (see chapter 2). This same passage in Ezra's Commentary also uses *histapqut* for satiation, a term derived from the same root (*s.p.q.*) as Zohar 2:256b-257a's *istapaq*.

70. For extensive reflections on Biblical use of the divine name *El*

Shaddai and its associations with both fertility and war, see David Biale, "The God with Breasts: El Shaddai in the Bible," *History of Religions* 21, no. 3 (1982): 240–56.

71. For discussions of the relationship between Joseph ben Abraham Gikatilla and Moses de León, see Liebes, *Studies in the Zohar*, 99–103; Scholem, *Major Trends in Jewish Mysticism*, 194–96.

72. Joseph ben Abraham Gikatilla, *Sha'arey Tzedeq*, trans. Raphael ben Avraham (Strasbourg, France: Gilen, 2007), 41–3. [Hebrew and French] For a fuller analysis of this passage and its surrounding context, including a detailed look at its suckling imagery, see Daniel Abrams, *The Female Body of God in Kabbalah*, 132–35.

73. A similar use of *Shaddai* is found in Gikatilla's work *Sha'arey Orah* (*Gates of Light*). In the text's section on *Yesod* (rather than *Ḥesed*, as in the Zoharic text), Gikatilla connects *El Shaddai* and the word *day* to sefirotic processes. In this case, the divine name *Adonay* (Lord) represents *Shekhinah*. However, the passage does not contain suckling imagery. Gikatilla writes, "The attribute *El Shaddai* gives sustenance to each and every creature and sends its blessings to *Adonay* until their lips are weary from saying, 'Enough!'" Gikatilla, *Sha'arey Orah*, vol. 1, 95–96.

74. Judgment and femininity are associated with the sefirotic structure's left side (which includes *Binah*, *Din* and *Hod*), while Mercy and masculinity are associated with the right (which includes *Hokhmah*, *Ḥesed*, and *Netzaḥ*). *Keter*, *Tif'eret*, *Yesod*, and *Shekhinah* are centrally located.

75. Much of the cognitive complexity associated with metaphoric connotations operates by means of metonymy. Alice Kehoe describes metonymy as "the contextual linking of concepts within a hierarchy of units (e.g., the "strong right arm" for "the powerful man")." See Alice B. Kehoe, "The Metonymic Pole and Social Roles," *Journal of Anthropological Research* 29, no. 4 (1973), 266. Metonymy's use of contiguity may be obvious, as in the part-for-whole relationship of Kehoe's example, or it may be more obscure, like the relationship between funerals and the color black (an example borrowed from Roman Jakobson's famous study). See Roman Jakobson, "Two Aspects of Language and Two Types of Aphasic Disturbances," in *Fundamentals of Language*, ed. Roman Jakobson and Morris Halle, 2d rev. ed., 67–96 (The Hague, The Netherlands: Mouton, 1971), 83–4.

76. Both texts rely on the root *g.l.y.* to discuss revelation.

77. Although this affective language is used mainly in descriptions of the *sefirot*, such passages often describe divine energy flowing into the world. This divine flow's positive emotional connotations help to demonstrate the world's ideal relationship with God.

Notes to Chapter 4

1. Mortimer Ostow has suggested that the very essence of mystical endeavor is the attempt to retrieve the mystic's "earliest feelings of being united with his mother or of being physically close to and intimate with either parent," effectively reversing the psychological process of "separation-individuation." While I'm not sure that I agree, this is certainly an interesting way to think about Kabbalah's nursing divine. Mortimer Ostow, "Introduction" in *Jewish Mystical Leaders and Leadership in the 13th Century*, ed. Moshe Idel and Mortimer Ostow (New York: Rowman and Littlefield Publishers, Inc., 2005), 4. For a more extensive presentation of Ostow's (and others') views on Kabbalah's psychological dimensions, see Mortimer Ostow, ed., *Ultimate Intimacy: The Psychodynamics of Jewish Mysticism* (London: Karnac Books, 1995).
2. For an example of *Shekhinah* channeling both Mercy and Judgment into the world, see Zohar 1:221a.
3. Of course, guilt, anxiety, and fear are also useful emotions, and have their own roles in kabbalistic tradition.
4. While these studies often focus on Ashkenazic Jewish culture, rather than on Spain's Sefardic communities, it is still possible to draw connections between the two groups since they communicated with each other extensively. The Spanish kabbalists shared a common body of halakhic literature related to women's issues with their northerly Jewish brethren, and they also shared a Christian cultural context with Ashkenazic Jews. However, it is difficult to know how closely related the two communities' cultural practices regarding women were, since we have almost no sources from late thirteenth-century Spain that describe the lives of Jewish women. As Avraham Grossman writes, "Not only is there no extant work created by a Jewish woman during the medieval period . . . but not so much as a single book from that period deals with her status in the family and society." Avraham Grossman, *Pious and Rebellious:*

Jewish Women in Medieval Europe, trans. Jonathan Chipman (Waltham, MA: Brandeis University Press, 2004), xiii.

5. See Ibid., xiii-xiv; Tova Rosen, *Unveiling Eve: Reading Gender in Medieval Hebrew Literature* (Philadelphia, PA: University of Pennsylvania Press, 2003), 3.

6. Elisheva Baumgarten, *Mothers and Children: Jewish Family Life in Medieval Europe* (Princeton, NJ: Princeton University Press, 2004), 22–4. Baumgarten's sources include the Babylonian Talmud, the Mishna, the Tosefta, a thirteenth-century commentary on the *piyyut Ta'alat zu kehafetz* for Rosh Hashanah, Rabbi Judah the Pious' commentary on Genesis, Rabbi Judah ben Samuel Hasid's *Sefer Hasidim,* and Rabbi Moses ben Jacob of Couçy's *Sefer Mitzvot ha-Gadol.* For specific citations, examples, and discussions, see her excellent book.

7. Much of the Genesis narrative's drama is rooted in tension over the next Israelite generation's birth and emphasis on divine reproductive control.

8. Ibid,, 158–59. For an example, see *Sefer Hasidim,* no. 589.

9. Ibid., 156–57.

10. Since pasteurization had not yet been discovered, human breast milk was critical to infants' survival. Ibid., 119–20, 164.

11. Although in this classical example breastfeeding is a metaphor for teaching Torah, medieval Jews studied Talmud extensively, and the idea that a female desired to give milk existed in the their cultural consciousness. For further reflections on this Talmudic citation and its association with Jewish mystical teachings, see Daniel Abrams, *The Female Body of God in Kabbalah: Embodied Forms of Love and Sexuality in the Divine Feminine* (Jerusalem: The Hebrew University Magnes Press Ltd., 2004), 125–26, 135–36. [Hebrew]

12. Baumgarten, *Mothers and Children,* 122–24. Christian literature of this period also presented breastfeeding as a motherly duty and obligation. Caroline Walker Bynum, *Jesus as Mother: Studies in the Spirituality of the High Middle Ages,* (Berkeley, CA: University of California Press, 1982), 117–18; Bernard of Clairvaux, *On the Song of Songs,* trans. Kilian Walsh, with an introduction by Jean Leclerq (Kalamazoo, MI.: Cistercian Publications Inc., 1983), 208.

13. Baumgarten, *Mothers and Children,* 133. Baumgarten notes that although we have documentation for this preference only from

Spain and Italy, this does not mean the belief was absent in other locations where such literature was less common.

14. Ibid., 126–27; Ivan Marcus, *Rituals of Childhood: Jewish Accultura-tion in Medieval Europe* (New Haven, CT: Yale University Press, 1996), 43.

15. Ibid., 13–14.

16. Marcus explains that both texts and teachers were regarded as met-aphorical nursing mothers. Ibid., 90–91.

17. See my analysis of BT *Eruvin* 54b, *Numbers Rabbah* 4:20, and *Exo-dus Rabbah* 30:9 in chapter 1, and Ezra's Commentary on Song 8:8 and Song 8:10 in chapter 2. Elliot Wolfson has written a helpful study of feminine Torah imagery in classical rabbinic texts through the Zohar, although his study focuses on erotic representations rather than on nurturing imagery. See Elliot Wolfson, "Female Imaging of the Torah: From Literary Metaphor to Religious Sym-bol," in *Circle in the Square: Studies of the Use of Gender in Kabbal-istic Symbolism* (Albany, NY: SUNY Press, 1995), 3–18.

18. The medievals' cultural assumptions about breastfeeding mothers and their children structure their ideas about God and themselves, "uniting them metonymically in their parallel structures" to create "a more concordant model of the world, a single, more encom-passing organization." See Deborah Durham and James Fernan-dez, "Tropical Dominions: The Figurative Struggle over Domains of Belonging and Apartness in Africa," in *Beyond Metaphor: The Play of Tropes in Culture*, ed. James Fernandez, 197–98 (Stanford, CA: Stanford University Press, 1991). Alice Kehoe has pointed out that metonymic alignments are critical to people's perception of their social roles—the specific qualities of themselves as human beings that they choose to foreground and enact in their daily lives. Alice B. Kehoe, "The Metonymic Pole and Social Roles," *Journal of Anthropological Research* 29, no. 4 (1973): 266.

19. Roy Rappaport. *Ecology, Meaning and Religion* (Berkeley, CA: North Atlantic Books, 1979), 127.

20. For "return to the whole," see James Fernandez, *Persuasions and Performances: The Play of Tropes in Culture* (Bloomington, IN: Indiana University Press, 1986), 191, 208. In terms of metaphor theory, the kabbalists' nursing divine is of interest because it can be understood as a "meta-metaphor." Metaphor is defined as a trope of "carrying over" meaning between seemingly unrelated

subjects, developing identity relationships between categories not recognized in other contexts as belonging to the same domain. This identification constitutes a new whole, in which entities that would otherwise remain conceptually separate become part of the same thing. When these domains are juxtaposed, meaning is transferred between the two categories, with each conditioning an understanding of the other. Anthropomorphic metaphors like the breastfeeding divine help to integrate human experience with the sociocultural environment, since physical experience of the body and the social categories through which the body is known cooperate in a continuous exchange of meaning. As a metaphor most specifically concerned with carrying over substance between beings, the nursing divine is a trope of carrying over *about* carrying over— in other words, a meta-metaphor. When the suckling mother image is applied to God, divinity and humanity are mutually relativized, becoming parts of the same organization. God is humanized to a point at which It can relate to humanity, while humanity is divinized to the extent that it can participate in an interactive relationship with God. Durham and Fernandez, "Tropical Dominions," 191–92; Terence Turner, ""We Are Parrots," "Twins Are Birds": Play of Tropes as Operational Structure," in *Beyond Metaphor: The Theory of Tropes in Anthropology*, ed. James W. Fernandez, 128 (Stanford, CA: Stanford University Press, 1991); Michael Jackson, "Thinking through the Body: An Essay on Understanding Metaphor." *Social Analysis* 14 (1983): 137; Mary Douglas, *Natural Symbols: Explorations in Cosmology*, with a new introduction (np: Barrie & Rockliff, 1970; reprint, New York: Routledge, 1996), 67.

21. Intellect also forms an important link between God and humanity in Kabbalah, which is heavily influenced by medieval Jewish philosophy despite the fact that it can be read as a reaction against philosophical spirituality. While attitudes toward philosophy among the thirteenth century Spanish kabbalists vary, they tend to be generally negative, viewing philosophy either as an inferior form of knowledge or as a dangerous lure away from religious observance and prayer. See Moshe Idel, *Kabbalah: New Perspectives* (New Haven, CT: Yale University Press, 1988), 46–49; Boaz Huss, "Mysticism versus Philosophy in Kabbalistic Literature," *Micrologus* 9 (2001): 125, 130–33; Mark Sendor, "The Emergence of Provençal Kabbalah: Rabbi Isaac the Blind's "Commentary on *Sefer*

Yetzirah," vol. 1 (PhD. diss., Harvard University, 1994), 28–35.

22. Moshe Idel, "Maimonides and Kabbalah," in *Studies in Maimonides*, ed. Isadore Twersky, 34–35, 50 (Cambridge, MA: Harvard University Press, 1990).

23. Moshe Idel (and to a certain extent Menachem Kellner) understand Maimonides as responding negatively to "proto-kabbalistic" elements in Jewish thought, which led him to reform Judaism from an intellectualist perspective, effectively defining Jewish esotericism as rationalism. In this view, Jewish thinkers who came after Maimonides then responded with their own kabbalistic efforts to defend Jewish esotericism from rationalizing tendencies. Still, philosophical language and thought played an important role in much of Kabbalah's development, as in the Gerona school's use of Neoplatonic ideas and terminology. Ibid., 34–7, 50; Menachem Kellner, *Maimonides' Confrontation with Mysticism*, with a Foreword by Moshe Idel (Portland, OR: The Littman Library of Jewish Civilization, 2006), 26; Moshe Idel, "Foreword," in *Maimonides' Confrontation with Mysticism*, Mehachem Kellner, viii (Portland, OR: The Littman Library of Jewish Civilization, 2006); Moshe Idel, "Naḥmanides: Kabbalah, Halakhah, and Spiritual Leadership," in *Jewish Mystical Leaders and Leadership in the Thirteenth Century*, ed. Moshe Idel and Mortimer Ostow (Lanham, Md.: Rowman & Littlefield Publishers, Inc., 2005), 59, 63, 84–85.

24. Charles Mopsik, "Late Judeo-Aramaic: The Language of Theosophic Kabbalah," translated by Ariel Klein, *Aramaic Studies* 4:1 (2006): 26–27; Daniel Abrams, "The Invention of the *Zohar* as a Book: On the Assumptions and Expectations of the Kabbalists and Modern Scholars," *Kabbalah: Journal for the Study of Jewish Mystical Texts* 19 (2009): 109–110.

25. See Maimonides' *Guide of the Perplexed* 1:35, in which the great philosopher expresses grave misgivings that anthropomorphic representations of God will lead to simplistic and misguided beliefs in divine corporeality or in divine likeness to created things. *Guide* 3:51 is also instructive. Moses Maimonides, *The Guide of the Perplexed*, trans. and with an introduction and notes by Shlomo Pines and with an introductory essay by Leo Strauss, 2 vols. (Chicago: The University of Chicago Press, 1963), vol 1, 79–81, vol. 2, 618–28. For kabbalistic involvement in the Maimonidean controversy, see Gershom Scholem, *Origins of the Kabbalah*, ed. R. J. Zwi

Werblowsky, trans. Allan Arkush, 1st English translation (np: The Jewish Publication Society, 1987; reprint, Princeton, NJ: Princeton University Press, 1990), 376–79; Idel, "Nahmanides: Kabbalah, Halakhah, and Spiritual Leadership," 63–64. For additional thoughts on medieval Kabbalah's engagement with philosophical ideas, see Elliot Wolfson, "Eunuchs Who Keep the Sabbath: Becoming Male and the Ascetic Ideal in Thirteenth-Century Jewish Mysticism," in *Becoming Male in the Middle Ages*, ed. Jeffrey Jerome Cohen and Bonnie Wheeler, 157 (New York: Garland Publishing, Inc., 2000); Elliot Wolfson, "By Way of Truth: Aspects of Nahmanides' Kabbalistic Hermeneutic," *AJS Review* 14:2 (1989): 156.

26. Maimonides, *Guide of the Perplexed*, vol. 2, 620.
27. Maimonides, *Guide of the Perplexed*, vol. 2, 621, 638.
28. Haviva Pedaya, "Aḥuzim ba-Dibbur: Li-Vruro shel ha-Defus ha-Mitpa'el etzel Rishonei ha-Mekubbalim," *Tarbitz* 65 (1996): 567, 580–81, 588. [Hebrew]
29. For an interesting example of Neoplatonism's influence on Ezra, see Moshe Idel, *Kabbalah and Eros* (New Haven, CT: Yale University Press, 2005), 183.
30. Melila Hellner-Eshed, *A River Flows from Eden: The Language of Mystical Experience in the Zohar* (Stanford,CA: Stanford University Press, 2005), 68–69, 189; Eitan Fishbane, "Tears of Disclosure: The Role of Weeping in Zoharic Narrative," *The Journal of Jewish Thought and Philosophy* 11:1 (2002): 25–47; Joel Hecker, *Mystical Bodies, Mystical Meals: Eating and Embodiment in Medieval Kabbalah* (Detroit, MI: Wayne State University Press, 2005), 130–39.
31. David Stern notes that such models weren't considered problematic until philosophy's growth in the Middle Ages. David Stern, "*Imitatio Hominis*: Anthropomorphism and the Character(s) of God in Rabbinic Literature," *Prooftexts: A Journal of Jewish Literary History* 12 (1992): 153–54.
32. Jeremy Cohen. *The Friars and the Jews: The Evolution of Medieval Anti-Judaism.* (Ithaca, NY: Cornell University Press, 1982), 63, 82–3, 109–110, 244–45, 249; Jeremy Cohen, "The Christian Adversary of Solomon ibn Adret," *The Jewish Quarterly Review* 71, no. 1 (1980): 52–53.
33. J. Cohen, *The Friars and the Jews*, 82, 109–110; J. Cohen, "The Christian Adversary of Solomon ibn Adret," 52.

34. This strategic appropriation of Jewish texts can be traced to Alan of Lille in the twelfth century. It was elaborated throughout the thirteenth century in Spain by Raymond de Peñafort (ca 1175–1275), Rodrigo Jiménez de Rada (archbishop of Toledo from 1209–1247), Paulus Christiani (active mid-thirteenth century), and Raymond Martini (ca.1215–1285), author of *Pugio fidei*. Although this strategy was developed in Aragon, rather than in Castile where the Zohar was composed, Lucy Pick identifies King Alfonso X of Castile (1221–1284) as carrying on many of Archbishop Rodrigo Jiménez de Rada's activities—including polemicizing against Judaism, while maintaining largely positive relationships with the Jewish community under his jurisdiction. Lucy Pick, *Conflict and Coexistence: Archbishop Rodrigo and the Muslims and Jews of Medieval Spain* (Ann Arbor, MI: The University of Michigan Press, 2004), vii, x, 5, 11–12, 172–73, 177–78, 206; J. Cohen, "The Christian Adversary of Solomon ibn Adret," 107; Robert Burns, "Jews and Moors in the *Siete Partidas* of Alfonso X the Learned: a Background Perspective," in *Medieval Spain: Culture, Conflict, and Coexistence: Studies in Honour of Angus MacKay*, ed., Roger Collins and Anthony Goodman, 48, 54 (Hampshire, UK: Palgrave Macmillan, 2002).

35. Yitzhak Baer, *From the Age of Reconquest to the Fourteenth Century*, trans. Louis Schoffman, with an introduction by Benjamin R Gampel, vol. 1 of *A History of the Jews in Christian Spain* (Philadelphia, PA: The Jewish Publication Society of America, 1961), 152, 155, 167–8; Robert Chazan, *Barcelona and Beyond: The Disputation of 1263 and Its Aftermath* (Berkeley, CA: University of California Press, 1992), 45; Robert Chazan, *Daggers of Faith: Thirteenth Century Christian Missionizing and Jewish Response* (Berkeley, CA: University of California Press, 1984), 14; David Berger, "The Attitude of St. Bernard of Clairvaux Toward the Jews," *Proceedings of the American Academy for Jewish Research* 40 (1972): 102; Pick, *Conflict and Coexistence*, 140; J. Cohen, *The Friars and the Jews*, 111.

36. Yehuda Liebes, *Studies in the Zohar*, trans. Arnold Schwartz, Stephanie Nakache, and Penina Peli (Albany, NY: SUNY Press, 1993), 139, 150, 160–61; Elliot Wolfson, *Language, Eros, Being: Kabbalistic Hermeneutics and Poetic Imagination* (New York: Fordham University Press, 2005), 259; Daniel Abrams, "The Virgin Mary as

the Moon That Lacks the Sun: A Zoharic Polemic Against the Veneration of Mary," *Kabbalah: Journal for the Study of Jewish Mystical Texts* 21 (2010): 16–17, 20–24.

37. Liebes, *Studies in the Zohar*, 141, 150, 160–61.
38. Mack notes that similar Jewish polemic traditions are preserved in Raymond Martini's *Pugio fidei*, providing an excellent example of how deeply entangled Jewish and Christian polemic literature were during this period. Ḥananel Mack, "Drashot Anti Notzri'ut Bamidrash Bamidbar Rabbah," *Proceedings of the Tenth World Congress of Jewish Studies* 3, no. 1 (1989): 134–37. [Hebrew]
39. For a text that provides examples of divine overflow sustaining the world *and* of this overflow being contingent on performing the commandments, see my analysis of Zohar 1:203a in chapter 3. The passage continues past the translated portion to describe the difficulties of inhabiting a world in which the Temple-related commandments can no longer be performed.
40. As Peter Schäfer notes, "'Proof' is not so much, or not only, the tangible physical evidence, materialized in this and that quotation adduced from this and that manuscript . . . but the realization of a close relationship between intertwined components in constantly changing configurations." Peter Schäfer, *Mirror of His Beauty: Feminine Images of God from the Bible to the Early Kabbalah* (Princeton, NJ: Princeton University Press, 2002), 232.
41. Arthur Green, "Shekhinah, the Virgin Mary, and the Song of Songs: Reflections on a Kabbalistic Symbol in Its Historical Context," *AJS Review* 26, no. 1 (2002): 21; Schäfer, *Mirror of His Beauty*, 12–13. It should be noted that Moshe Idel and Daniel Abrams are skeptical of this hypothesis, which relies on Gershom Scholem's understanding that the term *Shekhinah*, used in rabbinic literature for the divine presence, has no feminine connotations until the late twelfth century's early kabbalistic literature. Idel, *Kabbalah and Eros*, 46–49, 267–68; Abrams, "The Virgin Mary as the Moon That Lacks the Sun," 11–16, 21–24; Gershom Scholem, "Shekhinah: The Feminine Element in Divinity," in *On the Mystical Shape of the Godhead: Basic Concepts in the Kabbalah*, with a foreword by Joseph Dan, trans. Joachim Neugroschel and ed. Jonathan Chipman (New York: Schocken Books, 1991), 140–96.
42. Bynum, *Jesus as Mother*, 17, 138.
43. Caroline Walker Bynum, *Fragmentation and Redemption: Essays on*

Gender and the Human Body in Medieval Religion (New York: Zone Books, 1992), 58, 93; Bynum, *Jesus as Mother*, 112–13.

44. Bynum, *Jesus as Mother*, 115; Bynum, *Fragmentation and Redemption*, 93.

45. Bynum, *Jesus as Mother*, 115.

46. Bynum, *Fragmentation and Redemption*, 93, 115.

47. Bynum, *Jesus as Mother*, 124.

48. Rachel Fulton, *From Judgment to Passion: Devotion to Christ and the Virgin Mary, 800–1200* (New York: Columbia University Press, 2002), 348.

49. Ibid., 195, 292; Bynum, *Fragmentation and Redemption*, 58–59. Of course, Judaism has no equivalent of these officially recognized religious women. Nonetheless, it is interesting that in a religion where women did have the potential for a degree of religious authority and innovation, the suckling image remained the province of male clergy members.

50. See Arthur Green, "Editor's Note" in Seth Brody, ed. and trans., *Rabbi Ezra ben Solomon of Gerona: "Commentary on the Song of Songs" and Other Kabbalistic Commentaries*, with an introduction by Arthur Green (Kalamazoo, MI: Medieval Institute Publications for The Consortium for the Teaching of the Middle Ages, 1999), 7.

51. Fulton, *From Judgment to Passion*, 249.

52. Ibid., 289.

53. Bynum, *Jesus as Mother*, 117–119.

54. Christian theology at this time was concerned with interiority and personal experience, as well as with exteriority and performance. Fulton, *From Judgment to Passion*, 197.

55. Ibid., 197. Fulton sees this move as an "empathization:" a contemplative identification of the self with the Other. Ibid., 197, 397, 462.

56. Ibid., 4, 197.

57. Bynum, *Fragmentation and Redemption*, 158; Bynum, *Jesus as Mother*, 115, 160.

58. Bynum, *Jesus as Mother*, 129.

59. Rubin sees a link between this affective spirituality and increasing thirteenth-century anti-Judaism, since Christian empathetic literature often focused on Mary's distress and Jews were perceived as the cause of it. Miri Rubin, *Mother of God: A History of the Virgin*

Mary (New Haven, CT: Yale University Press, 2009), 249, 252.

60. E. Fishbane, "Tears of Disclosure," 30–34, 38–9; Hecker, *Mystical Bodies, Mystical Meals*, 130–31.

61. Hellner-Eshed, *A River Flows from Eden*, 189.

62. Bernard of Clairvaux, *On the Song of Songs*, vol. 1, 63. The selection is taken from Sermon 10, paragraph 3.

63. See Bynum, *Jesus as Mother*, 167–68. Also see the latter part of note 4 and note 5, above, for references on the scarcity of sources describing medieval Jewish women's lives.

64. Peter Schäfer has justifiably identified such influence as a topic for serious consideration. Schäfer, *Mirror of His Beauty*, 231–32.

65. Schäfer, *Mirror of His Beauty*, 239–40; Green, "Shekhinah, the Virgin Mary and the Song of Songs," 27.

66. Schäfer, *Mirror of His Beauty*, 215; Green, "Shekhinah, the Virgin Mary and the Song of Songs," 28; Wolfson, *Language, Eros, Being*, 258–60. Moshe Idel writes that one common medieval Jewish response to external challenges was arcanization. Moshe Idel, *Absorbing Perfections: Kabbalah and Interpretation*, with a foreword by Harold Bloom (New Haven, CT: Yale University Press, 2002), 253.

67. These ideas about observation and response correspond to Ivan Marcus' model of "inward acculturation," which explains that premodern Jews internalized aspects of surrounding culture "in a polemical, parodic or neutralized manner." Marcus, *Rituals of Childhood*, 12.

68. Bynum, *Jesus as Mother*, 12–14; Schäfer, *Mirror of His Beauty*, 147–8.

69. Schäfer, *Mirror of His Beauty*, 239–40.

70. Baer, *From the Age of Reconquest to the Fourteenth Century*, 150.

71. Ibid., 152, 155, 167–68; Chazan, *Barcelona and Beyond*, 45; Chazan, *Daggers of Faith*, 14.

72. Honorius was probably writing his Marian Song commentary around the year 1100, very shortly after the horrific episodes surrounding the First Crusade transpired. Fulton, *From Judgment to Passion*, 282.

73. Ibid., 281–84; Rubin, *Mother of God*, 162.

74. Ibid, 161–63, Pick, 140; Norman Roth, "Forgery and Abrogation of the Torah: A Theme in Muslim and Christian Polemic in Spain," *Proceedings of the American Academy for Jewish Research* 54

(1987): 227–8; Anna Sapir Abulafia, *Christians and Jews in the Twelfth-Century Renaissance* (New York: Routledge, 1995), 77.

75. Fulton, *From Judgment to Passion*, 281–4; Rubin, *Mother of God*, 164.

76. Rubin, *Mother of God*, 161–3.

77. Ibid., 161–68, 227–28.

78. Ibid., 168.

79. Schäfer, *Mirror of His Beauty*, 173–216.

80. Fulton, *From Judgment to Passion*, 284.

81. Bynum, *Jesus as Mother*, 244; Fulton, *From Judgment to Passion*, 384.

82. See my analysis of Zohar 3:65a-b, Zohar 2:122b and Zohar 3:17a in chapter 3 for examples.

83. Moshe Idel sees the Virgin's celibacy and the *Shekhinah*'s sexualization as a prime reason to question whether Marian theology influenced the *Shekhinah*'s development. Idel, *Kabbalah and Eros*, 48.

84. Bynum notes that by the thirteenth and fourteenth centuries, suckling imagery was associated with the blood of the Eucharist rather than with milk. Bynum, *Jesus as Mother*, 133, 151.

85. Daniel Abrams, "The Virgin Mary as the Moon That Lacks the Sun," 24.

86. See, for example, Wolfson, *Language, Eros, Being*, 81–83. Also see Elliot Wolfson, "Occultation of the Feminine and the Body of Secrecy in Medieval Kabbalah" in *Luminal Darkness: Imaginal Gleanings from Zoharic Literature* (Oxford: Oneworld Publications, 2007), 276. Similarly, Tova Rosen sees medieval Jews as participating in "the vast Western misogyny," in which, "Woman is identified with matter, body, and defiled sexuality." Rosen, *Unveiling Eve*, 23, 103–104.

87. Wolfson, *Language, Eros, Being*, 58, 265.

88. Ibid., 82.

89. Wolfson, *Circle in the Square*, 109. This statement is part of an extensive argument that the *Shekhinah* is in fact equated with the divine phallus' corona and that much of kabbalistic sexual symbolism is concerned with reconstituting an ideal divine androgyne. Moshe Idel disagrees with this view, while Arthur Green has also questioned Wolfson's phallic readings of kabbalistic texts. See Wolfson, *Circle in the Square*, 79–121; Idel, *Kabbalah and Eros*, 74, 121–25, 130, 143–44; Arthur Green, *Keter: The Crown of God*

in Early Jewish Mysticism (Princeton, NJ: Princeton University Press, 1997), 143.

90. Wolfson, "Eunuchs Who Keep the Sabbath," 157–58, 160–61; Wolfson, *Language, Eros, Being*, 45.

91. Wolfson, "Eunuchs Who Keep the Sabbath," 165, 173–74; Wolfson, *Language, Eros, Being*, 324–25, 331, 366–67. For Wolfson's most elaborate discussion of divine androgyny and the phallicized feminine, see his classic study: Elliot Wolfson, "Crossing Gender Boundaries in Kabbalistic Ritual and Myth," in *Circle in the Square: Studies in the Use of Gender in Kabbalistic Symbolism*, 79–121 (Albany, NY: SUNY Press, 1995).

92. See Wolfson, *Language, Eros, Being*, 81–82.

93. Daniel Abrams, "The Virgin Mary as the Moon That Lacks the Sun," 13, 18; Daniel Abrams, "The Condensation of the Symbol 'Shekhinah' in the Manuscripts of the *Book Bahir*," *Kabbalah: Journal for the Study of Jewish Mystical Texts* 16 (2007): 10, 36–7, 40–41.

94. Abrams, "The Condensation of the Symbol 'Shekhinah' in the Manuscripts of the *Book Bahir*," 10, 13–14, 40–41.

95. For Abrams' study of divine breastfeeding, see Abrams, *The Female Body of God in Kabbalah*, 123–39. (See 124–25 especially.)

96. Ibid,, 124, 128.

97. For example, Abrams reads a text by the kabbalist Isaac of Akko as a psychoanalytic fantasy of eradicating an intolerable distance between the self and the mother by containing the mother within the self. Abrams, *The Female Body of God in Kabbalah*, 126. Abrams' use of Freudian and Lacanian psychoanalysis is interesting. While the important psychoanalytic role Freud assigns to sexuality is well known, for Lacan the phallus represents the ultimate signifier. Their combined perspective seems to carry through much of Abrams' work. See especially Jacques Lacan, "The Meaning of the Phallus," in *Feminine Sexuality: Jacques Lacan and the École Freudienne*, trans. Jacqueline Rose, eds. Juliet Mitchell and Jacqueline Rose, 74–85 (np: 1982. Reprint, New York: W. W. Norton & Company and Pantheon Books, 1985).

98. Moshe Idel explains, "Kabbalistic manuscripts constitute a vast domain of eclectic compilation of diverse sources, which have been studied as if part of the same literary corpus." He calls for more attention devoted to individual strains of kabbalistic thought, a

position with which I agree. The Zohar has many sections, strata, and authors; it does not present a unified or systematic theology. The implication of Idel's assertion for this book is that while Wolfson's and Abrams' conclusions may be correct in the contexts they have explored, their correctness does not invalidate the conclusions I have drawn from the contexts that I have explored (and vice versa). See Idel, *Kabbalah and Eros*, 100.

99. For example, Moshe Idel has characterized Kabbalah as expressing a "sexually polarized ditheism," although he maintains that kabbalistic eroticism is part of a broader attempt to invest religious acts with increased ontological significance. Idel, *Kabbalah and Eros*, 49–50, 203, 234.

100. Hellner-Eshed, *A River Flows from Eden*, 74, 169.

101. Ibid, 170. Although I do not find Lacan in Hellner-Eshed's bibliography, it is interesting that her description of the Zohar's mystical experience as an "experiential wave" seems surprisingly similar to Lacan's discussion of mysticism and feminine *jouissance*. See Ibid., 309; Lacan, "God and the *Jouissance* of The Woman. A Love Letter," in *Feminine Sexuality*, 145–48.

102. Hellner-Eshed, *A River Flows from Eden*, 139–40, 219.

103. For example, see Hellner-Eshed's analysis of Zohar 3:136b from the *Idra' Rabba'*, in which she correlates abundance associated with expressing milk and abundance associated with discharging semen. The motherly and the erotic converge in her analysis, with eroticism eclipsing nurture. Ibid,, 273–4.

104. The Zohar often expresses divine unity through images of marriage and sexual relations between masculine and feminine *sefirot*. The kabbalists also write about how to conduct their own sex lives in religiously appropriate ways. For a few examples, see Zohar 1:49b-50a, Zohar 1:85b, Zohar 1:221a, Zohar 2:89a-89b, and Zohar 3:42a-b.

105. Wolfson, "Eunuchs Who Keep the Sabbath," 167–9, 171–73; Hellner-Eshed, *A River Flows from Eden*, 64–73; E. Fishbane, "*Tears of Disclosure*," 36.

106. For additional sources on kabbalistic erotics, see Moshe Idel, *Kabbalah and Eros*; Yehuda Liebes, "Zohar ve-Eros," *Alpayim* 9 (1994): 67–119; Elliot Wolfson, *Through a Speculum that Shines: Vision and Imagination in Medieval Jewish Mysticism* (Princeton,

     NJ: Princeton University Press, 1994); Wolfson, *Circle in the Square.*

107. Green, "Shekhinah, the Virgin Mary and the Song of Songs," 25–26; Wolfson, "Eunuchs Who Keep the Sabbath," 173.

108. Abrams, *The Female Body of God in Kabbalah*, 124.

109. Hellner-Eshed, *A River Flows from Eden*, 360.

110. George Lakoff and Mark Johnson, *Metaphors We Live By* (Chicago: The University of Chicago Press, 1981) 40; Victor Turner, *The Forest of Symbols: Aspects of Ndembu Ritual* (Ithaca NY: Cornell University Press, 1967), 142, 150; Fernandez, *Persuasions and Performances*, 92; Douglas, *Natural Symbols*, 67. Also see Jackson, Thinking through the Body," 137. As the reader has undoubtedly noticed, I rely mainly on anthropological literature for my understanding of religious symbol and imagery. I believe this may be one reason why my opinions diverge from scholars who ground their understanding in psychoanalytic thought, which tends to place greater emphasis on sexual symbolism. In my opinion, anthropological literature is an important but underappreciated resource in this field of study.

111. Rachel Fulton also believes it is prudent to look beyond overtly sexual explanations for the feminine religious images of the Middle Ages. She writes, "It has been fashionable for some time now . . . to see almost every expression of love for Christ's Mother Mary (or Christ, for that matter) as in some way a manifestation of repressed sexual desire. . . . Nevertheless, this vision is, I would insist, much too monolithic, not to say reductive, to take account of the medieval devotion to Mary as a whole and should be resisted." Fulton, *From Judgment to Passion* 242.

112. "There is reason to think that medieval viewers saw bared breasts . . . not primarily as sexual but as the food with which they were iconographically associated." Bynum, *Fragmentation and Redemption*, 86.

113. Bernard of Clairvaux, *On the Song of Songs* vol. 2, 208. The citation is from Sermon 41, paragraph 6. It reflects on the task of preaching, which may seem a burdensome activity to the soul that prefers to bask in divine intimacy. The sixteenth-century kabbalist Isaac Luria also compared his teaching to the act of breastfeeding. See Abrams, *The Female Body of God in Kabbalah*, 138.

114. Abrams has also suggested this, but has not fully explored the ramifications of such an alternative to sexual imagery. Abrams, *The Female Body of God in Kabbalah*, 125.

115. Of course, if you are a Freudian, you may well believe that very young children do experience sexual desires directed toward their parents of the opposite sex. See, for example, Sigmund Freud, *The Interpretation of Dreams*, trans. Joyce Crick, with an introduction and notes by Ritchie Robertson (Oxford: Oxford University Press, 1999), 198. I am not a Freudian, and I believe that Freud's findings are constrained by his cultural context, like the work of all great thinkers. I see no reason why a psychoanalytic sexual formula developed by a man living in the nineteenth and twentieth centuries should hold true for medievals, whose lives and culture were very different from those of the people Freud examined in his case studies. While Freud's other theories may provide fruitful lenses for understanding kabbalistic symbolism, I find the application of his perspectives on sexuality to the kabbalists unconvincing. However, for an interesting and helpful use of less sexualized Freudian theory, see Abrams, The Condensation of the Symbol "Shekhinah" in the Manuscripts of the Book Bahir," 14–15.

116. Moshe Idel also finds it likely that the kabbalists would valorize female breastfeeding. He writes, "Mothers give birth to male babies and remain females. Surely the kabbalists were also, quite naturally, acquainted with this fact. They might also have been acquainted with the fact that their sons suckled from their mother's breast, and though she was described as the source of a flow, this biological fact did not transform her into a male, from either a sexual or a gendered point of view." Idel, *Kabbalah and Eros*, 130.

117. As with many kabbalistic symbols, this positive association is not always consistent. Suckling can transmit positive or negative qualities, both in Kabbalah (in which it can transmit both Mercy and Judgment) and in rabbinic literature (in which negative spiritual qualities can be transmitted by suckling from the wrong woman). However, positive associations with divine breastfeeding do comprise a consistent kabbalistic theme.

118. I am not attempting to invalidate kabbalistic relational models different from the one I present in this work. They are all important and complementary aspects of kabbalistic thought.

119. Caroline Bynum asserts that medieval Christians' tendency to imagine God as a female parent served as a corrective to the confusion of applying sexual imagery to relationships between humanity and divinity. She suggests that parental imagery was employed to emphasize the concept of unity between God and human beings. It seems likely that the image of God as nursing mother serves a similar purpose in Judaism. Bynum, *Jesus as Mother*, 161.

120. Isaac the Blind, *Commentary on Sefer Yetzirah*, chapter 1. Hellner-Eshed has also identified mystical experience in the Zohar as encompassing an experience that goes beyond language. Hellner-Eshed, *A River Flows from Eden*, 350.

121. Rosen, *Unveiling Eve*, 103–117. Also see Grossman, *Pious and Rebellious*, 12, 14.

122. David Biale, *Eros and the Jews: From Biblical Israel to Contemporary America* (Berkeley, CA: University of California Press, 1997), 97–98; Rosen, *Unveiling Eve*, 119. The Albigensian heresy was centered in southern France: the same area in which the earliest kabbalists lived and wrote.

123. For example, in Maimonides' *Guide of the Perplexed*, the great Aristotelian philosopher groups women in the same intellectual category as children below the age of reason, primitive people, and men incapable of becoming philosophers. Collette Sirat, *A History of Jewish Philosophy in the Middle Ages* (Paris: Cambridge University Press, 1985), 163. Also see Biale, *Eros and the Jews*, 100.

124. See Ruth Mazzo Karras, *Sexuality in Medieval Europe: Doing Unto Others* (New York: Routledge, 2005), 66–67, 158; Joyce Salisbury, "Gendered Sexuality" in *Handbook of Medieval Sexuality*, eds. Vern Bullough and James Brundage (New York: Garland Publishing, Inc., 1996), 84–85. As pointed out by David Biale, this conflict is directly addressed in the thirteenth century kabbalistic manual on sexuality, *Iggeret ha-Qodesh*. Biale, *Eros and the Jews*, 101, 106. See also Charles Chavel, ed., *"Iggeret ha-Qodesh,"* in *Kitve Rabenu Moshe ben Naḥman*, vol. 2 (Jerusalem: Mosad ha-Rav Kook, 2002), 323. *Iggeret's* anonymous author rejects Maimonides' Aristotelian view, preferring earlier reproductive science derived from Galenic medicine. (As with Ezra's *Commentary on the Song of Songs*, *Iggeret ha-Qodesh* is conveniently but incorrectly grouped with Naḥmanides' works in Chavel's volume.)

125. David Nirenberg, *Communities of Violence: Persecution of Minorities in the Middle Ages* (Princeton CA: Princeton University Press, 1996), 151–52, 157.

126. Rosen, *Unveiling Eve*, 122–23; Baumgarten, *Mothers and Children*, 26–27.

127. Grossman, *Pious and Rebellious*, 79–80, 83–84. See Zohar 3:69a for a parable about a king who diminishes himself by cleaving to a concubine rather than to his royal wife.

128. The anonymous thirteenth-century kabbalistic text *Iggeret ha-Qodesh* (*The Holy Letter*) devotes itself to explaining and defending marital sexuality's virtues. Similarly, Zohar 1:49b–50a questions whether it would be better for men to forsake their wives in favor of relating exclusively to *Shekhinah*, and responds by asserting that the kabbalists' relationships to this divine aspect are *dependent upon* their relationships with their wives. However, some thirteenth-century kabbalists chose to enact modified forms of abstinence within the context of marriage. Elliot Wolfson has analyzed kabbalistic texts that advocate temporary physical celibacy within marriage in order to enhance spiritual relationships with God. The presence of such trends provides further evidence of the cultural tensions regarding women and marriage during this period, while demonstrating that the kabbalists were thoroughly engaged in this debate. See Wolfson, "Eunuchs Who Keep the Sabbath."

129. Biale, *Eros and the Jews*, 95–98; Baer, *From the Age of Reconquest to the Fourteenth Century*, 250, 259–60. Moshe Idel sees *Iggeret ha-Qodesh*'s defense of marriage and sexuality as reacting against medieval Aristotelianism's presentation of sexuality, particularly as it appears in Maimonides' *Guide of the Perplexed*. Idel, "Maimonides and Kabbalah," 43–44.

130. Baumgarten, *Mothers and Children*, 163. In fact, without wives kabbalistic men were considered incomplete human beings. See Zohar 3:81b and Zohar 2:122a for examples.

131. Eva Feder Kittay notes that women serve as symbolic Others to men in many ways that extend beyond the sexual. She asserts that because "Mother as Other" is "man's first and most significant attempt to define himself and to establish his relationships . . . women serve metaphorically to represent those activities and domains in which man will redefine himself . . .

This conceptual move is facilitated by the structure of metaphor itself. Because it the very structure of metaphor to exploit such relationships, woman's situation as Other is solidified through the metaphorization of these early experiences and their metaphorical transposition on to man's later life." Eva Feder Kittay, "Woman as Metaphor," in *Feminist Social Thought: A Reader*, ed. Diana Tietjens Meyers, 270 (New York: Routledge, 1997). Caroline Bynum has shown that femininity plays a similar role in medieval Christian religious writings, occupying a liminal position that serves as a gateway between masculine states of being. Bynum, *Fragmentation and Redemption*, 29–32, 137. It is certainly the case that the feminine *sefirot* associated with suckling imagery in the Zohar occupy such liminal positions, with the *Shekhinah* mediating between the divine and human worlds and *Binah* mediating between the three upper and the seven lower *sefirot*.

132. For examples of scholars concerned with exposing misogyny in medieval Jewish literature, see Rosen, *Unveiling Eve*, 8, 26; Wolfson, *Language, Eros, Being*, 49, 53.

Bibliography

Abrams, Daniel. *The Book Bahir: An Edition Based on the Earliest Manuscripts.* With an introduction by Moshe Idel. Los Angeles, CA: Cherub Press, 1994.

———. "The Boundaries of Divine Ontology: The Inclusion and Exclusion of Metatron in the Godhead." *Harvard Theological Review* 87, no. 3 (1994): 291–321.

———. "The Condensation of the Symbol 'Shekhinah' in the Manuscripts of the *Book Bahir*," *Kabbalah: Journal for the Study of Jewish Mystical Texts* 16 (2007): 7–82.

———. *The Female Body of God in Kabbalah: Embodied Forms of Love and Sexuality in the Divine Feminine.* Jerusalem: The Hebrew University Magnes Press Ltd., 2004. [Hebrew]

———. "The Invention of the *Zohar* as a Book: On the Assumptions and Expectations of the Kabbalists and Modern Scholars." *Kabbalah: Journal for the Study of Jewish Mystical Texts* 19 (2009): 7–142.

———. *R. Asher ben David: His Complete Works and Studies in His Kabbalistic Thought.* Los Angeles, CA: Cherub Press, 1996.

———. "The Virgin Mary as the Moon That Lacks the Sun: A Zoharic Polemic Against the Veneration of Mary." *Kabbalah: Journal for the Study of Jewish Mystical Texts* 21 (2010): 7–56.

Abulafia, Anna Sapir. "Bodies in the Jewish-Christian Debate." In *Framing Medieval Bodies*, edited by Sarah Kay and Miri Rubin, 123–37. New York: Manchester University Press, 1994.

————. *Christians and Jews in the Twelfth-Century Renaissance*. New York: Routledge, 1995.

Altmann, A. and S. M. Stern. *Isaac Israeli: A Neoplatonic Philosopher of the Early Tenth Century*, np. Oxford University Press, 1958. Reprint, Westport, CT: Greenwood Press, Publishers, 1979.

Baer, Yitzhak. *From the Age of Reconquest to the Fourteenth Century*. Translated by Louis Schoffman. With an introduction by Benjamin R. Gampel. Vol. 1 of *A History of the Jews in Christian Spain*. Philadelphia, PA: The Jewish Publication Society of America, 1961.

Barthes, Roland. *Mythologies*. Translated by Annette Lavers. First American edition. New York: Hill and Wang, 1972.

Bataille, Georges. *Inner Experience*. Translated and with an introduction by Leslie Ann Boldt. SUNY Series Intersections: Philosophy and Critical Theory, ed. Rodolphe Gasché and Mark C. Taylor. Albany, NY: SUNY Press, 1988.

Baumgarten, Elisheva. *Mothers and Children: Jewish Family Life in Medieval Europe*. Princeton, NJ: Princeton University Press, 2004.

Beck, Brenda. "The Symbolic Merger of Body, Space and Cosmos." *Contributions to Indian Sociology* 10, no. 2 (1976): 213–43.

Ben-Porat, Ziva. "The Poetics of Literary Allusion." *PTL: A Journal for Descriptive Poetics and Theory of Literature* 1 (1976): 105–28.

Berger, David. "The Attitude of St. Bernard of Clairvaux Toward the Jews." *Proceedings of the American Academy for Jewish Research* 40 (1972): 89–108.

Berger, Michael. "Two Models of Medieval Jewish Marriage: A Preliminary Study." *Journal of Jewish Studies* 52, no. 1 (2001): 73–84.

Bernard of Clairvaux. *On the Song of Songs*. Translated by Kilian Walsh with an introduction by Jean Leclerq. Cistercian Fathers Series: Number Seven, 3 vols. Kalamazoo, MI: Cistercian Publications Inc., 1983.

Biale, David. *Eros and the Jews: From Biblical Israel to Contemporary America*. Berkeley, CA: University of California Press, 1997.

————. "The God with Breasts: El Shaddai in the Bible." *History of Religions* 21, no. 3 (1982): 240–56.

Blanchot, Maurice. *The Infinite Conversation*. Translated and with a foreword by Susan Hanson. Theory and History of Literature, ed. Wlad Godzich and Jochen Schulte-Sasse, no. 82. Minneapolis, MN: University of Minnesota Press, 1993.

Bloom, Harold. *The Anxiety of Influence: A Theory of Poetry*. 2nd ed. New York: Oxford University Press, Inc., 1997.

Boyarin, Daniel. *Intertextuality and the Reading of Midrash*. np. Bloomington, IN: Indiana University Press, 1990. Reprint, Eugene, OR: Wipf and Stock Publishers, 2001.

Braude, William G. *Jewish Proselytizing in the First Five Centuries of the Common Era, the Age of the Tannaim and Amoraim*. Brown University Studies, no. 6. Providence, RI: Brown University, 1940.

Bregman, Marc. "Mordekhai the Milkman." Lecture, The University of North Carolina at Greensboro, Greensboro, NC, Fall, 2008.

Brody, Seth, trans. *Rabbi Ezra ben Solomon of Gerona: "Commentary on the Song of Songs" and Other Kabbalistic Commentaries*. With an introduction by Arthur Green. Commentary Series, ed. E. Ann Matter. Kalamazoo, MI: Medieval Institute Publications for The Consortium for the Teaching of the Middle Ages, 1999.

Burns, Robert Ignatius. "Jews and Moors in the *Siete Partidas* of Alfonso X the Learned: a Background Perspective." In *Medieval Spain: Culture, Conflict, and Coexistence: Studies in Honour of Angus MacKay*. edited by Roger Collins and Anthony Goodman, 46–62. Hampshire, UK: Palgrave Macmillan, 2002.

———. *Muslims, Christians and Jews in the Crusader Kingdom of Valencia: Societies in Symbiosis*. Cambridge Iberian and Latin America Studies. New York: Cambridge University Press, 1984.

Butler, Judith. *Bodies That Matter: On the Discursive Limits of "Sex."* New York: Routledge, 1993.

Bynum, Caroline Walker. *Fragmentation and Redemption: Essays on Gender and the Human Body in Medieval Religion*. New York: Zone Books, 1992.

———. *Jesus as Mother: Studies in the Spirituality of the High Middle Ages*. Publications of the UCLA Center for Medieval and Renaissance Studies, no. 16. Berkeley, CA: University of California Press, 1982.

Camille, Michael. "The Image and the Self: Unwriting Late Medieval Bodies." In *Framing Medieval Bodies*, edited by Sarah Kay and Miri Rubin, 62–99. New York: Manchester University Press, 1994.

Carruthers, Mary. *The Craft of Thought: Meditation, Rhetoric, and the Making of Images, 400–1200*. Cambridge Studies in Medieval Literature, edited by Alastair Minnis, no. 34. New York: Cambridge University Press, 1998.

Chavel, Charles, ed. *"Iggeret ha-Qodesh"* and *"Perush le-Shir ha-Shirim."* In *Kitve Rabenu Moshe ben Nachman*, vol. 2., 321–37, 473–518. Jerusalem: Mosad ha-Rav Kook, 2002.

Chazan, Robert. *Barcelona and Beyond: The Disputation of 1263 and Its Aftermath*. Berkeley, CA: University of California Press, 1992.

———. *Daggers of Faith: Thirteenth Century Christian Missionizing and Jewish Response*. Berkeley, CA: University of California Press, 1989.

Chernus, Ira. *Mysticism in Rabbinic Judaism: Studies in the History of Midrash*. Studia Judaica, ed. E. L. Ehrlich, no. 11. New York: Walter de Gruyter, 1982.

Cohen, Jeremy. "The Christian Adversary of Solomon ibn Adret." *The Jewish Quarterly Review* 71, no. 1 (1980): 48–55.

———. *The Friars and the Jews: The Evolution of Medieval Anti-Judaism*. Ithaca, NY: Cornell University Press, 1982.

Cohen, Shaye J. D. *The Beginnings of Jewishness: Boundaries, Varieties, Uncertainties*. Hellenistic Culture and Society no. 31, edited by Anthony W. Bulloch, Erich S. Gruen, A. A. Long, and Andrew F. Stewart,. Berkeley, CA: University of California Press, 1999.

Derrida, Jacques. "White Mythology: Metaphor in the Text of Philosophy." *New Literary History* 6, no. 1 (1974): 5–74.

Dishon, Judith. "Images of Women in Medieval Jewish Literature." In *Women of the Word: Jewish Women and Jewish Writing*, edited by Judith R. Baskin, 335–49. Detroit, MI: Wayne State University Press, 1994.

Douglas, Mary. *Natural Symbols: Explorations in Cosmology*. With a new introduction. np London: Barrie & Rockliff, 1970. Reprint, New York: Routledge, 1996.

———.*Purity and Danger: An Analysis of Concept Pollution and Taboo*. With a new preface by the author. London: Routledge & Kegan Paul, 1966. Reprint, New York: Routledge Classics, 2002.

Edge, David. "Technological Metaphor and Social Control." *New Literary History* 6, no. 1 (1974): 135–47.

Eilberg-Schwartz, Howard. *God's Phallus and Other Problems for Men and Monotheism*. Boston: Beacon Press, 1994.

———, ed. *People of the Body: Jews and Judaism from an Embodied Perspective*. SUNY Series, The Body in Culture, History, and Religion, ed. Howard Eilberg-Schwartz. Albany, NY: SUNY Press, 1992.

———. *The Savage in Judaism: An Anthropology of Israelite Religion and Ancient Judaism*. Bloomington, IN: Indiana University Press, 1990.

Feldman, Louis H. *Jew and Gentile in the Ancient World: Attitudes and Interactions from Alexander to Justinian*. Princeton, NJ: Princeton University Press, 1993.

———. "Jewish "Sympathizers" in Classical Literature and Inscriptions." *Transactions and Proceedings of the American Philological Association* 81 (1950): 200–208.

Fernandez, James. *Persuasions and Performances: The Play of Tropes in Culture*. Bloomington, IN: Indiana University Press, 1986.

———, ed. *Beyond Metaphor: The Theory of Tropes in Anthropology*. Stanford, CA: Stanford University Press, 1991.

Fishbane, Eitan. "Tears of Disclosure: The Role of Weeping in Zoharic Narrative." *The Journal of Jewish Thought and Philosophy* 11, no. 1 (2002): 25–47.

Fishbane, Michael. *Biblical Myth and Rabbinic Mythmaking*. New York: Oxford University Press, 2003.

———. *The Exegetical Imagination: On Jewish Thought and Theology*. Cambridge, MA: Harvard University Press, 1998.

———. *The Kiss of God: Spiritual and Mystical Death in Judaism*. The Samuel and Althea Stroum Lectures in Jewish Studies. Seattle, WA: University of Washington Press, 1994.

———. "The Well of Living Water: A Biblical Motif and Its Ancient Transformations." In *"Sha'arei Talmon:" Studies in the Bible, Qumran, and the Ancient Near East Presented to Shemaryahu Talmon*, edited by Michael Fishbane and Emanuel Tov with Weston W. Fields, 3–16. Winona Lake, IN.: Eisenbrauns, 1992.

Fonrobert, Charlotte Elisheva. *Menstrual Purity: Rabbinic and Christian Reconstructions of Biblical Gender*. Stanford, CA: Stanford University Press, 2000.

Fraade, Steven D. *From Tradition to Commentary: Torah and Its Interpretation in the Midrash "Sifre to Deuteronomy."* SUNY Series in Judaica: Hermeneutics, Mysticism, and Religion, edited by Michael Fishbane, Robert Goldenberg, and Arthur Green. Albany, NY: SUNY Press, 1991.

Freud, Sigmund. *The Interpretation of Dreams*. Translated by Joyce Crick with an introduction and notes by Ritchie Robertson. Oxford: Oxford University Press, 1999.

Fulton, Rachel. *From Judgment to Passion: Devotion to Christ and the Virgin Mary, 800–1200*. New York: Columbia University Press, 2002.

Gikatilla, Joseph ben Abraham. *Sha'arey Orah.* 2 vols. Jerusalem: Mosad Bialik, 1980.

——. *Sha'arey Tzedeq.* Translated by Raphael ben Avraham. Strasbourg, France: Gilen, 2007. [Hebrew and French]

Goldberg, Harriet. "Two Parallel Medieval Commonplaces: Antifeminism and Antisemitism in the Hispanic Literary Tradition." In *Aspects of Jewish Culture in the Middle Ages,* edited by Paul E. Szarmach, 85–119. Albany, NY: SUNY Press, 1979.

Goldberg, Yechiel. "Spiritual Leadership and the Popularization of Kabbalah in Medieval Spain." *The Journal for the Study of Sephardic and Mizrahi Jewry* 2, no. 2 (2009): 1–59.

Goodman, Martin. *Mission and Conversion: Proselytizing in the Religious History of the Roman Empire.* Oxford: Clarendon Press, 1994.

Green, Arthur. *Keter: The Crown of God in Early Jewish Mysticism.* Princeton, NJ: Princeton University Press, 1997.

——. "Shekhinah, the Virgin Mary, and the Song of Songs: Reflections on a Kabbalistic Symbol in Its Historical Context." *AJS Review* 26, no. 1 (2002): 1–52.

Grossman, Avraham. *Pious and Rebellious: Jewish Women in Medieval Europe.* Translated by Jonathan Chipman. Waltham, MA: Brandeis University Press, 2004.

Gruber, Mayer I. "Matrilineal Determination of Jewishness: Biblical and Near Eastern Roots." In *Pomegranates and Golden Bells: Studies in Biblical, Jewish, and Near Eastern Ritual, Law, and Literature in Honor of Jacob Milgrom,* edited by David P. Wright, David Noel Freedman, and Avi Hurvitz, 437–43. Winona Lake, IN: Eisenbrauns, 1995.

Halbertal, Moshe. *Concealment and Revelation: Esotericism in Jewish Thought and Its Philosophical Implications.* Translated by Jackie Feldman. Princeton, NJ: Princeton University Press, 2007.

Haskell, Ellen. "Bathed in Milk: Metaphors of Suckling and Spiritual Transmission in Thirteenth-Century Kabbalah." In *Figuring Religions: Comparing Ideas, Images, and Activities,* edited by Shubha Pathak. Albany, NY: SUNY Press, forthcoming.

——. "Metaphor, Transformation and Transcendence: Toward an Understanding of Kabbalistic Imagery in *Sefer hazohar.*" *Prooftexts: A Journal of Jewish Literary History* 28, no. 3 (2008): 335–62.

Hayman, A. Peter. *Sefer Yeṣira: Edition, Translation and Text-Critical Commentary.* Tübingen, Germany: Mohr Siebeck, 2004.

Hecker, Joel. "Eating Gestures and the Ritualized Body in Medieval Jewish Mysticism." *History of Religions* 40, no. 2 (2002): 125–51.

———. *Mystical Bodies, Mystical Meals: Eating and Embodiment in Medieval Kabbalah*. Raphael Patai Series in Jewish Folklore and Anthropology, edited by Dan Ben-Amos. Detroit, MI: Wayne State University Press, 2005.

Hellner-Eshed, Melila. *A River Flows from Eden: The Language of Mystical Experience in the Zohar*. Translated by Nathan Wolski. Stanford, CA: Stanford University Press, 2009.

Huss, Boaz. *Like the Radiance of the Sky: Chapters in the Reception History of the Zohar and the Construction of Its Symbolic Value*. Jerusalem: Mosad Bialik, 2008. [Hebrew]

———. "Mysticism versus Philosophy in Kabbalistic Literature." *Micrologus* 9 (2001): 125–35.

———. "*Sefer ha-Zohar* as Canonical, Sacred and Holy Text: Changing Perspectives of the Book of Splendor between the Thirteenth and the Eighteenth Centuries." *The Journal of Jewish Thought and Philosophy* 7 (1998): 257–307.

Idel, Moshe. *Absorbing Perfections: Kabbalah and Interpretation*. With a foreword by Harold Bloom. New Haven, CT: Yale University Press, 2002.

———. *Ascensions on High in Jewish Mysticism: Pillars, Lines, Ladders*. Pasts Incorporated: CEI Studies in the Humanities, Vol. 2, edited by Sorin Antohi and László Kontler. New York: Central European University Press, 2005.

———. "Enoch is Metatron." *Immanuel* 24/5 (1990): 220–40.

———. *Kabbalah: New Perspectives*. New Haven, CT: Yale University Press, 1988.

———. *Kabbalah and Eros*. New Haven, CT: Yale University Press, 2005.

———. "Maimonides and Kabbalah." In *Studies in Maimonides*, edited by Isadore Twersky, 31–81. Cambridge, MA: Harvard University Press, 1990.

———. "Nahmanides: Kabbalah, Halakhah, and Spiritual Leadership." In *Jewish Mystical Leaders and Leadership in the Thirteenth Century*, edited by Moshe Idel and Mortimer Ostow, 15–96. Lanham, MD: Rowman & Littlefield Publishers, Inc., 2005.

Jackson, Michael. "Thinking through the Body: An Essay on Understanding Metaphor." *Social Analysis* 14 (1983): 127–48.

Jakobson, Roman. "Two Aspects of Language and Two Types of Apha-
    sic Disturbances." In *Fundamentals of Language*, edited by Roman
    Jakobson and Morris Halle, 2nd rev. ed., 67–96. The Hague, The
    Netherlands: Mouton, 1971.
Kaplan, Aryeh. *Sefer Yetzirah: The Book of Creation in Theory and Prac-
    tice*. York Beach, ME: Samuel Weiser, Inc., 1990.
Karras, Ruth Mazzo. *Sexuality in Medieval Europe: Doing Unto Others*.
    New York: Routledge, 2005.
Kehoe, Alice B. "The Metonymic Pole and Social Roles." *Journal of
    Anthropological Research* 29, no. 4 (1973): 266–74.
Kellner, Menachem. *Maimonides' Confrontation with Mysticism*. With
    a foreword by Moshe Idel. Portland, OR: The Littman Library of
    Jewish Civilization, 2006.
Kittay, Eva Feder. "Woman as Metaphor." In *Feminist Social Thought:
    A Reader*, edited by Diana Tietjens Meyers, 265–85. New York:
    Routledge, 1997.
Kittay, Eva Feder and Adrienne Lehrer. "Semantic Fields and the Struc-
    ture of Metaphor." *Studies in Language* 5, no. 1 (1981): 31–63.
Kofman, Sarah. *Camera Obscura of Ideology*. Translated by Will Straw,
    np. Ithaca, NY: Cornell University Press, 1999.
Kosman, Admiel. "The Female Breast and the Male Mouth: A Talmu-
    dic Vignette (BT *Bava Batra* 9a-b)." *Jewish Studies Quarterly* 11,
    no. 4 (2004): 293–312.
Lacan, Jacques. *Feminine Sexuality: Jacques Lacan and the École
    Freudienne*. Translated by Jacqueline Rose and edited by Juliet
    Mitchell and Jacqueline Rose. np: 1982. Reprint, New York: W.
    W. Norton & Company and Pantheon Books, 1985.
Lakoff, George and Mark Johnson. *Metaphors We Live By* Chicago: The
    University of Chicago Press, 1981.
Laskaris, Julie. "Nursing Mothers in Greek and Roman Medicine."
    American Journal of Archaeology 112 (2008): 459–64.
Levinas, Emmanuel. *Totality and Infinity: An Essay on Exteriority*.
    Translated by Alphonso Lingis. Pittsburgh, PA: Duquesne Univer-
    sity Press, 1969.
Liebes, Yehuda. "Hebrew and Aramaic as Languages of the Zohar."
    Translated by Daphne Freedman and Ada Rapoport-Albert. *Ara-
    maic Studies* 4, no. 1 (2006): 35–52.
———. *Studies in the Zohar*. Translated by Arnold Schwartz, Stephanie
    Nakache, and Penina Peli. SUNY Series in Judaica: Hermeneutics,

Mysticism, and Religion, edited by Michael Fishbane, Robert Goldenberg, and Arthur Green. Albany, NY: SUNY Press, 1993.

————. *Torat ha-Yetzirah shel Sefer Yetzirah*. Tel Aviv: Schocken Publishing House Ltd., 2000. [Hebrew]

————. "Zohar ve-Eros." *Alpayim* 9 (1994): 67–119. [Hebrew]

Lovejoy, Arthur. "Reflections on the History of ideas." In *Ideas in Cultural Perspective*, edited Philip Wiener and Aaron Noland, 3–23. New Brunswick, NJ: Rutgers University Press, 1962.

Mack, Ḥananel. "Drashot Anti Notzri'ut Bamidrash Bamidbar Rabbah." *Proceedings of the Tenth World Congress of Jewish Studies* 3, no. 1 (1989): 134–37. [Hebrew]

————. "Midrash Bamidbar Rabbah and the Beginning of Kabbalah in Provence." In *Myth in Judaism*, ed. Haviva Pedaya, 78–94, Vol. 4 of *Eshel Beer-Sheva: Occasional Publications in Jewish Studies*. Jerusalem: Mosad Bialik for Ben-Gurion University of the Negev Press, 1996.

Maimonides, Moses. *The Guide of the Perplexed*. Translated with an introduction and notes by Shlomo Pines and with an introduction by Leo Strauss. 2 vols. Chicago: The University of Chicago Press, 1963.

Marcus, Ivan. *Rituals of Childhood: Jewish Acculturation in Medieval Europe*. New Haven, CT: Yale University Press, 1996.

Margaliot, Reuven Moshe, ed. *Sefer ha-Bahir*. Jerusalem: Mosad ha-Rav Kook, 1994.

————, ed. *Sefer ha-Zohar al Ḥamishah Ḥumshei Torah*. 3 vols. Jerusalem: Mosad ha-Rav Kook, 1999.

Matt, Daniel, trans. *The Zohar: Pritzker Edition*. With an introduction by Arthur Green. vol. 1. Stanford, CA: Stanford University Press for Zohar Education Project, Inc., 2004.

Meltzer, Françoise. *For Fear of the Fire: Joan of Arc and the Limits of Subjectivity*. Chicago: The University of Chicago Press, 2001.

Merleau-Ponty, Maurice. *Phenomenology of Perception*. Translated by Colin Smith, np. Routledge & Kegan Paul, 1958. Reprint, New York: Routledge, 2003.

Meroz, Ronit. "And I Was Not There?: The Complaints of Rabbi Simeon bar Yohai According to an Unknown Zoharic Story." *Tarbitz* 71 (2002): 163–93.

————. "On the Time and Place of Some Passages in *Sefer ha-Bahir*." *Da'at* 49 (2002): 137–80. [Hebrew].

————. "The Path of Silence: An Unknown Story from a Zohar Manuscript." *European Journal of Jewish Studies* 1, no. 2 (2008): 319–42.

————. "Zoharic Narratives and Their Adaptations." *Hispania Judaica* 3 (2000): 3–63.

Moore, R. I. *The Formation of a Persecuting Society: Power and Deviance in Western Europe, 950–1250.* Cambridge, MA: Blackwell Publishers Inc., 1990.

Mopsik, Charles. "Late Judeo-Aramaic: The Language of Theosophic Kabbalah." Translated by Ariel Klein. *Aramaic Studies* 4, no. 1 (2006): 21–33.

Nirenberg, David. *Communities of Violence: Persecution of Minorities in the Middle Ages.* Princeton, NJ: Princeton University Press, 1996.

Orlov, Andrei. *The Enoch-Metatron Tradition.* Texts and Studies in Ancient Judaism 107, edited by Martin Hengel and Peter Schäfer. Tübingen, Germany: Mohr Siebeck, 2005.

————. "Titles of Enoch-Metatron in *2 Enoch.*" *Journal for the Study of the Pseudepigrapha* 18 (1998): 71–86.

Ortner, Sherry. "On Key Symbols." *American Anthropologist* 75 (1973): 1338–435.

Ostow, Mortimer. "Introduction." In *Jewish Mystical Leaders and Leadership in the 13th Century,* edited by Moshe Idel and Mortimer Ostow, 1–13. New York: Rowman and Littlefield Publishers, Inc., 2005.

————, ed. *Ultimate Intimacy: The Psychodynamics of Jewish Mysticism.* London: Karnac Books, 1995.

Pedaya, Haviva. "Ahuzim ba-Dibbur: Li-Vruro shel ha-Defus ha-Mitpa'el etzel Rishonei ha-Mekubbalim." *Tarbitz* 65 (1996): 565–636. [Hebrew]

Pick, Lucy. *Conflict and Coexistence: Archbishop Rodrigo and the Muslims and Jews of Medieval Spain.* History, Languages, and Cultures of the Spanish and Portuguese Worlds, edited by Sabine MacCormack. Ann Arbor, MI: The University of Michigan Press, 2004.

Rapoport-Albert, Ada and Theodore Kwasman. "Late Aramaic: The Literary and Linguistic Context of the Zohar." *Aramaic Studies* 4, no. 1 (2006): 5–19.

Rappaport, Roy. *Ecology, Meaning, and Religion.* Berkeley, CA: North Atlantic Books, 1979.

Ricoeur, Paul. *The Rule of Metaphor: Multi-Disciplinary Studies of the Creation of Meaning in Language.* Translated by Robert Czerny with Kathleen McLaughlin and John Costello. Toronto: University of Toronto Press, 1977.

Rosen, Tova. *Unveiling Eve: Reading Gender in Medieval Hebrew Literature.* Philadelphia, PA: University of Pennsylvania Press, 2003.

Rosenbloom, Joseph R. *Conversion to Judaism: From the Biblical Period to the Present.* Cincinnati, OH: Hebrew Union College Press, 1978.

Roth, Norman. "Forgery and Abrogation of the Torah: A Theme in Muslim and Christian Polemic in Spain." *Proceedings of the American Academy for Jewish Research* 54 (1987): 203–36.

———. "A Note on Research into Jewish Sexual Identity in the Medieval Period." In *Handbook of Medieval Sexuality*, edited by Vern L. Bullough and James A. Brundage, 309–17. Garland Reference Library of the Humanities, no. 1696. New York: Garland Publishing, Inc., 1996.

———. "The "Wiles of Women" Motif in the Medieval Hebrew Literature of Spain." *Hebrew Annual Review: A Journal of Studies of Hebrew Language and Literature* 2 (1978): 145–65.

Rubin, Miri. *Mother of God: A History of the Virgin Mary.* New Haven, CT: Yale University Press, 2009.

Salisbury, Joyce. "Gendered Sexuality." In *Handbook of Medieval Sexuality*, edited by Vern Bullough and James Brundage, 81–102. Garland Reference Library of the Humanities, no. 1696. New York: Garland Publishing, Inc., 1996.

Schäfer, Peter. "Daughter, Sister, Bride, and Mother: Images of the Femininity of God in the Early Kabbala." *Journal of the American Academy of Religion* 68, no. 2 (2000): 221–42.

———. *Mirror of His Beauty: Feminine Images of God from the Bible to the Early Kabbalah.* Princeton, NJ: Princeton University Press, 2002.

Scholem, Gershom. *Major Trends in Jewish Mysticism.* With a foreword by Robert Alter. Jerusalem: Schocken Publishing House, Ltd., 1941. Reprint, New York: Schocken Books Inc., 1995.

———. *On the Kabbalah and Its Symbolism.* With a foreword by Bernard McGinn. Translated by Ralph Manheim. New York: Schocken Books Inc., 1965. Reprint, New York: Schocken Books, 1996.

———. *On the Mystical Shape of the Godhead: Basic Concepts in the Kabbalah.* With a foreword by Joseph Dan. Translated by Joachim Neugroschel and edited by Jonathan Chipman. New York: Schocken Books, 1991.

————. *Origins of the Kabbalah*. Edited by R.J. Zwi Werblowsky and translated by Allan Arkush. 1st English translation, np. Philadelphia, PA: The Jewish Publication Society, 1987. Reprint, Princeton, NJ: Princeton University Press, 1990.

————, ed. *"Perush Sefer Yetzirah."* In *Ha-Kabbalah bi-Provans: Ḥug ha-Rabad u-Veno R. Yitzḥak Sagi Nahor*, appendix 1: 1–18. Jerusalem: Akademon, 1969.

Sendor, Mark. "The Emergence of Provençal Kabbalah: Rabbi Isaac the Blind's "Commentary on *Sefer Yetzirah*." 2 vols. PhD. diss., Harvard University, 1994.

Schwartz, Seth. "Language, Power and Identity in Ancient Palestine." *Past and Present* 148 (1995): 3–47.

Schwartzmann, Julia. "Gender Concepts of Medieval Jewish Thinkers and the Book of Proverbs." *Jewish Studies Quarterly* 7, no. 3 (2000): 183–202.

Sirat, Collette. *A History of Jewish Philosophy in the Middle Ages*. Paris: Cambridge University Press, 1985.

Stern, David. *"Imitatio Hominis*: Anthropomorphism and the Character(s) of God in Rabbinic Literature." *Prooftexts: A Journal of Jewish Literary History* 12 (1992): 151–74.

————. *Parables in Midrash: Narrative and Exegesis in Rabbinic Literature*. Cambridge, MA: Harvard University Press, 1991.

Strack, H. L. and Günter Stemberger. *Introduction to the Talmud and Midrash*. Translated and edited by Markus Bockmuehl, np. Edinburgh, UK: T & T Clark Ltd., 1991. Reprint, Minneapolis, MN: Fortress Press, 1996, with emendations and updates.

Talmage, Frank. "Apples of Gold: The Inner Meaning of Sacred Texts in Judaism." In *Jewish Spirituality*. vol 1, *From the Bible through the Middle Ages*, edited by Arthur Green, 313–55. World Spirituality, no. 13. New York: Crossroad, 1986.

Theodor, J. *Bereschit Rabbah: mit Kritischem Apparat und Kommentar*. 2nd printing with additional corrections by Ch. Albeck. 3 vols. Jerusalem: Wahrmann Books, 1965.

Tishby, Isaiah and Fischel Lachower, ed. *The Wisdom of the Zohar: An Anthology of Texts*. Translated by David Goldstein. 3 vols. Washington DC: The Littman Library of Jewish Civilization, 1989.

Turner, Victor. *The Forest of Symbols: Aspects of Ndembu Ritual*. Ithaca, NY: Cornell University Press, 1967.

Urbach, Ephraim E. *The Sages: Their Concepts and Beliefs*. Translated by Israel Abrahams. Jerusalem: The Magnes Press, 1975. Reprint, Cambridge, MA: Harvard University Press, 1979.

Vajda, Georges. *L'amour de Dieu dans la Théologie Juive du Moyen Age.* Études de Philosophie Médiévale, edited by Étienne Gilson, no. 46. Paris: Librairie Philosophique J. Vrin, 1957.

Verman, Mark. *The Books of Contemplation: Medieval Jewish Mystical Sources.* SUNY Series in Judaica. Albany, NY: SUNY Press, 1992.

Wasserstrom, Steven. "Further Thoughts on the Origins of Sefer Yesirah." *Aleph: Historical Studies in Science and Judaism* 2 (2002): 201–21.

White, Hayden V. *Metahistory: The Historical Imagination in Nineteenth-Century Europe.* Baltimore, MD: The Johns Hopkins University Press, 1973.

Whorf, Benjamin Lee. *Collected Papers on Metalinguistics.* Washington, DC: Department of State for the Foreign Service Institute, 1952.

Wiener, Philip. "Some Problems and Methods in the History of Ideas." In *Ideas in Cultural Perspective*, edited by Philip Wiener and Aaron Noland, 24–41. New Brunswick, NJ: Rutgers University Press, 1962.

Wolfson, Elliot. "The Anonymous Chapters of the Elderly Master of Secrets: New Evidence for the Early Activity of the Zoharic Circle." *Kabbalah: Journal for the Study of Jewish Mystical Texts* 19 (2009): 143–94.

———. *Along the Path: Studies in Kabbalistic Myth, Symbolism, and Hermeneutics.* Albany, NY: SUNY Press, 1995.

———. "By Way of Truth: Aspects of Nahmanides' Kabbalistic Hermeneutic." *AJS Review* 14, no. 2 (1989): 103–78.

———. *Circle in the Square: Studies in the Use of Gender in Kabbalistic Symbolism.* Albany, NY: SUNY Press, 1995.

———. "Eunuchs Who Keep the Sabbath: Becoming Male and the Ascetic Ideal in Thirteenth-Century Jewish Mysticism." In *Becoming Male in the Middle Ages*, edited by Jeffrey Jerome Cohen and Bonnie Wheeler, 151–85. New York: Garland Publishing, Inc., 2000.

———. *Language, Eros, Being: Kabbalistic Hermeneutics and Poetic Imagination.* New York: Fordham University Press, 2005.

———. "Metatron and Shi'ur Qomah in the Writings of Haside Ashkenaz." In *Mysticism, Magic, and Kabbalah in Ashkenazic Judaism: International Symposium Held in Frankfurt a.M. 1991*, edited by

Karl Erich Grözinger and Joseph Dan, 60–92. New York: Walter de Gruyter, 1995.

———. "Occultation of the Feminine and the Body of Secrecy in Medieval Kabbalah." In *Luminal Darkness: Imaginal Gleanings from Zoharic Literature* (Oxford: Oneworld Publications, 2007), 258–94.

———. "The Theosophy of Shabbetai Donnolo, with Special Emphasis on the Doctrine of *Sefirot* in His *Sefer Hakhmoni*." *Jewish History* 6, no. 1 and 2, The Frank Talmage Memorial Volume (1992): 281–316.

———. *Through a Speculum that Shines: Vision and Imagination in Medieval Jewish Mysticism*, Princeton, NJ: Princeton University Press, 1994.

Yates, Frances. *The Art of Memory*. Chicago: The University of Chicago Press, 1966.

Index

Abraham (patriarch), 6, 13, 15, 17–20, 26, 31, 36, 50–51, 83, 84, 86–87, 154n68, 127n51–52
Abraham Abulafia, 71
Abraham ben David of Posquières, 99, 108, 131n3
Adam of Perseigne, 7, 96
adoption, 18, 20, 25
affectivity, 7, 51–52, 56, 60, 62, 65, 73, 76–77, 81, 93–94, 96–97, 100–101, 164n59; affective language, 40, 48, 58, 65, 68, 81, 88, 100, 156n77; affective spirituality, 7, 93, 97, 164n59. *See also* emotion
Ahavah. See Ḥesed
aquatic imagery, 8, 73, 76; fountain, 21, 26 54, 55, 149n36; lake, 72–73; river, 11, 21, 28, 65, 72–77, 79, 149n34, 151n45; spring, 18, 19, 21, 149n36; stream, 72, 151n48; well, 21, 73, 149n36
Assembly of Israel. *See Shekhinah*
Atika' Kadisha', 77–78

Avinu Malkenu (prayer), 10–11, 62, 57, 79
Azriel of Gerona, 28, 41, 49, 95, 129n57, 138nn49–51

Babylonian Talmud, 5, 17, 19, 20–21, 24, 30, 82, 84, 85, 91, 128, 121n4, 122n14, 124n29, 126n43, 127n50, 126n45, 142n74, 153n58, 154n63, 157n6, 157n11, 158n17
Bernard of Clairvaux, 96–98, 105
Binah, 8, 11, 49, 66–67, 74–78, 80–82, 87, 89, 100, 133n14, 137n38, 148n26, 150n44, 151n48, 154n62, 155n74, 173n131

celibacy, 102, 104, 107, 166n83, 172n128
Christians, 5, 7, 94, 96–101, 107, 171n119
Christian thought, 5–7, 14, 24, 46, 94–98, 99–101, 116n36, 163n38, 164n54, 171n119, 173n131

189